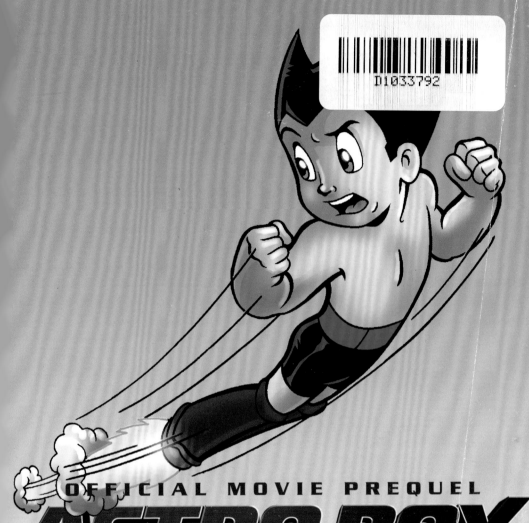

OFFICIAL MOVIE PREQUEL

ASTRO BOY®

THE MOVIE

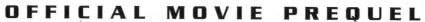

OFFICIAL MOVIE PREQUEL

ASTRO BOY THE MOVIE

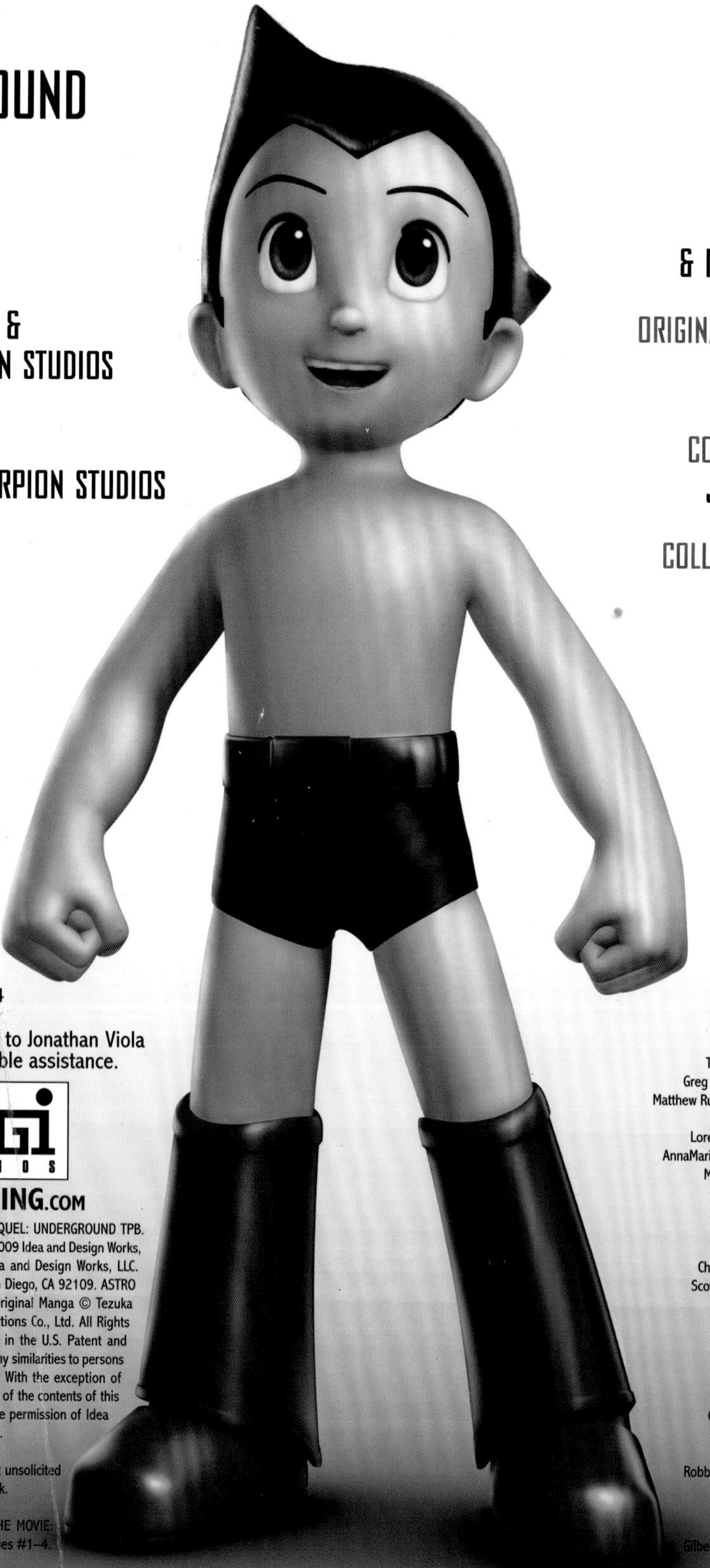

UNDERGROUND

WRITER
SCOTT TIPTON

ARTIST
DIEGO JOURDAN &
JORGE SANTILLAN STUDIOS

COLORIST
TOM SMITH/SCORPION STUDIOS

LETTER
NEIL UYET
& ROBBIE ROBB

ORIGINAL SERIES EDIT
TOM WA

COLLECTION EDIT
JUSTIN EISING

COLLECTION DESIGN
NEIL UYETA

ISBN: 978-1-60010-518-0
12 11 10 09   1 2 3 4

Special thanks to Jonathan Viola for his invaluable assistance.

www.IDWPUBLISHING.com

Originally published as ASTRO BOY THE MOVIE: OFFICIAL PREQUEL: UNDERGROUND Issues #1–4.

IDW Publish
Operatic
Ted Adams, Chief Executive Offi
Greg Goldstein, Chief Operating Offi
Matthew Ruzicka, CPA, Chief Financial Offi
Alan Payne, VP of Sa
Lorelei Bunjes, Dir. of Digital Servi
AnnaMaria White, Marketing & PR Mana
Marci Hubbard, Executive Assist
Alonzo Simon, Shipping Mana
Angela Loggins, Staff Account

Editori
Chris Ryall, Publisher/Editor-in-Ch
Scott Dunbier, Editor, Special Proje
Andy Schmidt, Senior Edit
Justin Eisinger, Edit
Kris Oprisko, Editor/Foreign L
Denton J. Tipton, Edit
Tom Waltz, Edit
Mariah Huehner, Associate Edit
Carlos Guzman, Editorial Assista

Desig
Robbie Robbins, EVP/Sr. Graphic Arti
Neil Uyetake, Art Directo
Chris Mowry, Graphic Artis
Amauri Osorio, Graphic Artis
Gilberto Lazcano, Production Assista

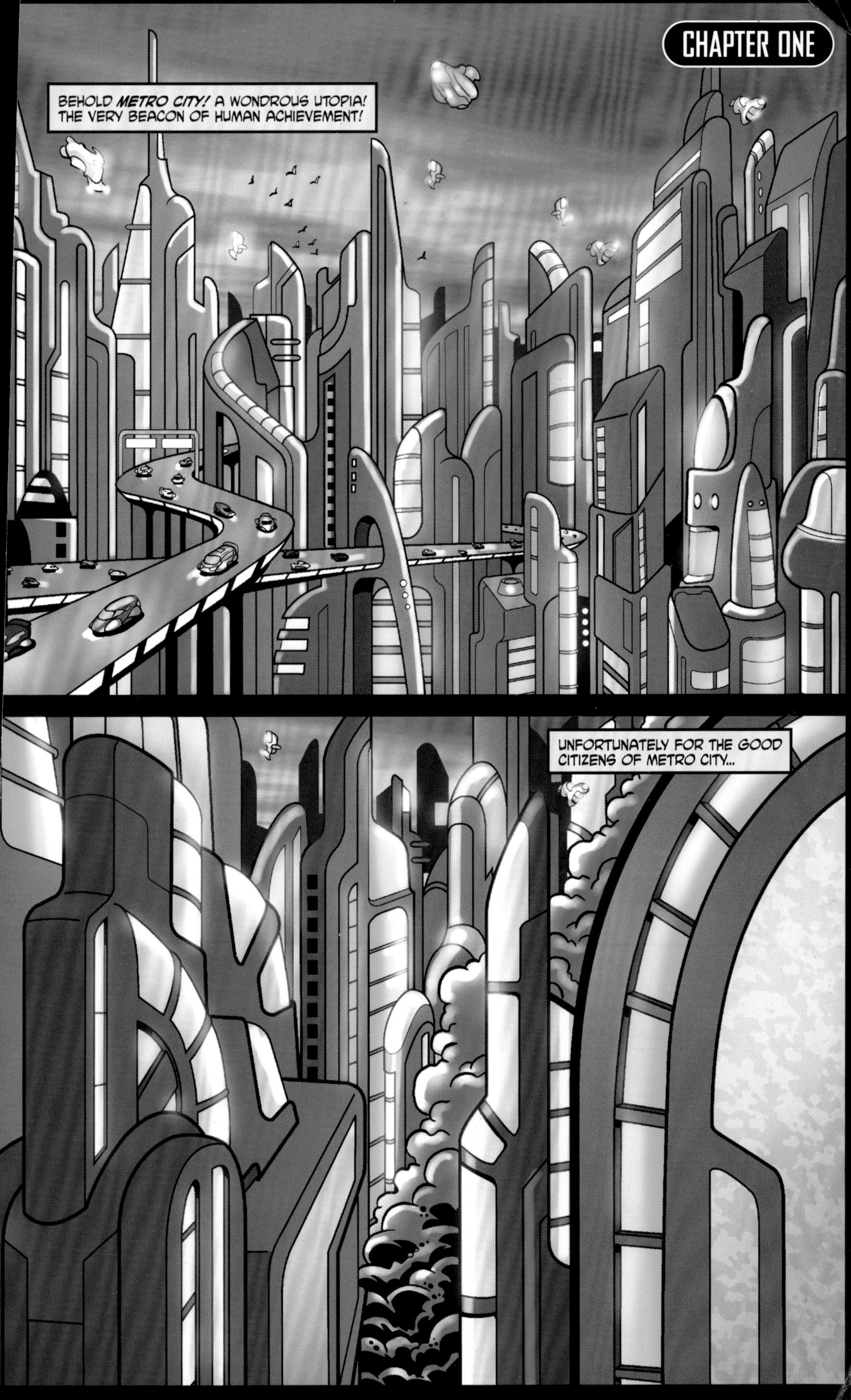
CHAPTER ONE
BEHOLD METRO CITY! A WONDROUS UTOPIA! THE VERY BEACON OF HUMAN ACHIEVEMENT!
UNFORTUNATELY FOR THE GOOD CITIZENS OF METRO CITY...

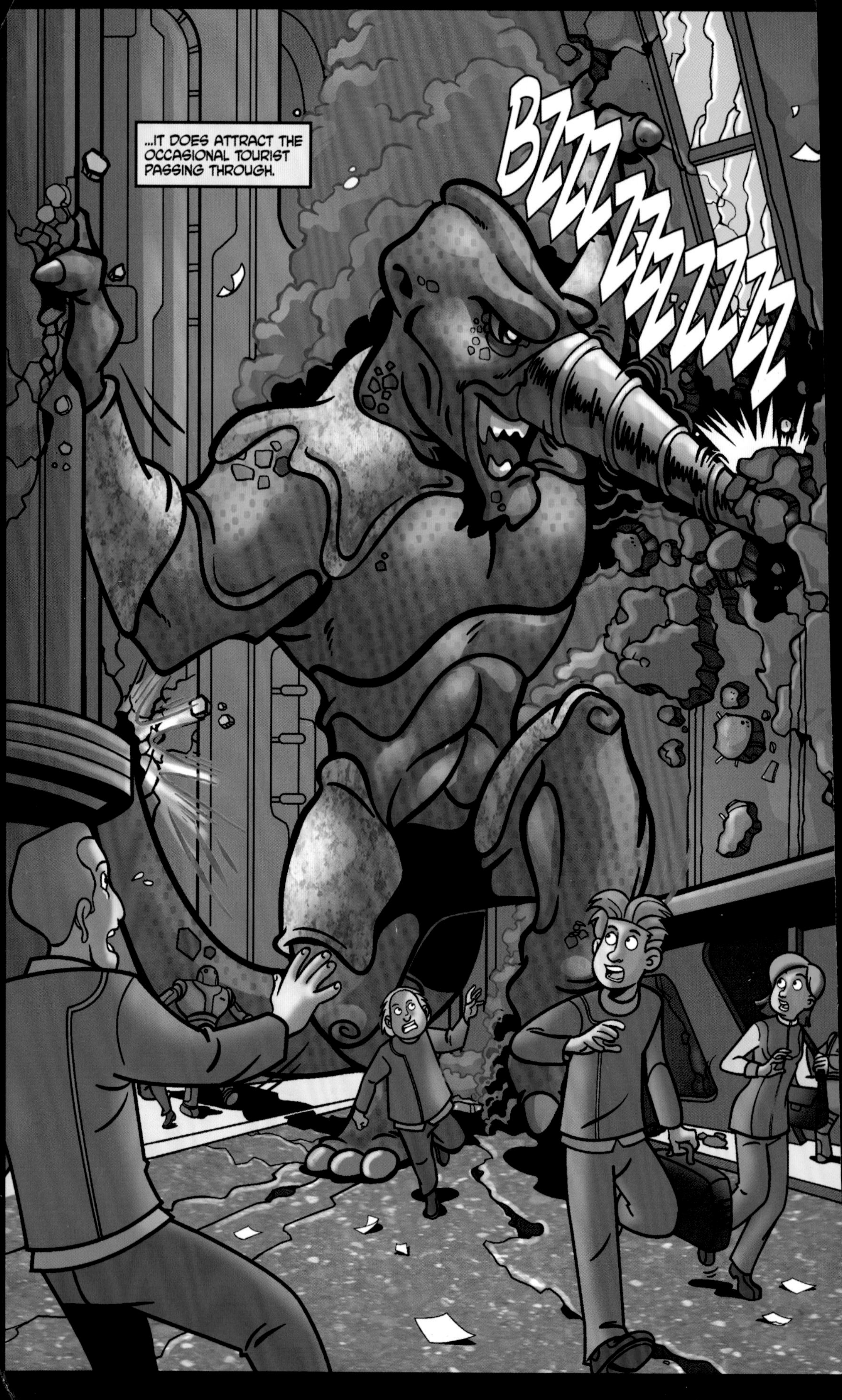
...IT DOES ATTRACT THE OCCASIONAL TOURIST PASSING THROUGH.
BZZZZZZZZZZZ

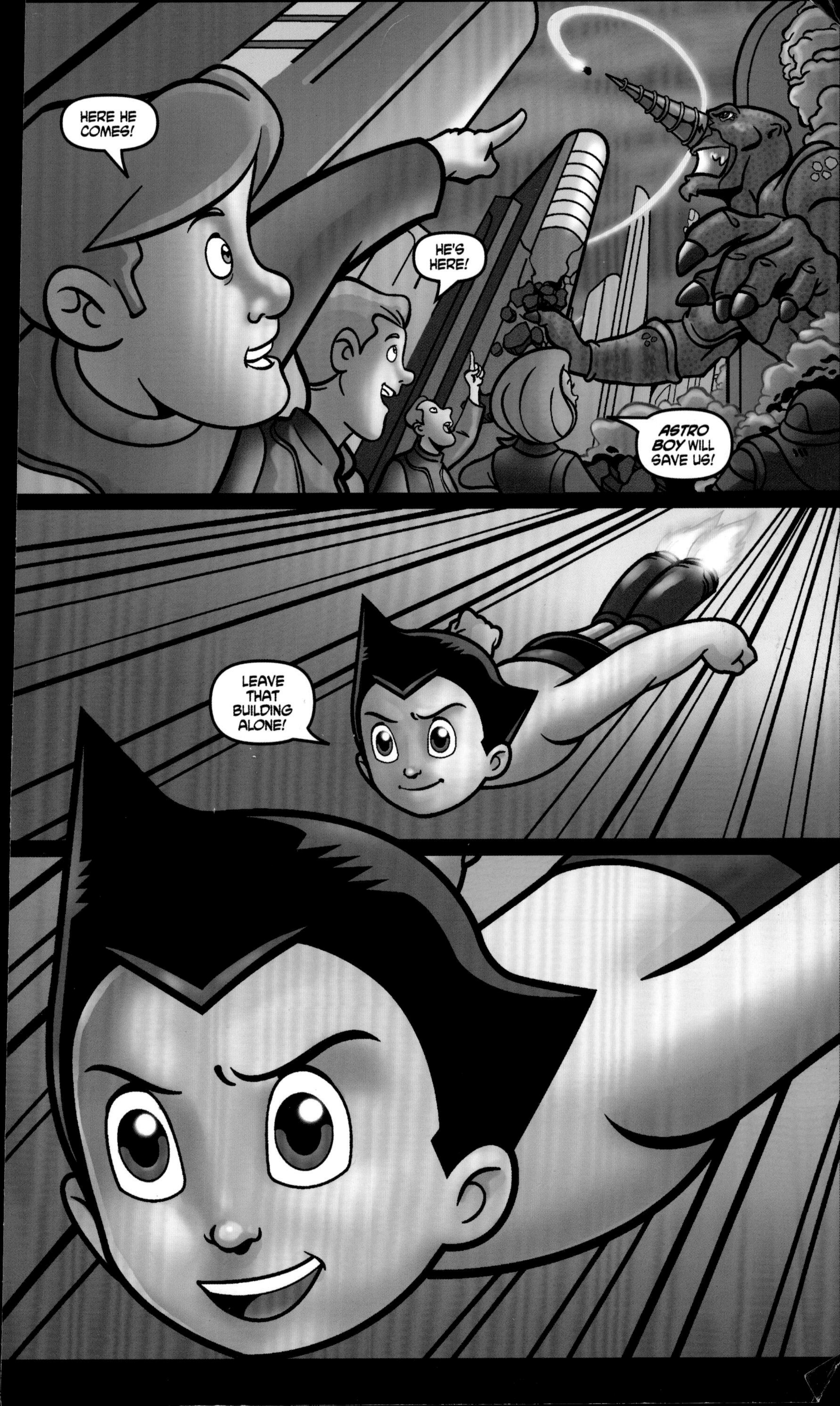
HERE HE COMES!
HE'S HERE!
ASTRO BOY WILL SAVE US!
LEAVE THAT BUILDING ALONE!

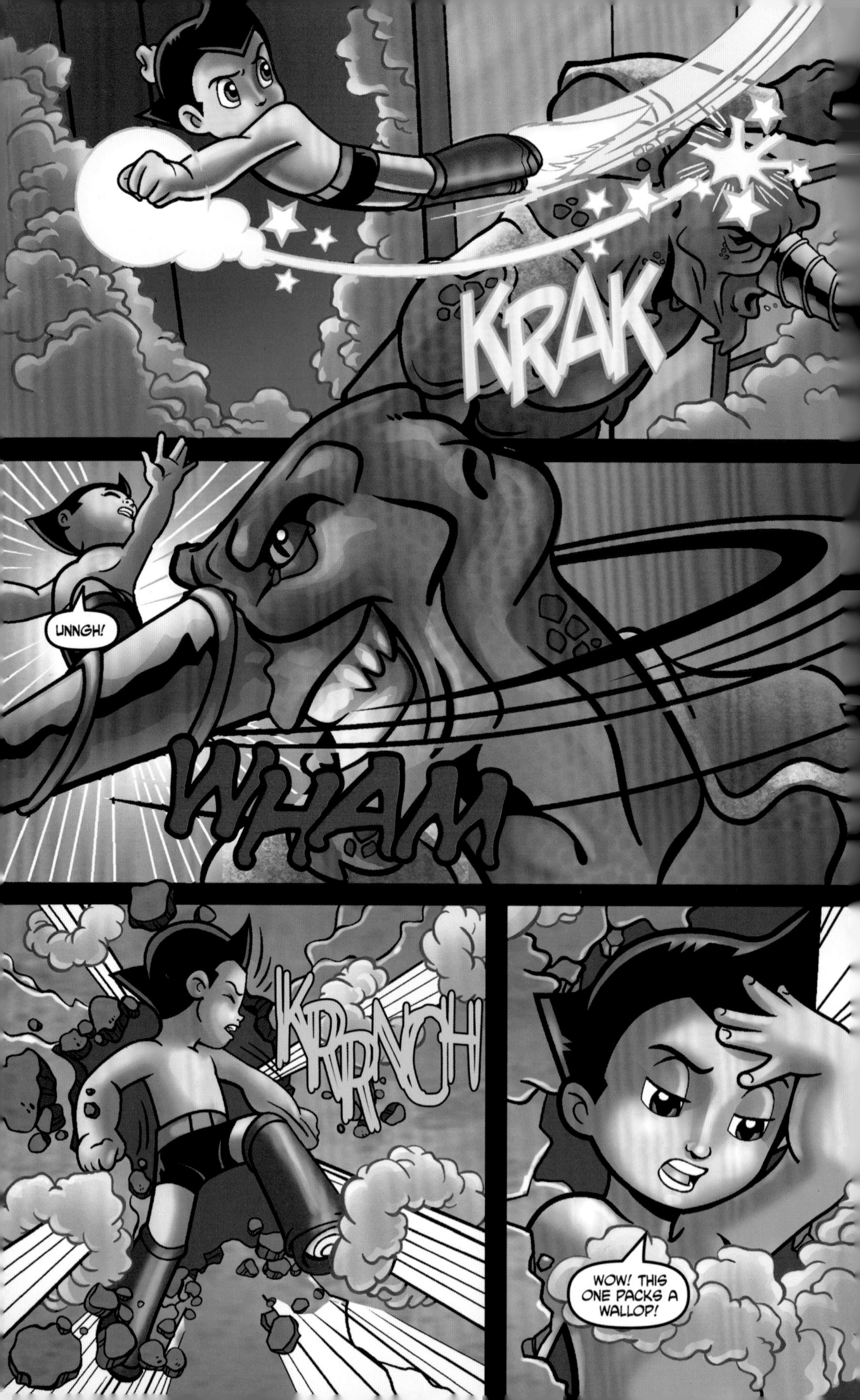
KRAK
UNNGH!
WHAM
KRRNCH
WOW! THIS ONE PACKS A WALLOP!

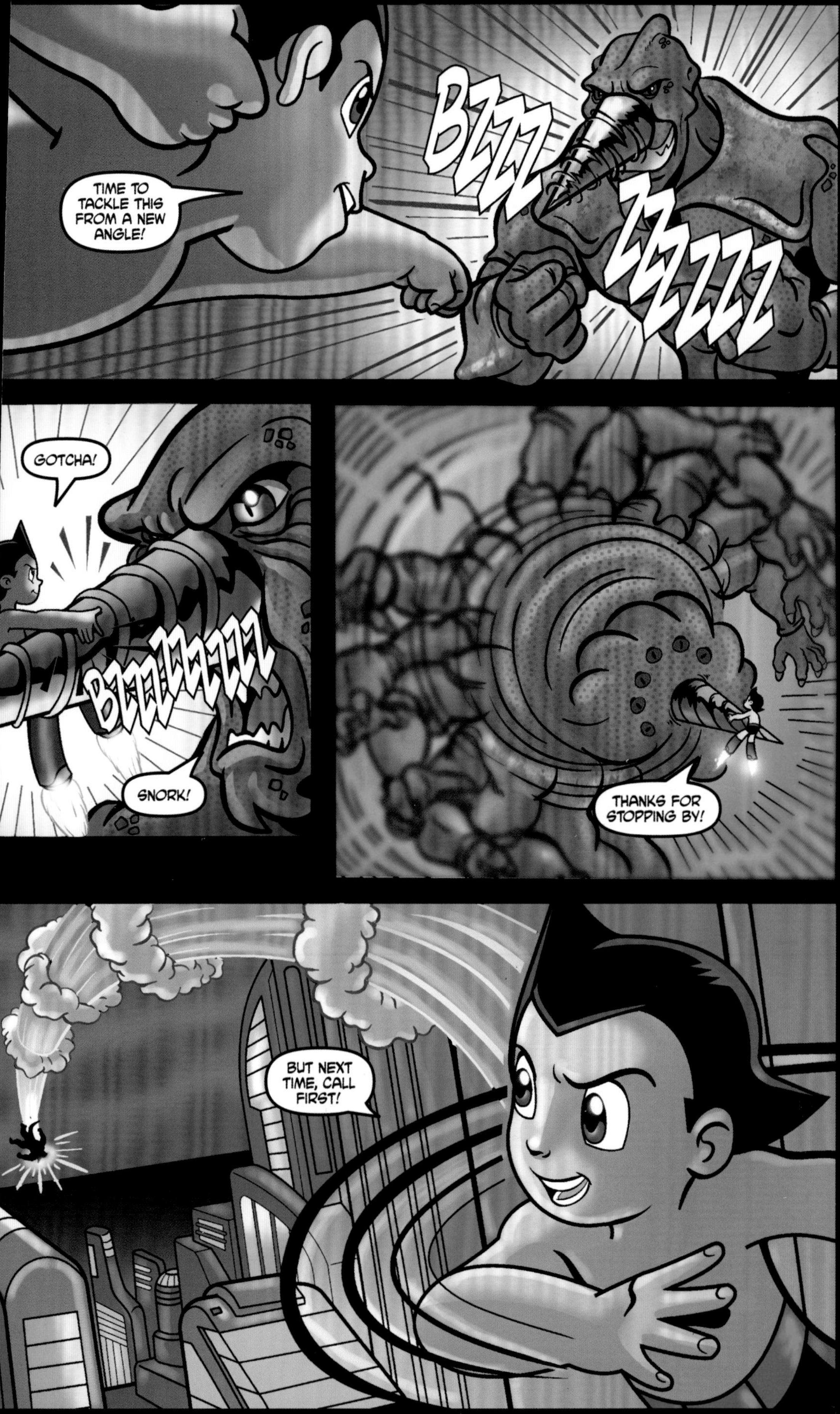
TIME TO TACKLE THIS FROM A NEW ANGLE!
BZZZ
ZZZZZZ
GOTCHA!
BZZZZZZZZZ
SNORK!
THANKS FOR STOPPING BY!
BUT NEXT TIME, CALL FIRST!

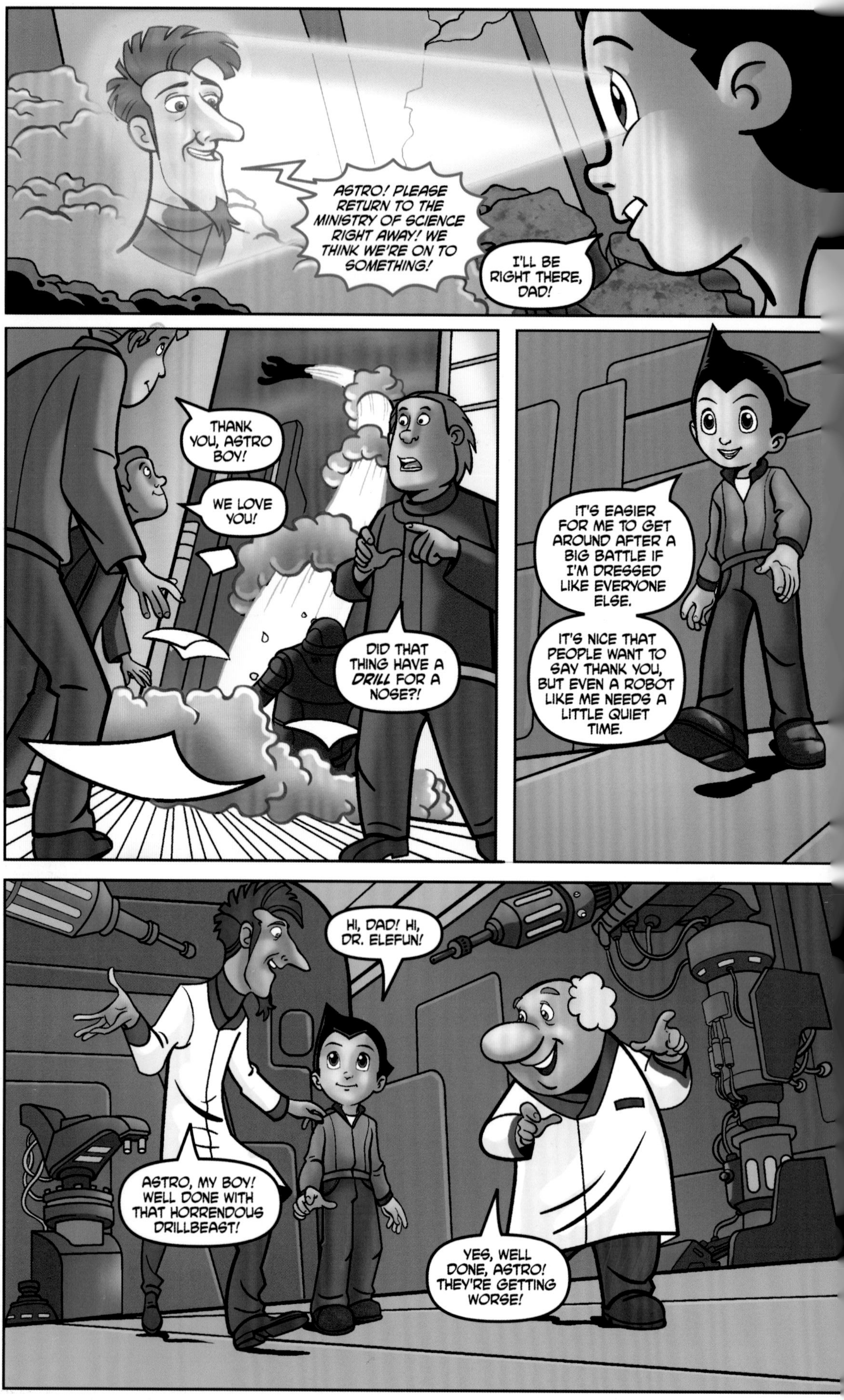
ASTRO! PLEASE RETURN TO THE MINISTRY OF SCIENCE RIGHT AWAY! WE THINK WE'RE ON TO SOMETHING!
I'LL BE RIGHT THERE, DAD!
THANK YOU, ASTRO BOY!
WE LOVE YOU!
DID THAT THING HAVE A *DRILL* FOR A NOSE?!
IT'S EASIER FOR ME TO GET AROUND AFTER A BIG BATTLE IF I'M DRESSED LIKE EVERYONE ELSE.
IT'S NICE THAT PEOPLE WANT TO SAY THANK YOU, BUT EVEN A ROBOT LIKE ME NEEDS A LITTLE QUIET TIME.
HI, DAD! HI, DR. ELEFUN!
ASTRO, MY BOY! WELL DONE WITH THAT HORRENDOUS DRILLBEAST!
YES, WELL DONE, ASTRO! THEY'RE GETTING WORSE!

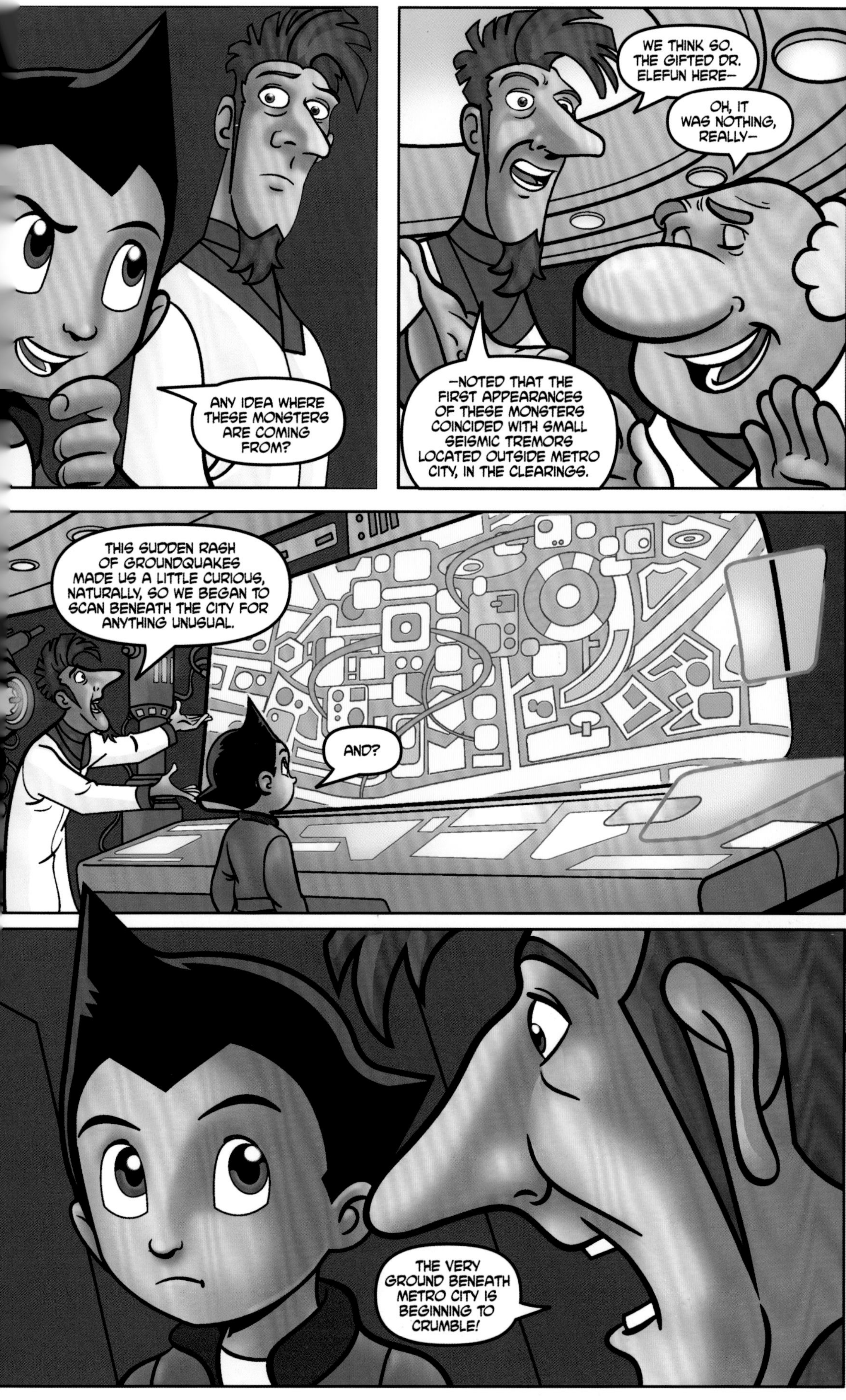

ANY IDEA WHERE THESE MONSTERS ARE COMING FROM?
WE THINK SO. THE GIFTED DR. ELEFUN HERE–
OH, IT WAS NOTHING, REALLY–
–NOTED THAT THE FIRST APPEARANCES OF THESE MONSTERS COINCIDED WITH SMALL SEISMIC TREMORS LOCATED OUTSIDE METRO CITY, IN THE CLEARINGS.
THIS SUDDEN RASH OF GROUNDQUAKES MADE US A LITTLE CURIOUS, NATURALLY, SO WE BEGAN TO SCAN BENEATH THE CITY FOR ANYTHING UNUSUAL.
AND?
THE VERY GROUND BENEATH METRO CITY IS BEGINNING TO CRUMBLE!

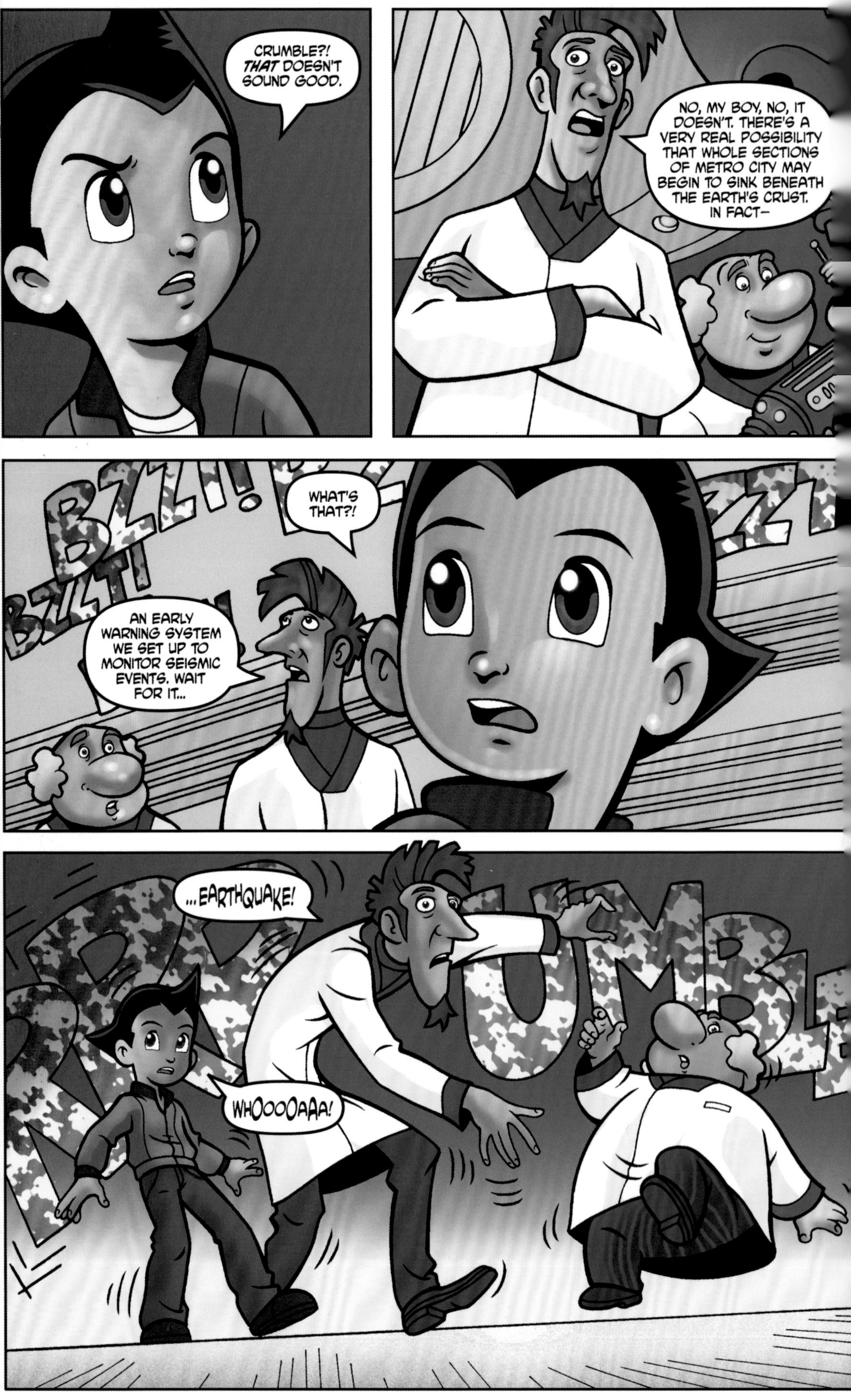
CRUMBLE?! THAT DOESN'T SOUND GOOD.
NO, MY BOY, NO, IT DOESN'T. THERE'S A VERY REAL POSSIBILITY THAT WHOLE SECTIONS OF METRO CITY MAY BEGIN TO SINK BENEATH THE EARTH'S CRUST. IN FACT—
WHAT'S THAT?!
AN EARLY WARNING SYSTEM WE SET UP TO MONITOR SEISMIC EVENTS. WAIT FOR IT...
...EARTHQUAKE!
WHOOOOAAA!

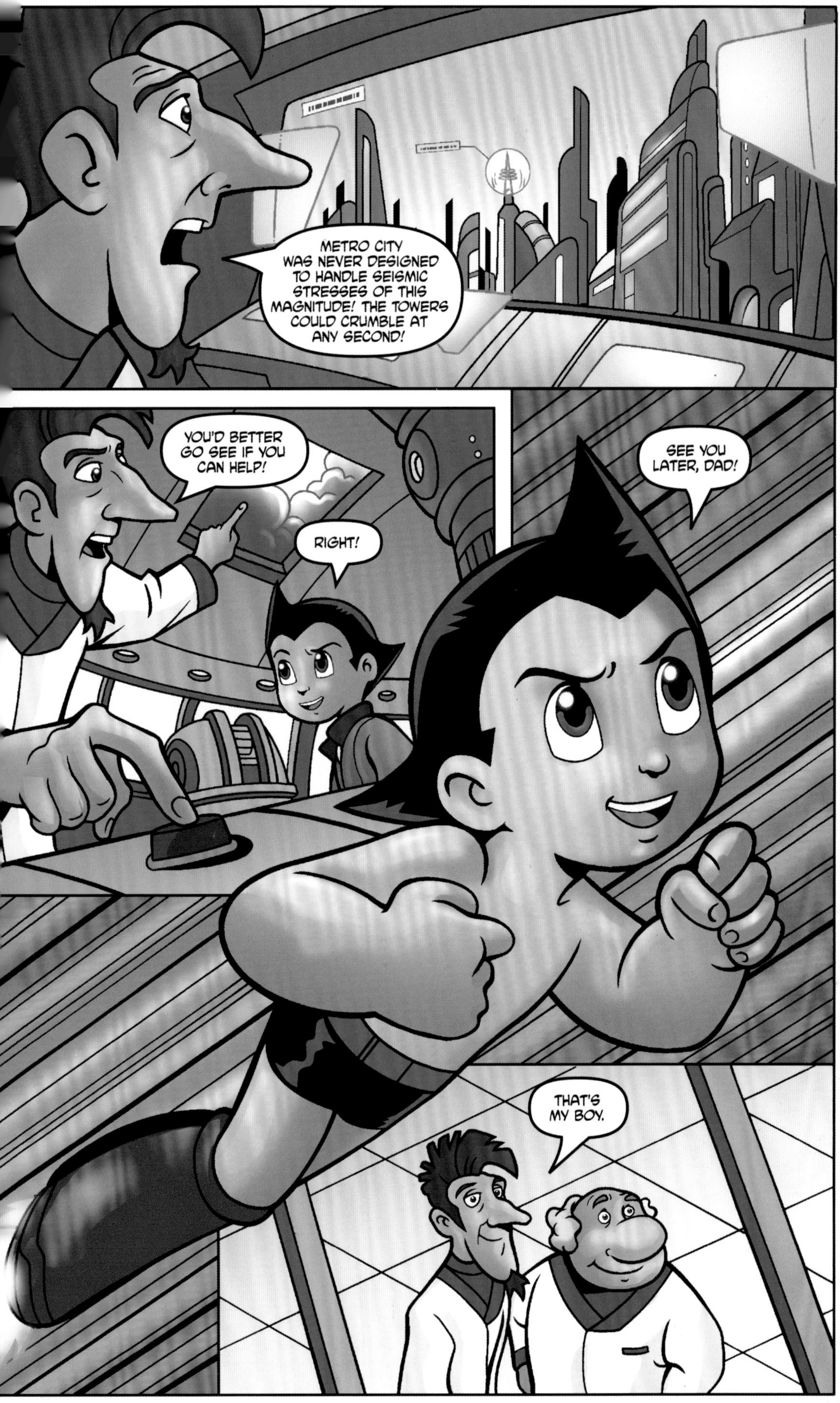
METRO CITY WAS NEVER DESIGNED TO HANDLE SEISMIC STRESSES OF THIS MAGNITUDE! THE TOWERS COULD CRUMBLE AT ANY SECOND!
YOU'D BETTER GO SEE IF YOU CAN HELP!
RIGHT!
SEE YOU LATER, DAD!
THAT'S MY BOY.

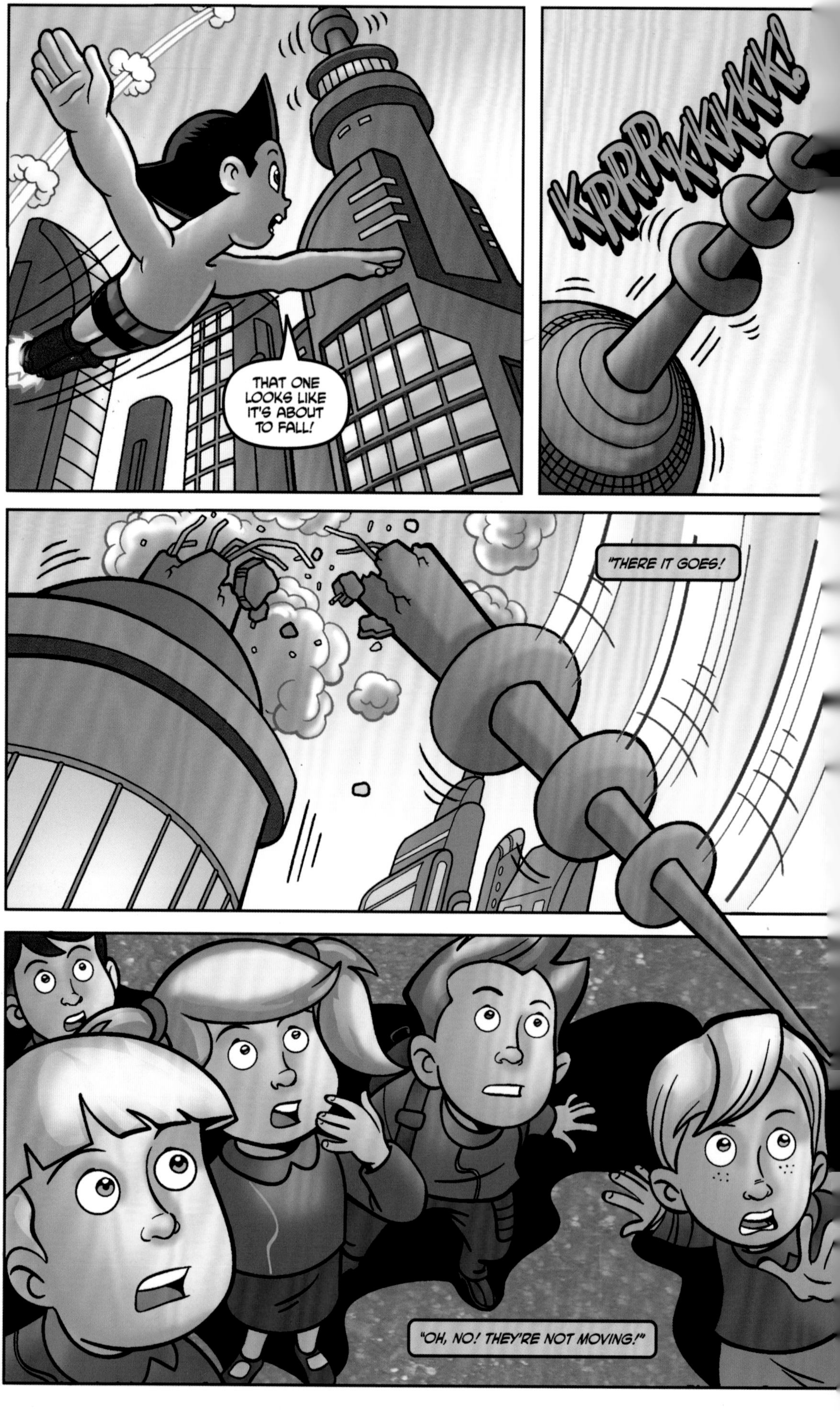
THAT ONE LOOKS LIKE IT'S ABOUT TO FALL!
KRRRKKKK!
"THERE IT GOES!
"OH, NO! THEY'RE NOT MOVING!"

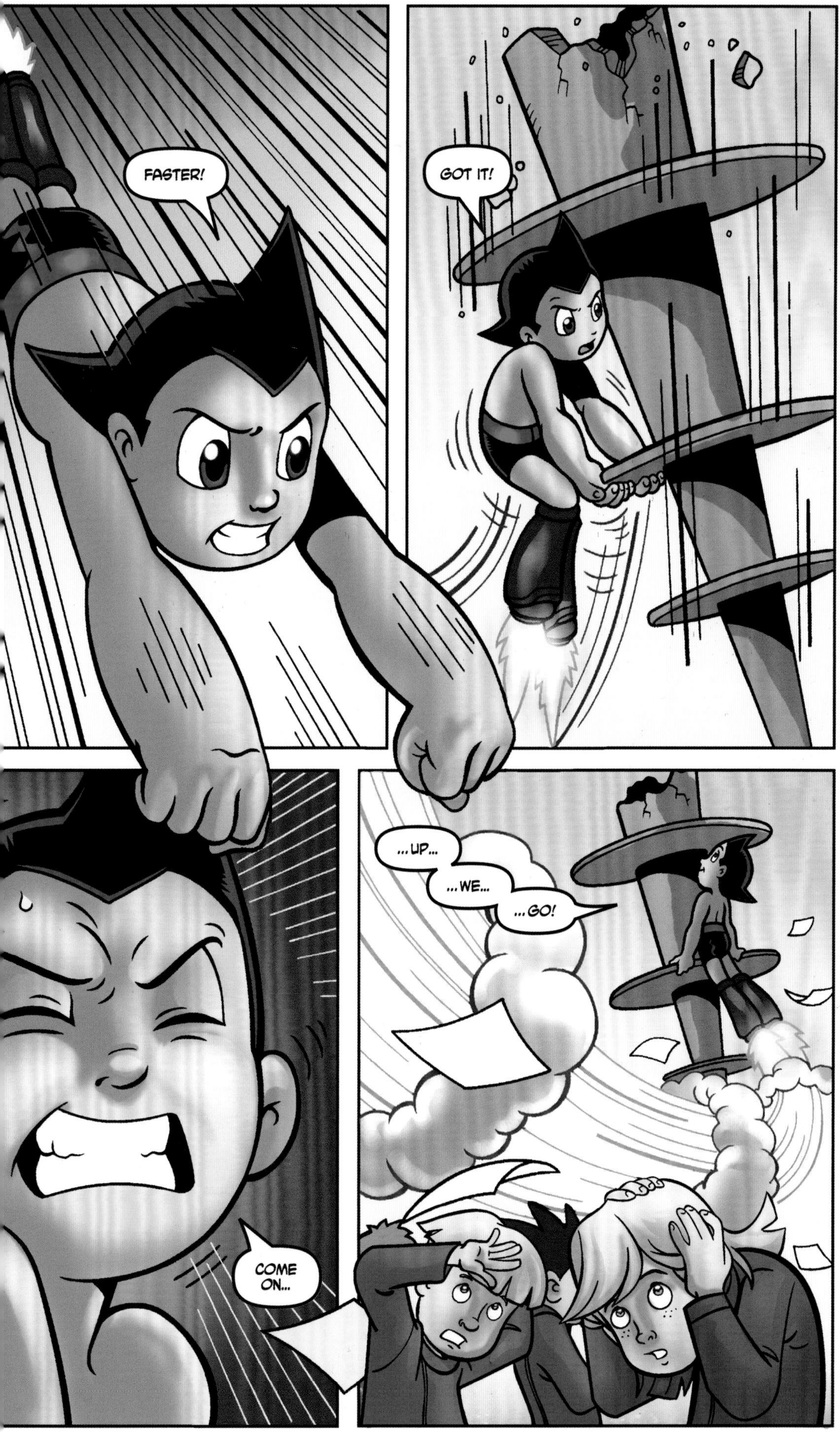
FASTER!
GOT IT!
COME ON...
...UP...
...WE...
...GO!

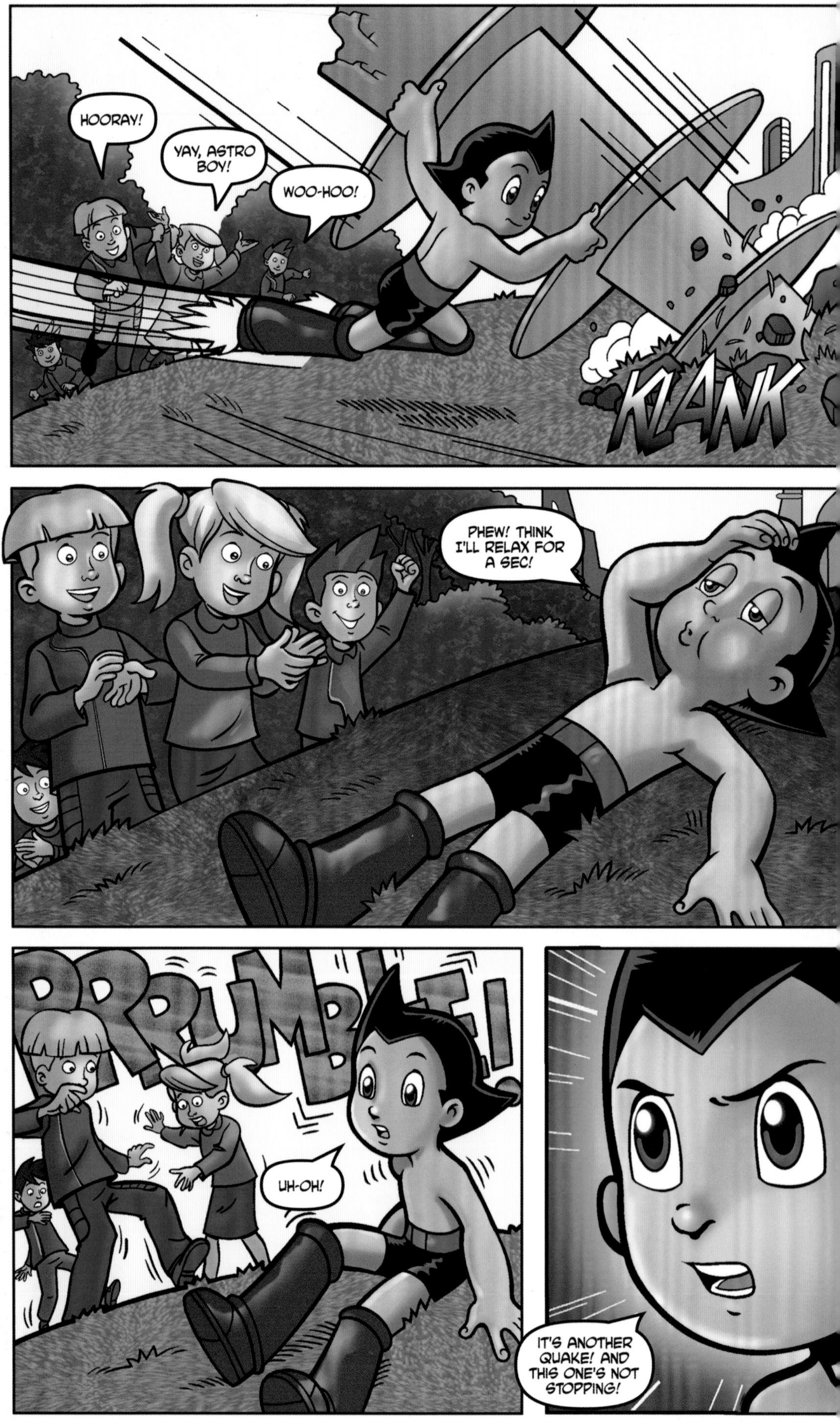
HOORAY!
YAY, ASTRO BOY!
WOO-HOO!
KLANK
PHEW! THINK I'LL RELAX FOR A SEC!
UH-OH!
IT'S ANOTHER QUAKE! AND THIS ONE'S NOT STOPPING!

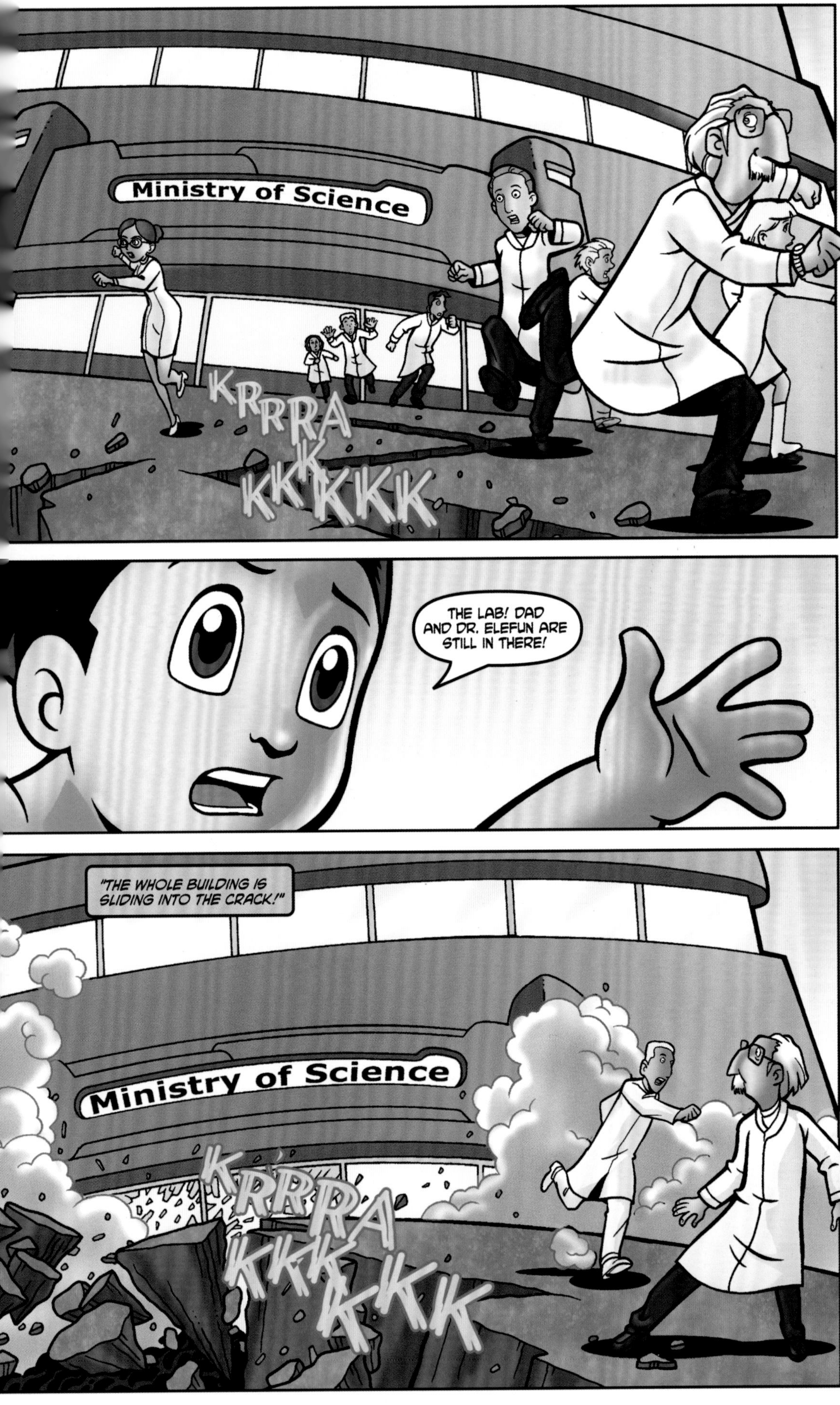
Ministry of Science
KRRRAKKKKKK
THE LAB! DAD AND DR. ELEFUN ARE STILL IN THERE!
"THE WHOLE BUILDING IS SLIDING INTO THE CRACK!"
Ministry of Science
KRRRAKKKKKK

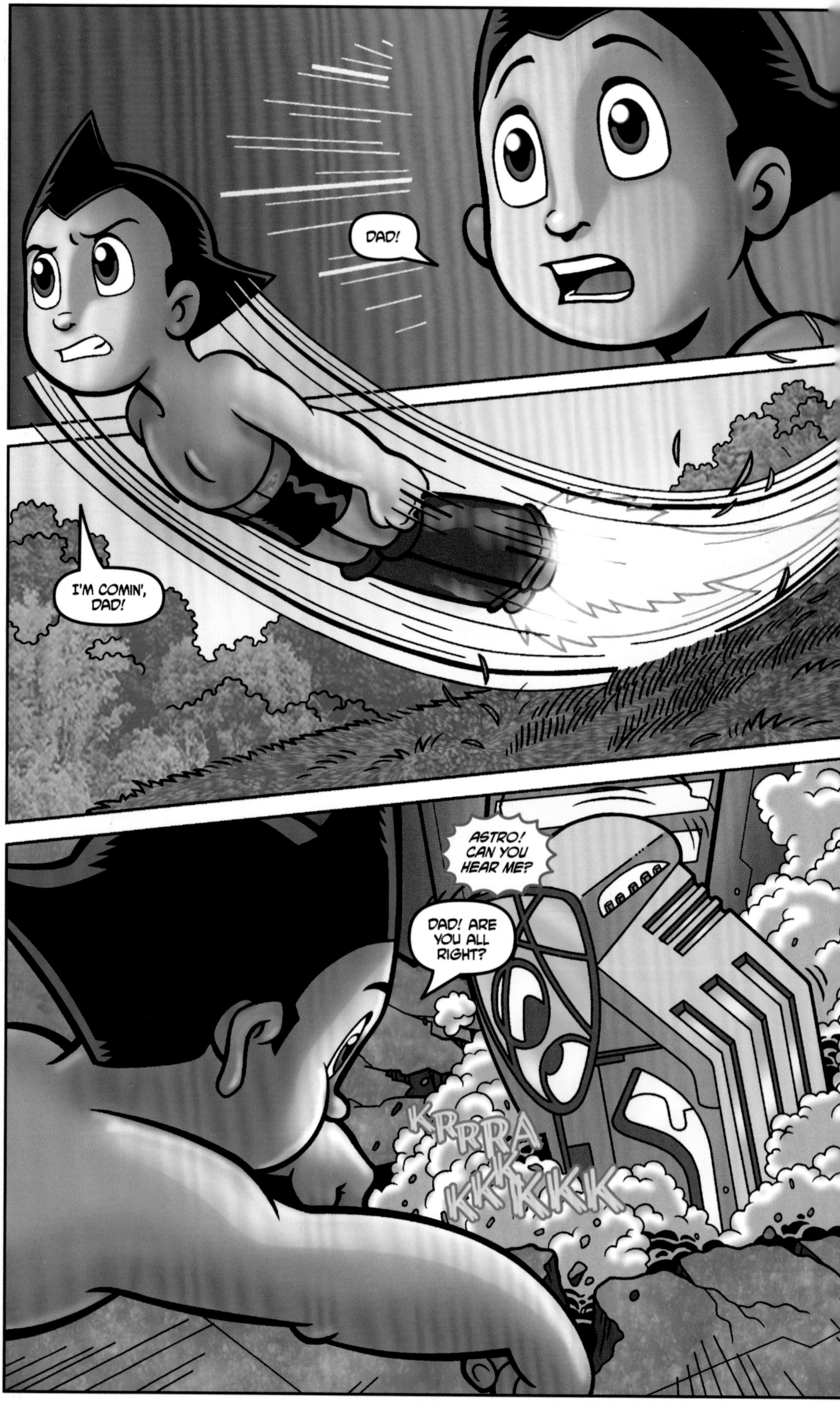
DAD!
I'M COMIN', DAD!
ASTRO! CAN YOU HEAR ME?
DAD! ARE YOU ALL RIGHT?
KRRRAKKKKKK

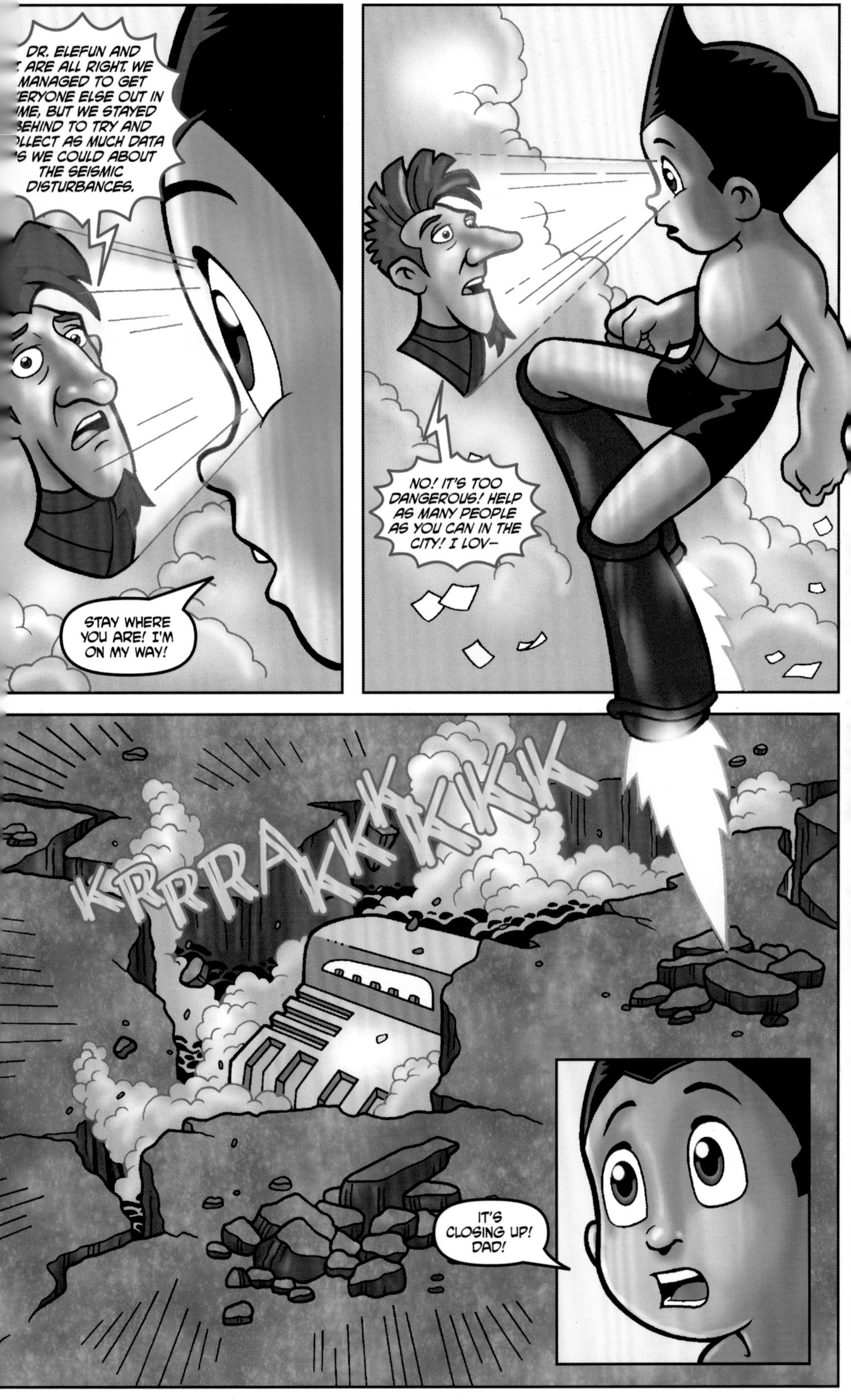
DR. ELEFUN AND
ARE ALL RIGHT. WE MANAGED TO GET
ERYONE ELSE OUT IN
ME, BUT WE STAYED
BEHIND TO TRY AND
LLECT AS MUCH DATA
S WE COULD ABOUT THE SEISMIC DISTURBANCES.
STAY WHERE YOU ARE! I'M ON MY WAY!
NO! IT'S TOO DANGEROUS! HELP AS MANY PEOPLE AS YOU CAN IN THE CITY! I LOV–
KRRRAKKKKKK
IT'S CLOSING UP! DAD!

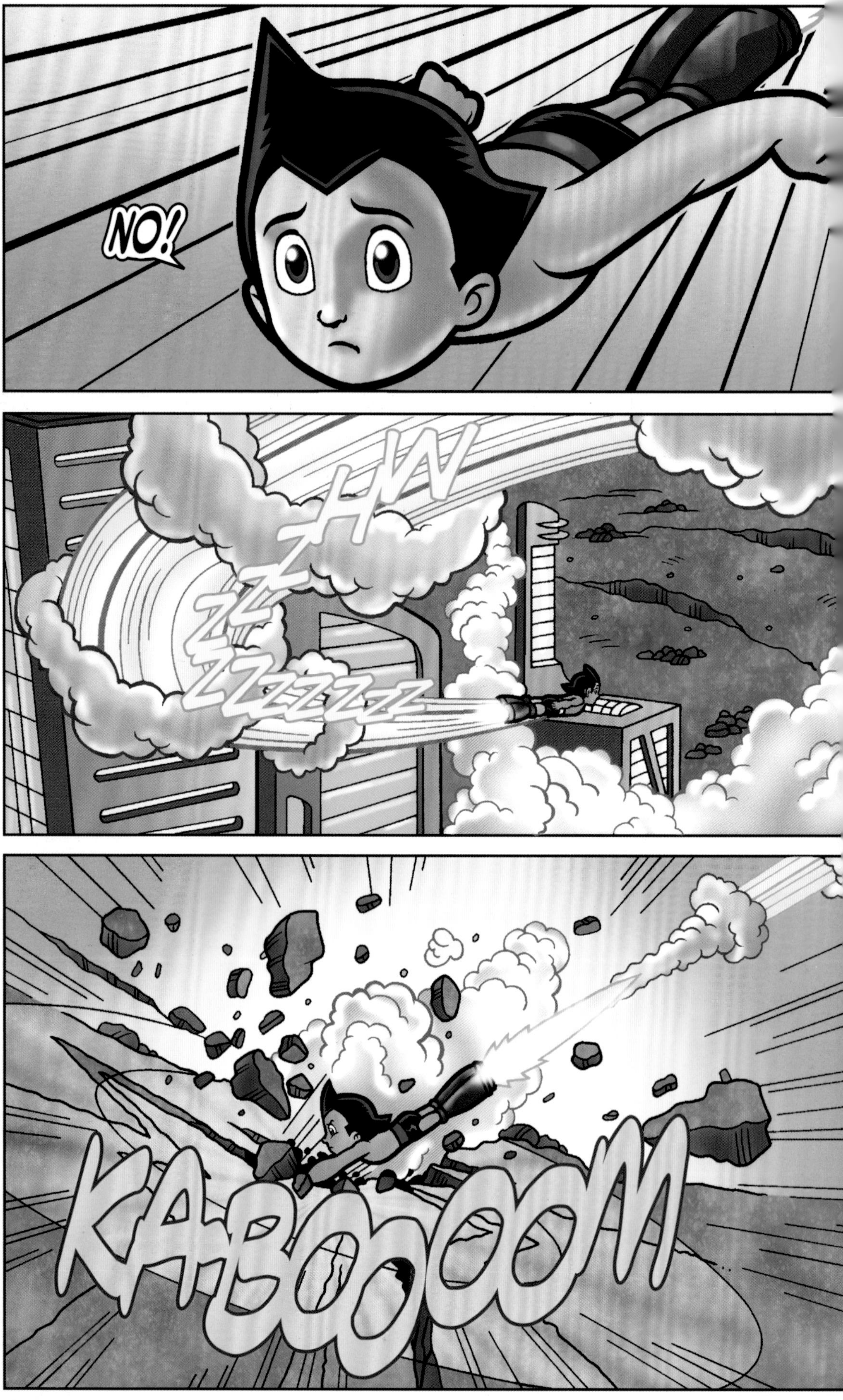
NO!
HWZZZZZZZZZ
KABOOOOM

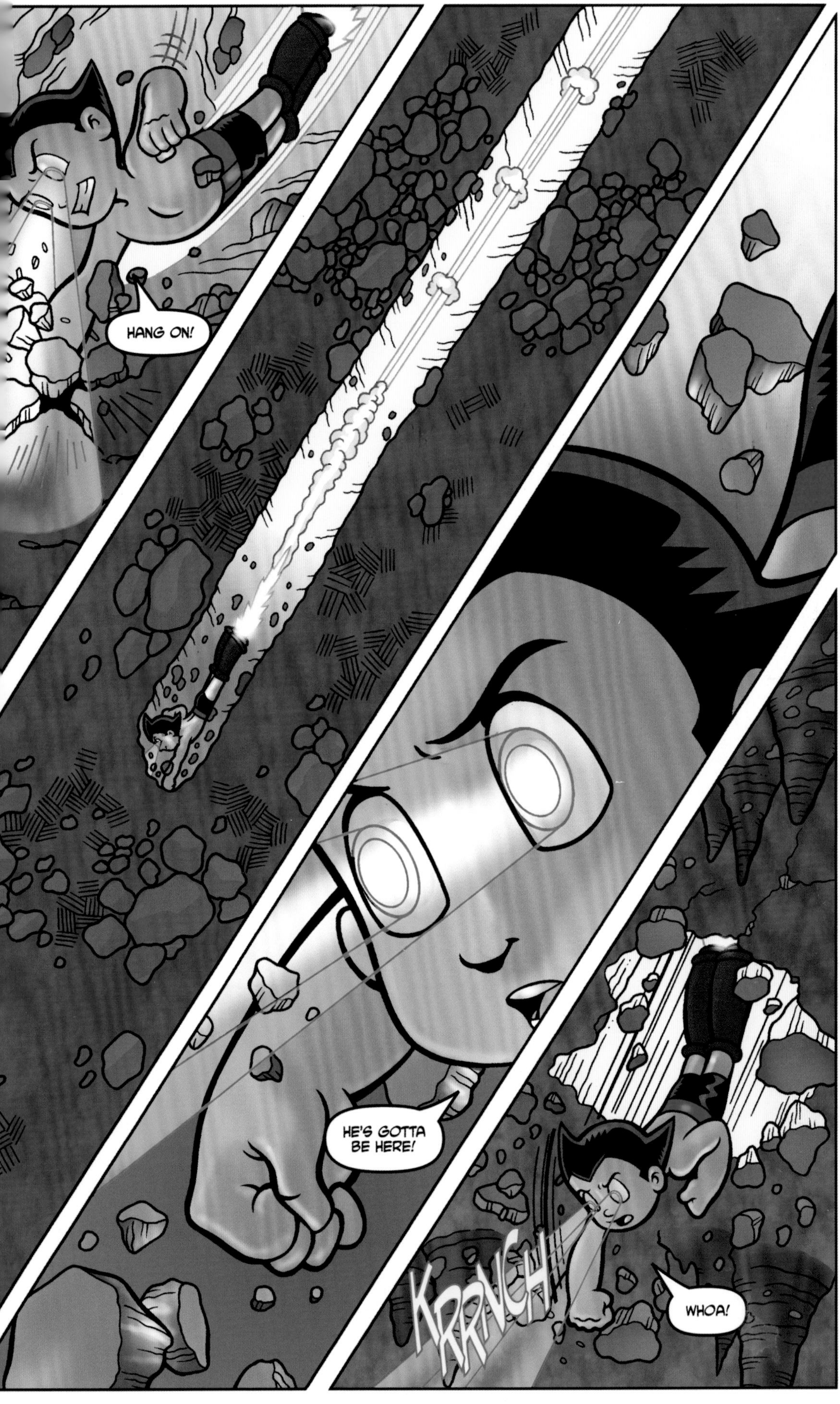
HANG ON!
HE'S GOTTA BE HERE!
KRRNCH
WHOA!

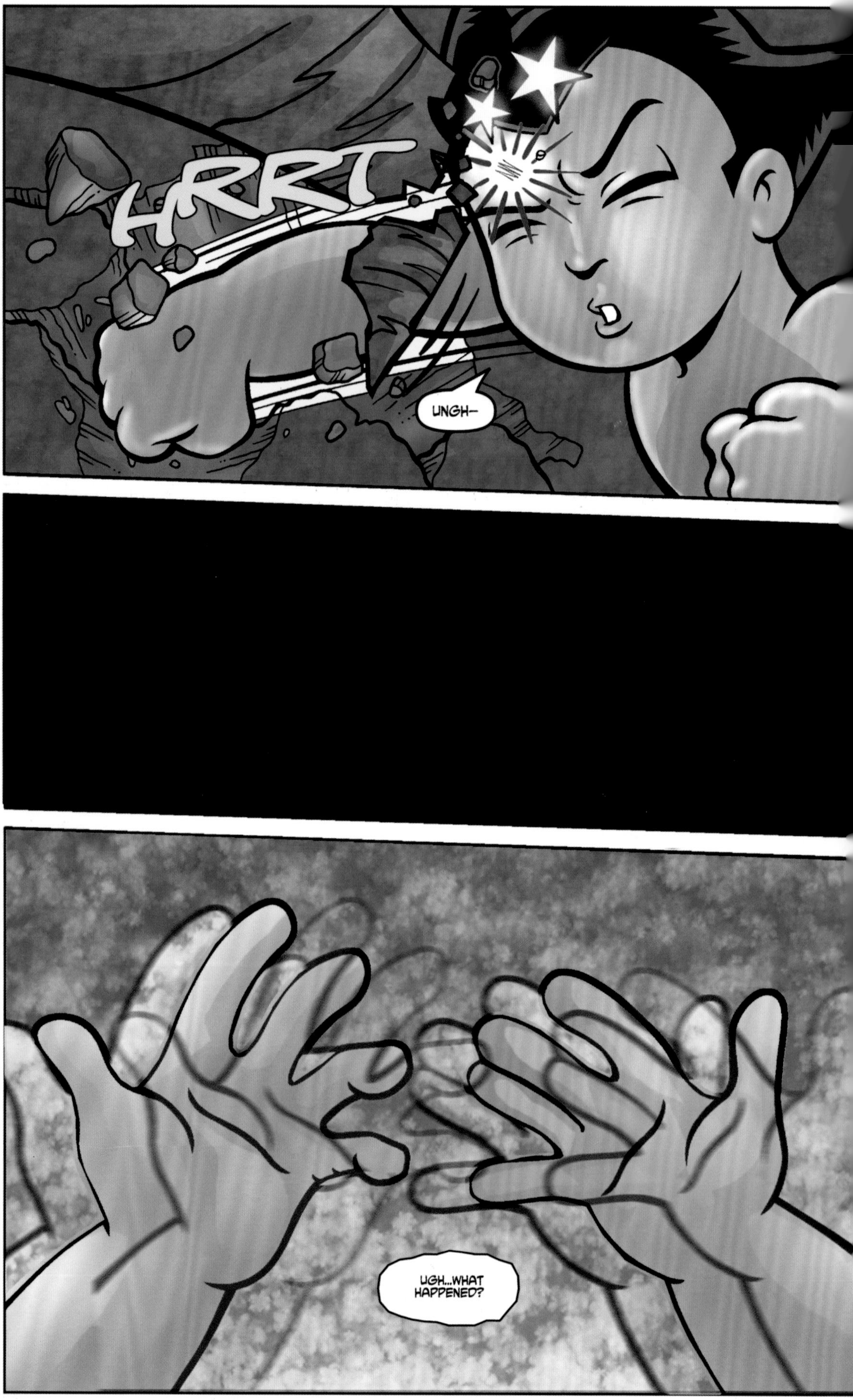
HRRT
UNGH–
UGH...WHAT HAPPENED?

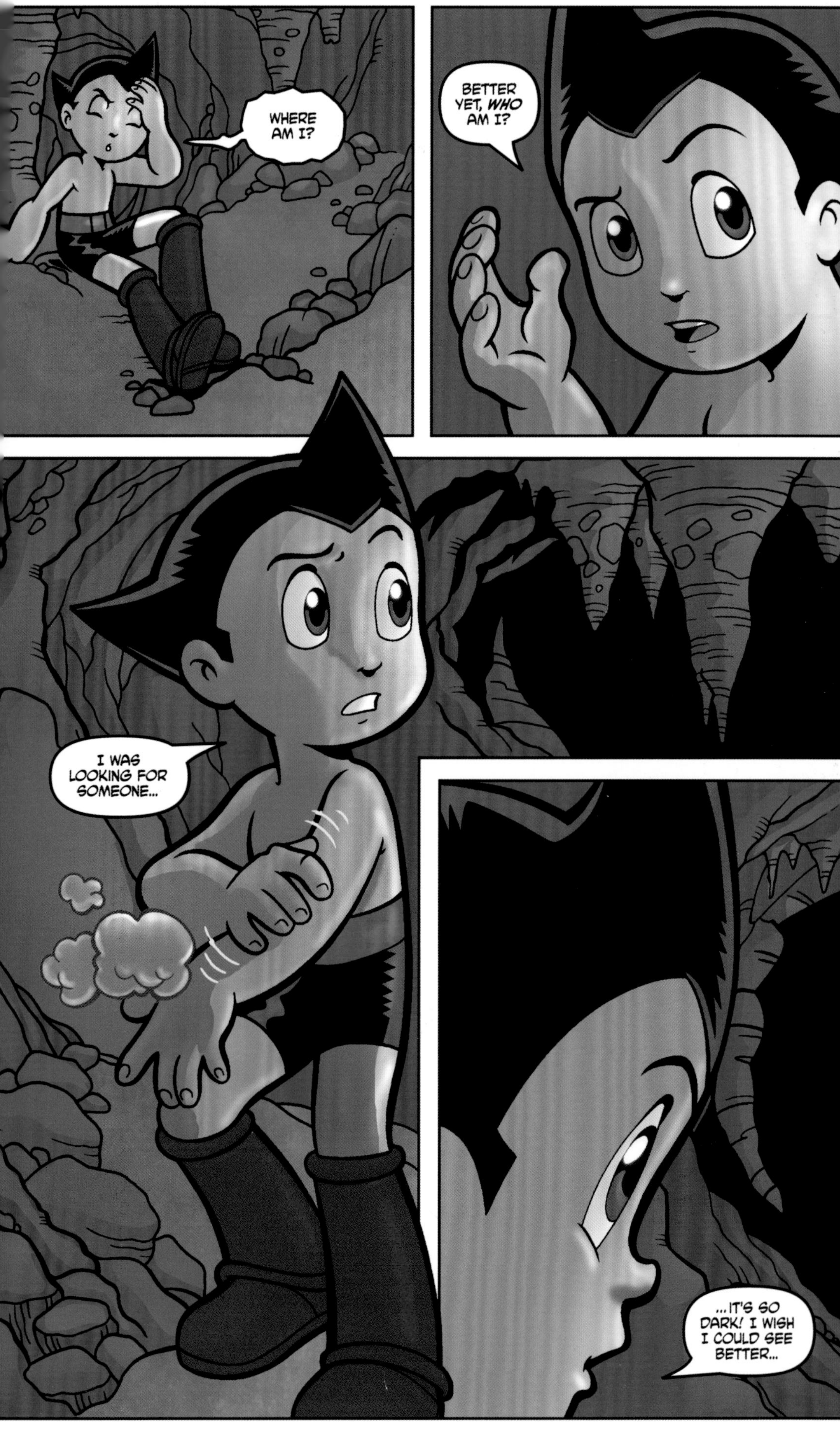
WHERE AM I?
BETTER YET, *WHO* AM I?
I WAS LOOKING FOR SOMEONE...
...IT'S SO DARK! I WISH I COULD SEE BETTER...

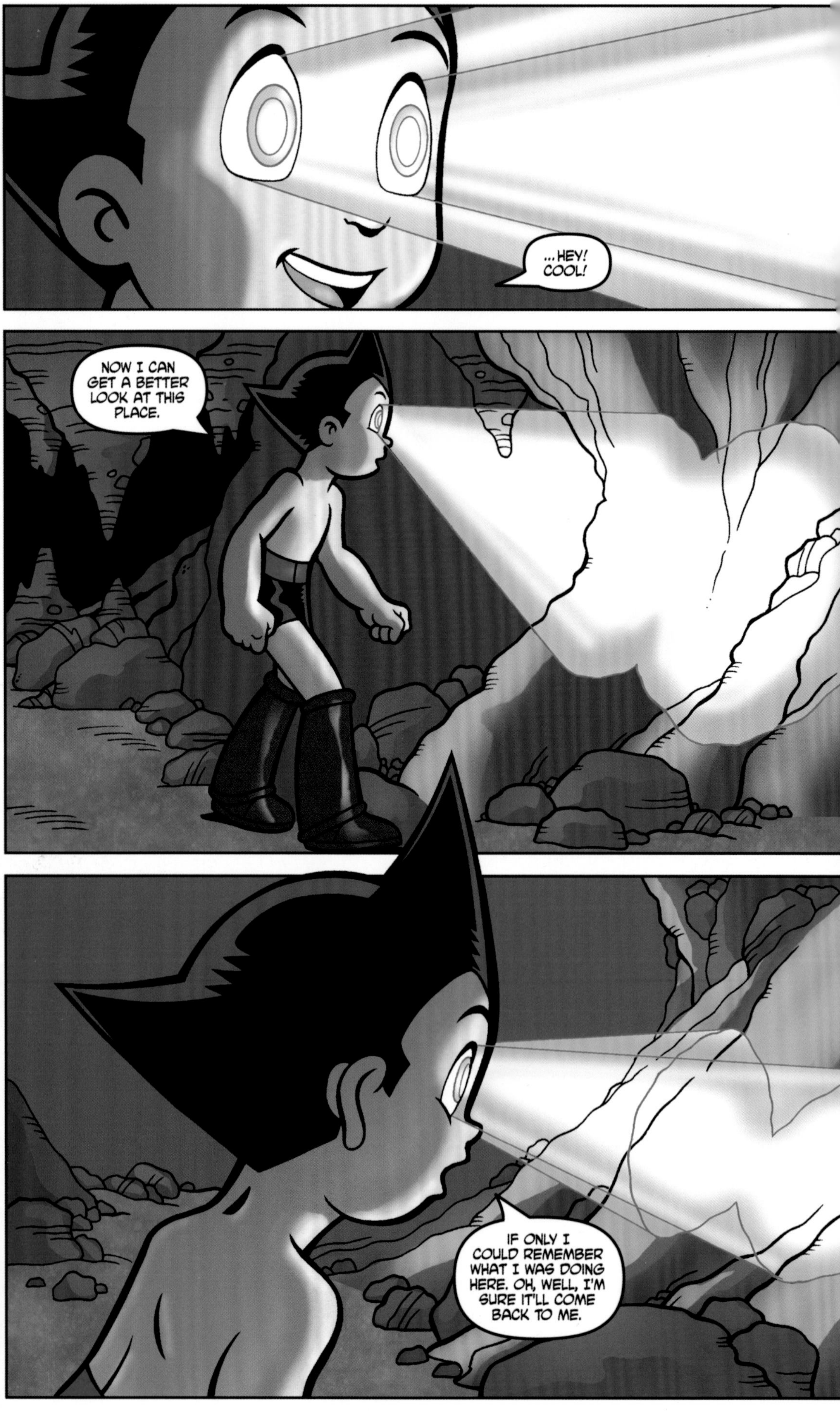
...HEY! COOL!
NOW I CAN GET A BETTER LOOK AT THIS PLACE.
IF ONLY I COULD REMEMBER WHAT I WAS DOING HERE. OH, WELL, I'M SURE IT'LL COME BACK TO ME.

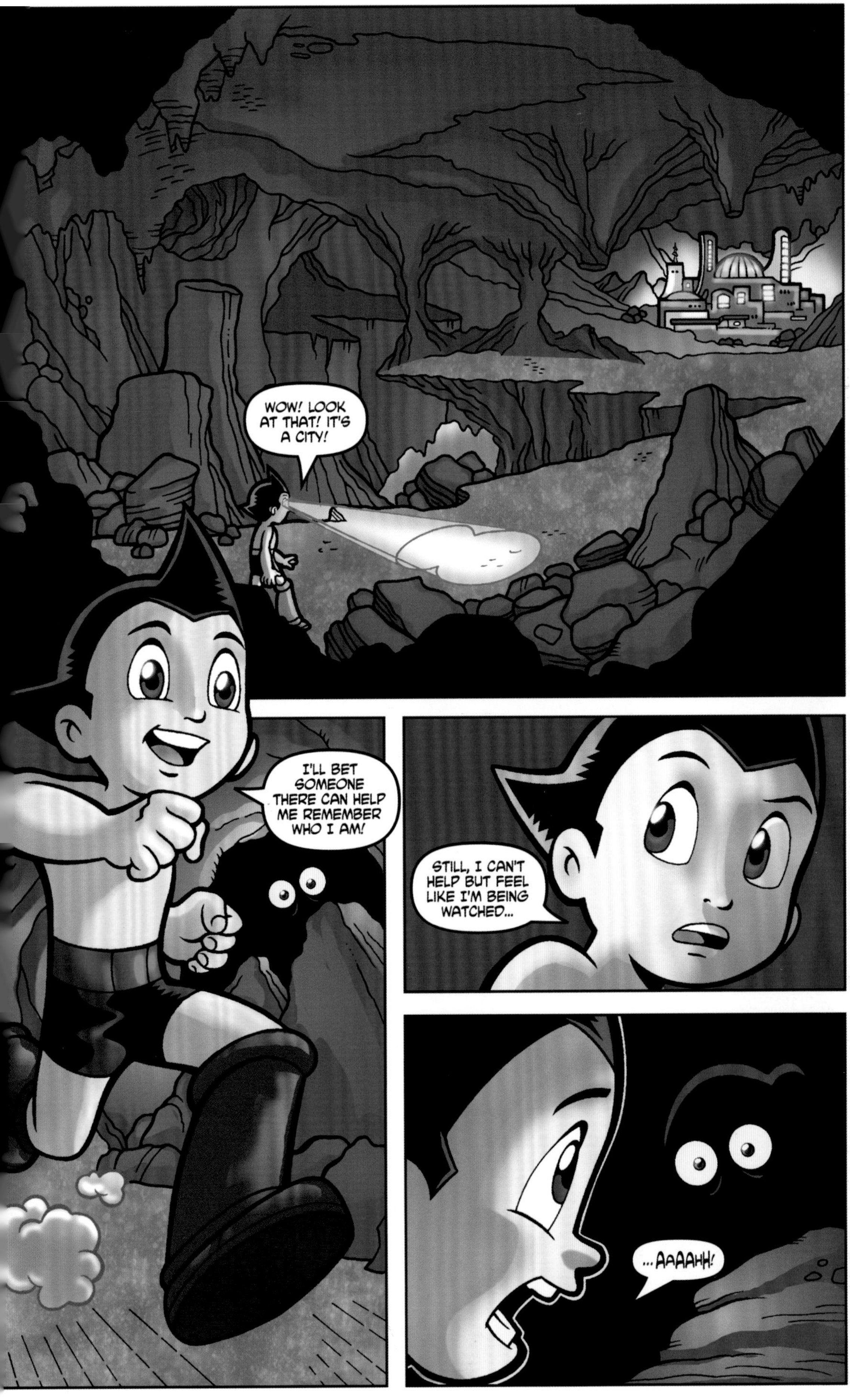
WOW! LOOK AT THAT! IT'S A CITY!
I'LL BET SOMEONE THERE CAN HELP ME REMEMBER WHO I AM!
STILL, I CAN'T HELP BUT FEEL LIKE I'M BEING WATCHED...
...AAAAHH!

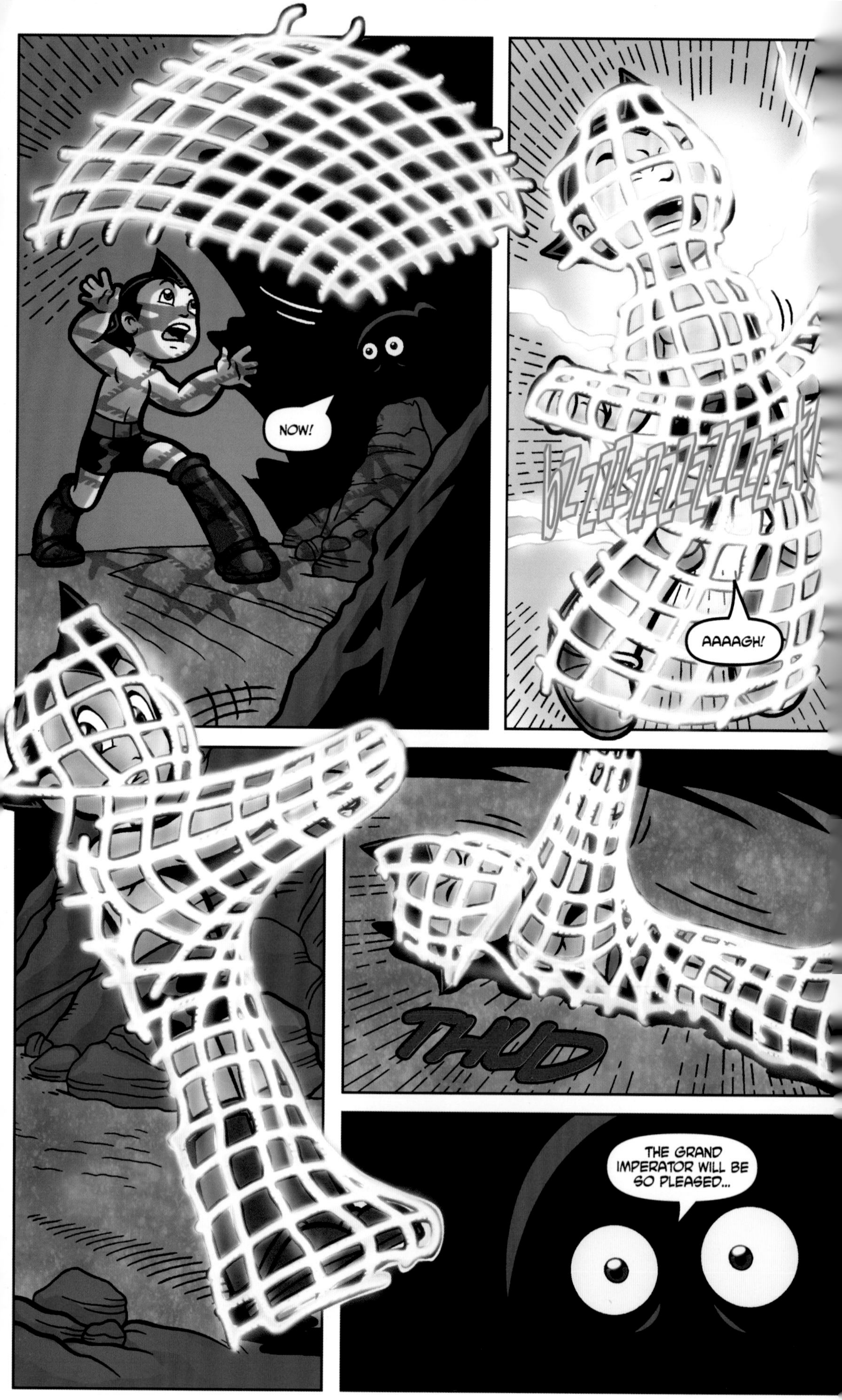
NOW!
BZZZZZZZZZZZZZZZZZT!
AAAAGH!
THUD
THE GRAND IMPERATOR WILL BE SO PLEASED...

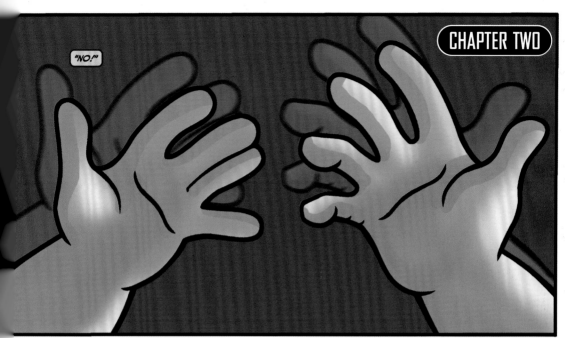

CHAPTER TWO

"NO!"

NO!

WHOA... WHERE AM I?

KNOK KNOK KNOK

HOW ARE YOU FEELING?

UHH... OKAY, I GUESS...

MOST EXCELLENT. THE GRAND IMPERATOR REQUESTS YOUR PRESENCE.

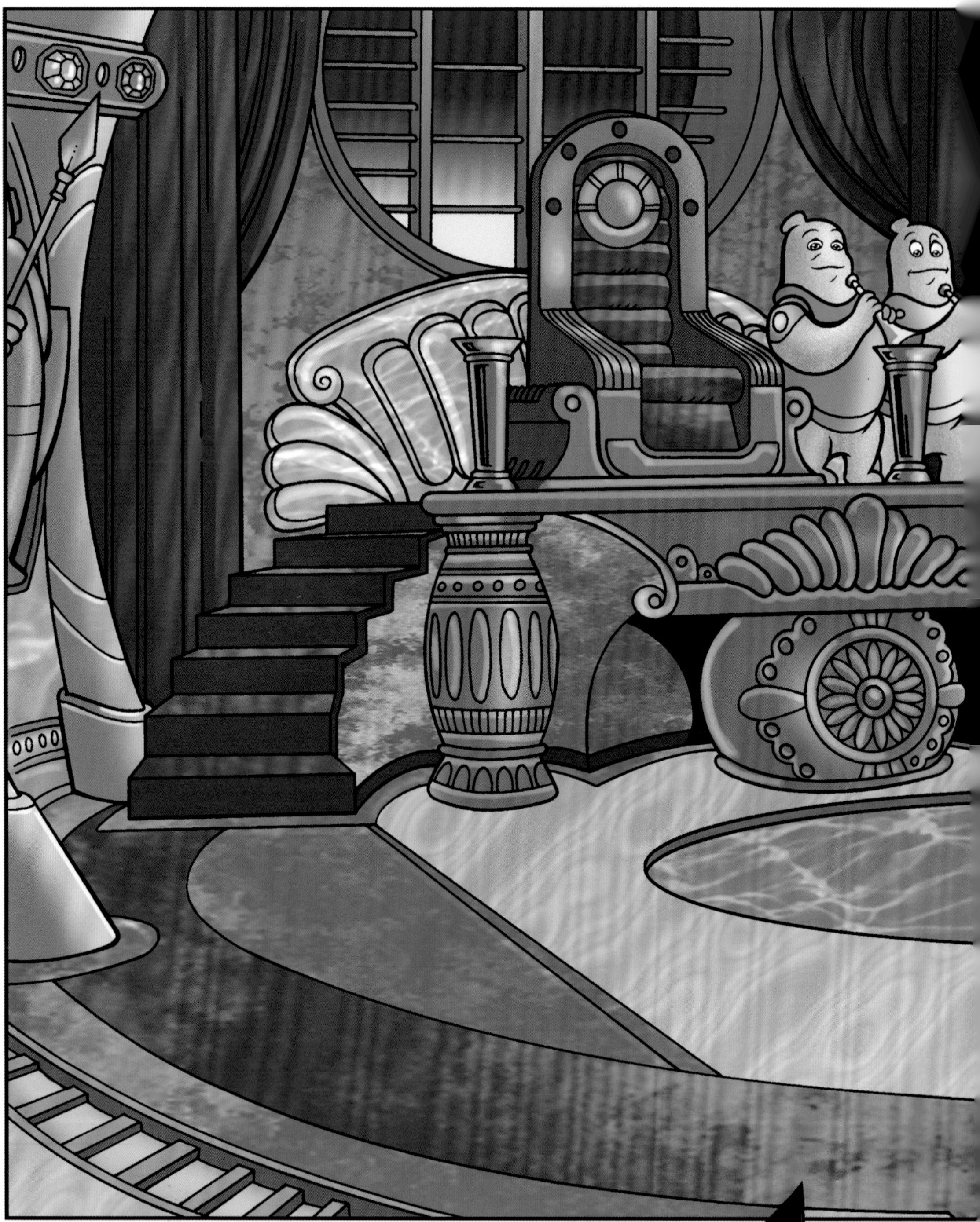

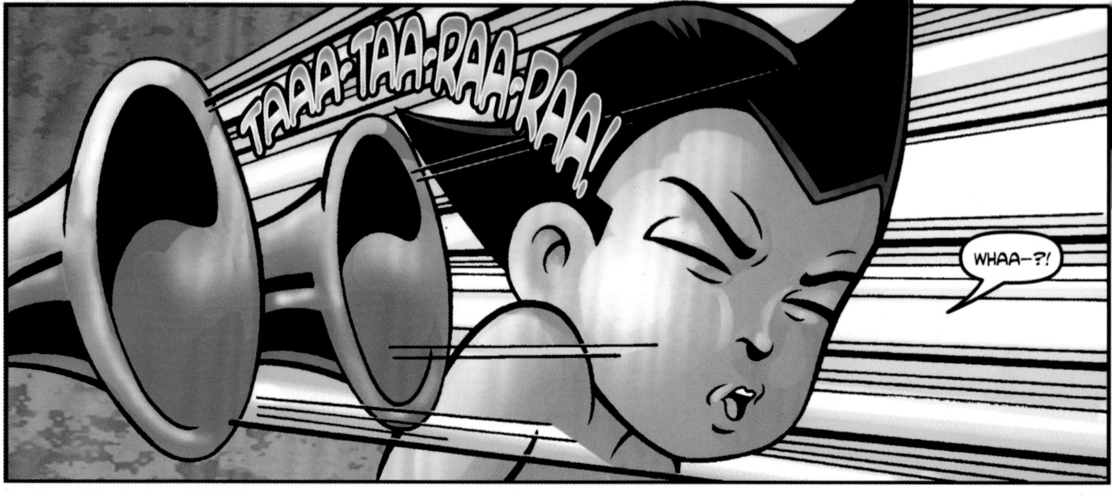
TAAA-TAA-RAA-RAA!
WHAA--?!

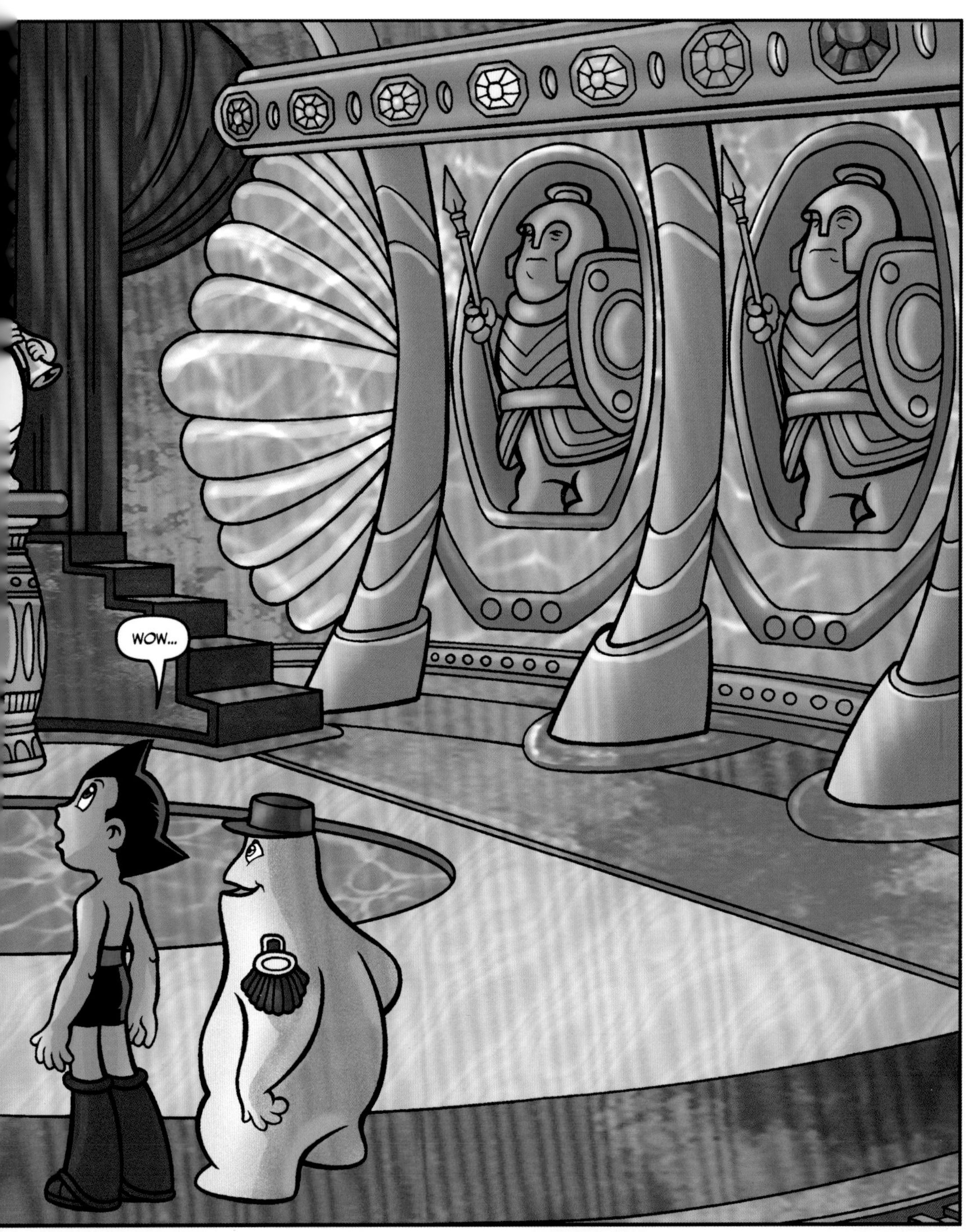
WOW...

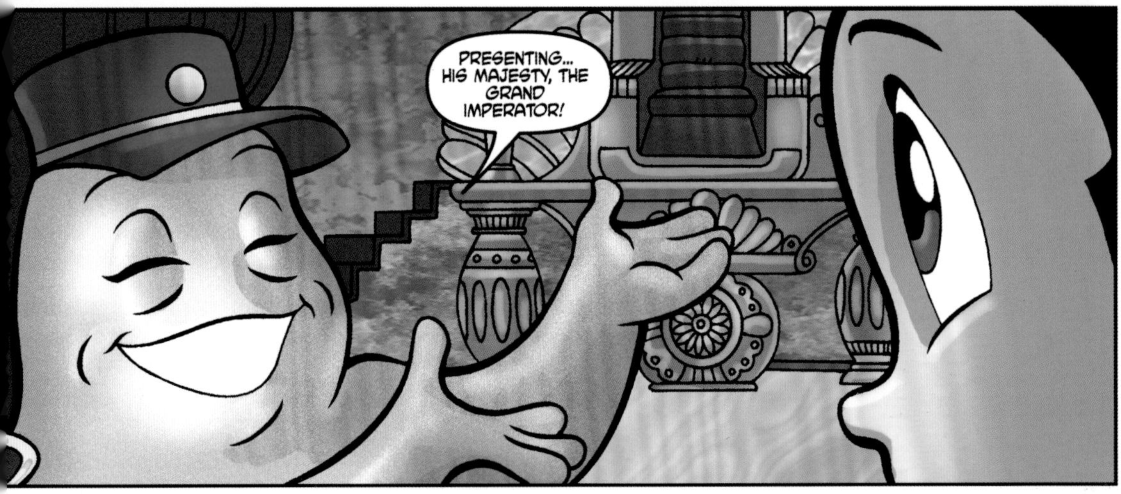
PRESENTING... HIS MAJESTY, THE GRAND IMPERATOR!

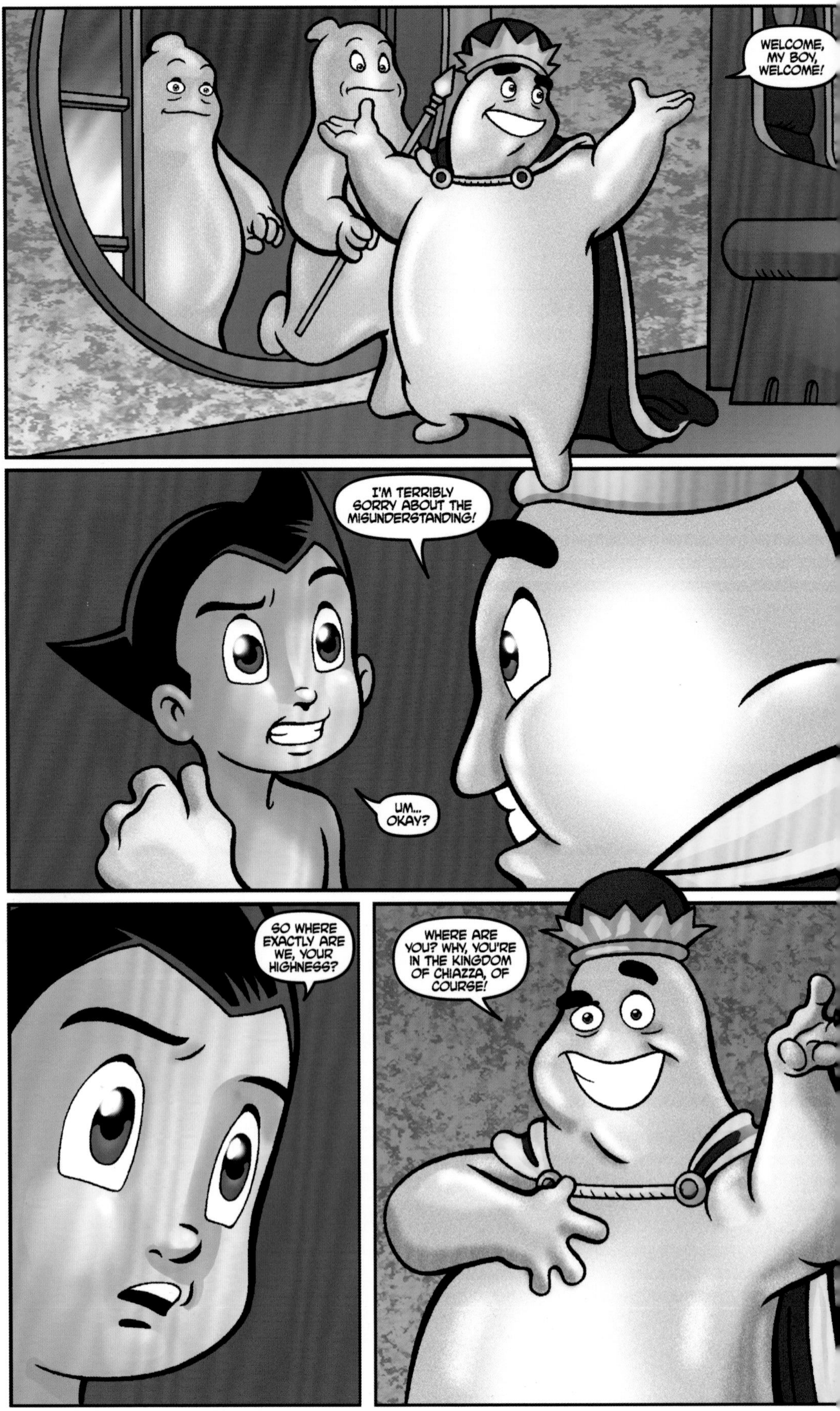

WELCOME, MY BOY, WELCOME!
I'M TERRIBLY SORRY ABOUT THE MISUNDERSTANDING!
UM... OKAY?
SO WHERE EXACTLY ARE WE, YOUR HIGHNESS?
WHERE ARE YOU? WHY, YOU'RE IN THE KINGDOM OF CHIAZZA, OF COURSE!

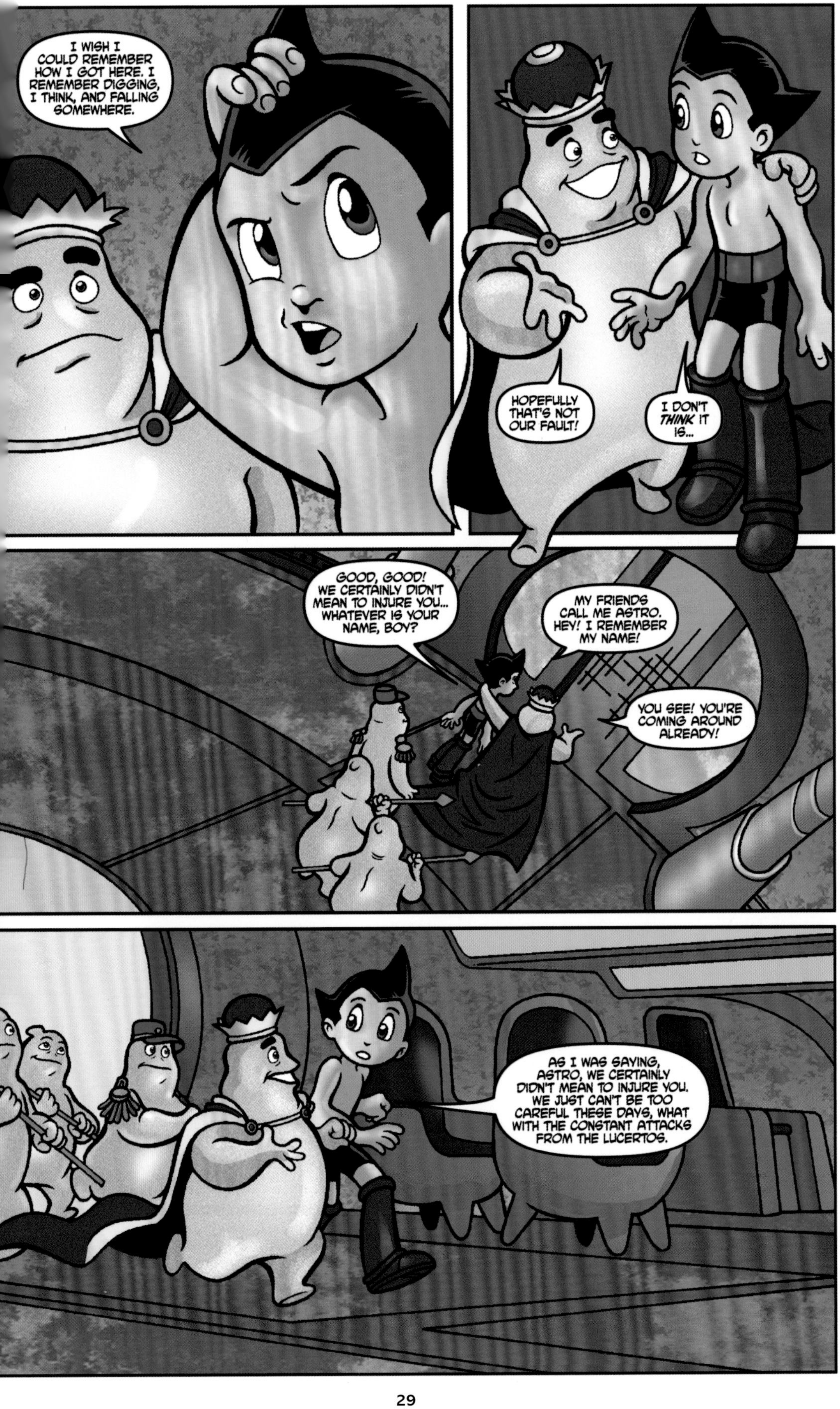
I WISH I COULD REMEMBER HOW I GOT HERE. I REMEMBER DIGGING, I THINK, AND FALLING SOMEWHERE.
HOPEFULLY THAT'S NOT OUR FAULT!
I DON'T *THINK* IT IS...
GOOD, GOOD! WE CERTAINLY DIDN'T MEAN TO INJURE YOU... WHATEVER IS YOUR NAME, BOY?
MY FRIENDS CALL ME ASTRO. HEY! I REMEMBER MY NAME!
YOU SEE! YOU'RE COMING AROUND ALREADY!
AS I WAS SAYING, ASTRO, WE CERTAINLY DIDN'T MEAN TO INJURE YOU. WE JUST CAN'T BE TOO CAREFUL THESE DAYS, WHAT WITH THE CONSTANT ATTACKS FROM THE LUCERTOS.

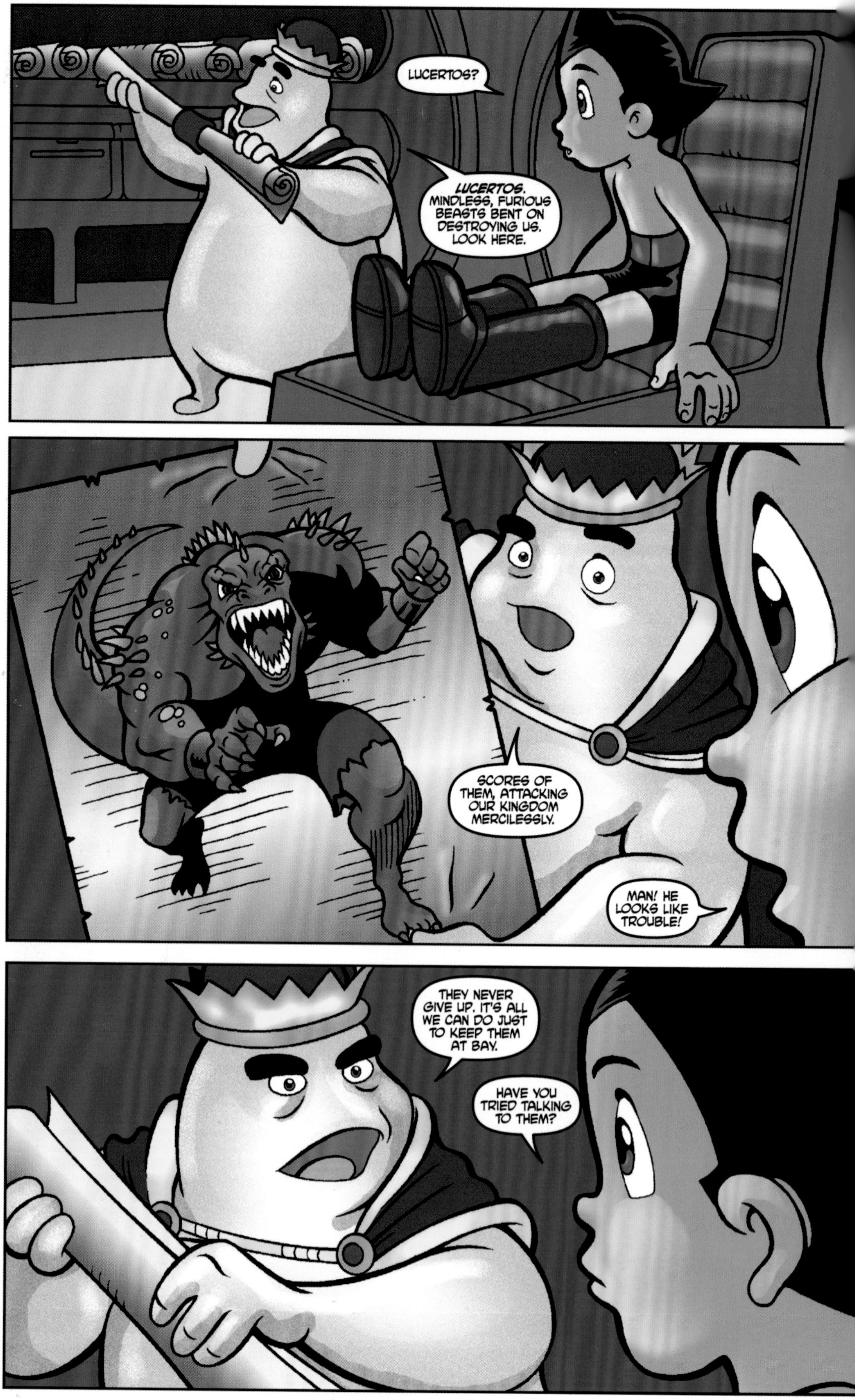
LUCERTOS?
LUCERTOS. MINDLESS, FURIOUS BEASTS BENT ON DESTROYING US. LOOK HERE.
SCORES OF THEM, ATTACKING OUR KINGDOM MERCILESSLY.
MAN! HE LOOKS LIKE TROUBLE!
THEY NEVER GIVE UP. IT'S ALL WE CAN DO JUST TO KEEP THEM AT BAY.
HAVE YOU TRIED TALKING TO THEM?

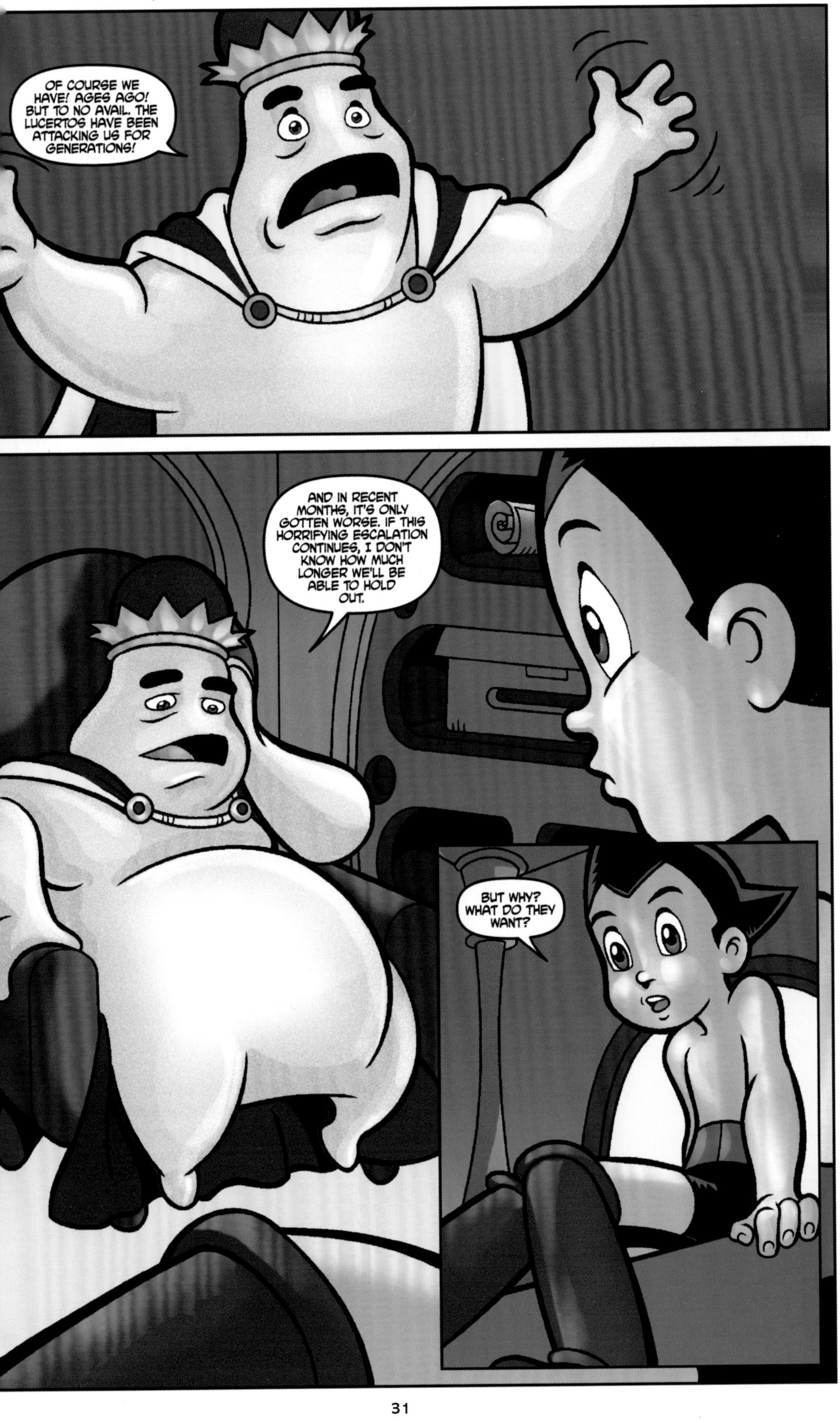
OF COURSE WE HAVE! AGES AGO! BUT TO NO AVAIL. THE LUCERTOS HAVE BEEN ATTACKING US FOR GENERATIONS!
AND IN RECENT MONTHS, IT'S ONLY GOTTEN WORSE. IF THIS HORRIFYING ESCALATION CONTINUES, I DON'T KNOW HOW MUCH LONGER WE'LL BE ABLE TO HOLD OUT.
BUT WHY? WHAT DO THEY WANT?

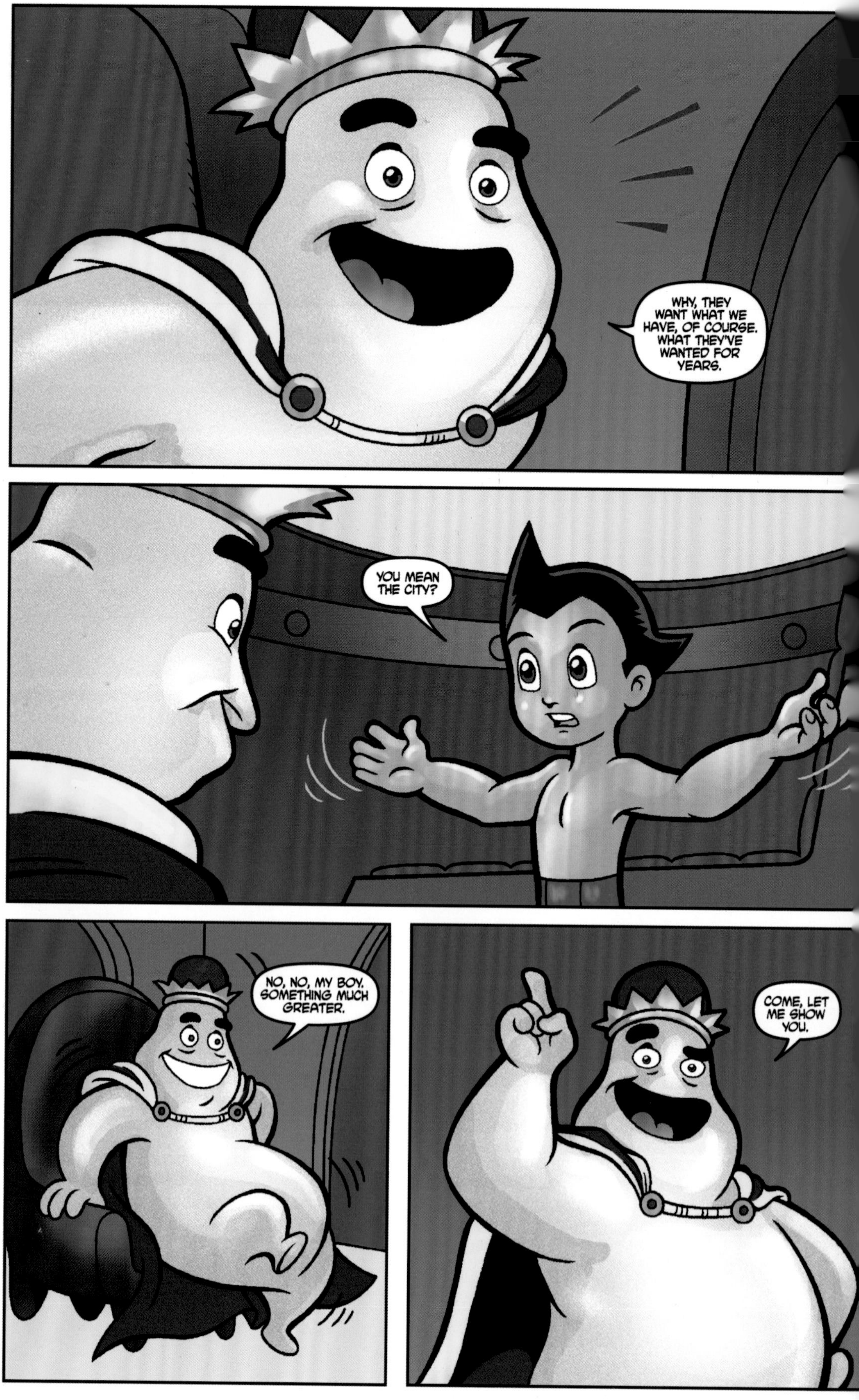
WHY, THEY WANT WHAT WE HAVE, OF COURSE. WHAT THEY'VE WANTED FOR YEARS.
YOU MEAN THE CITY?
NO, NO, MY BOY. SOMETHING MUCH GREATER.
COME, LET ME SHOW YOU.

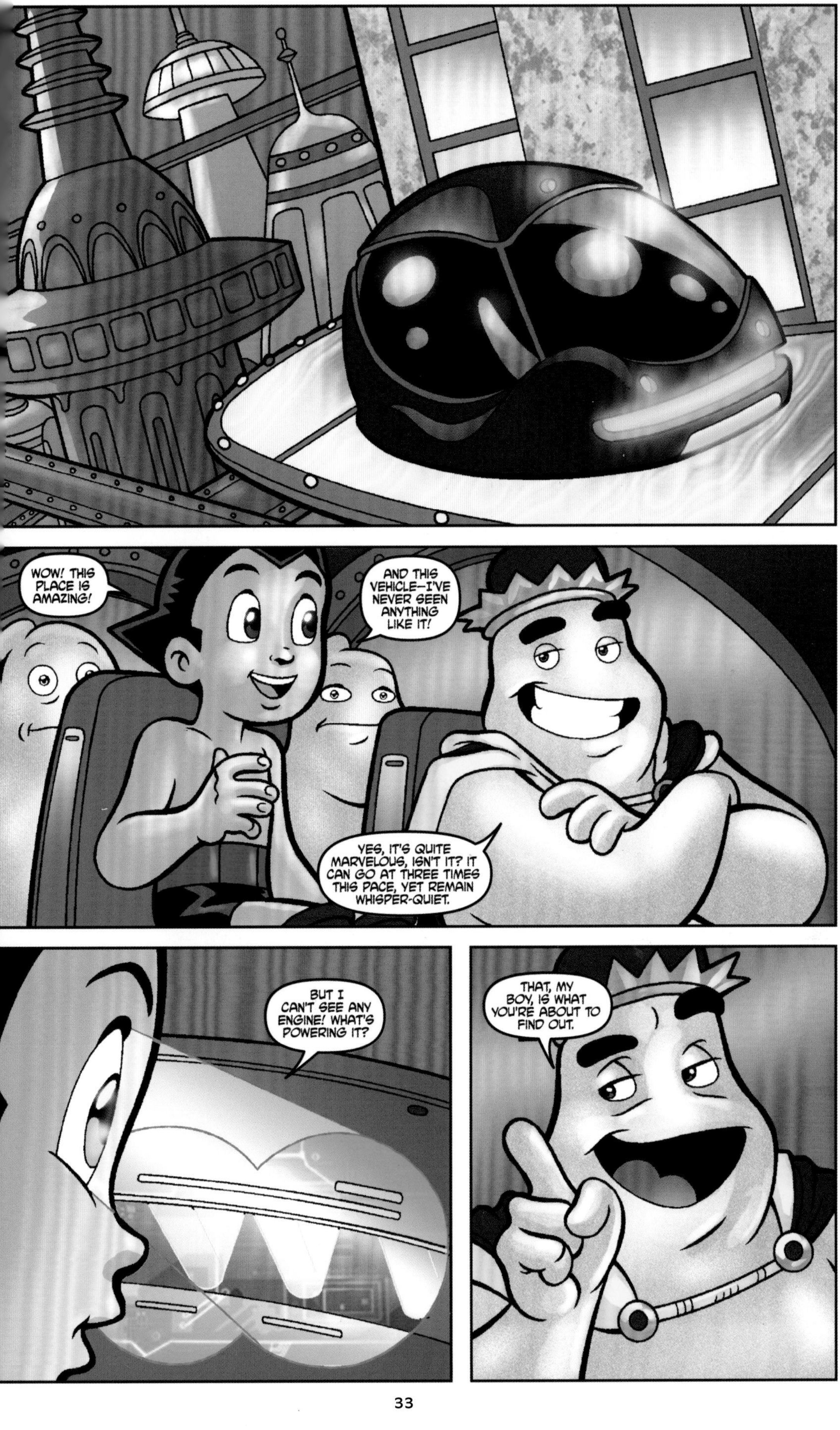
WOW! THIS PLACE IS AMAZING!
AND THIS VEHICLE--I'VE NEVER SEEN ANYTHING LIKE IT!
YES, IT'S QUITE MARVELOUS, ISN'T IT? IT CAN GO AT THREE TIMES THIS PACE, YET REMAIN WHISPER-QUIET.
BUT I CAN'T SEE ANY ENGINE! WHAT'S POWERING IT?
THAT, MY BOY, IS WHAT YOU'RE ABOUT TO FIND OUT.

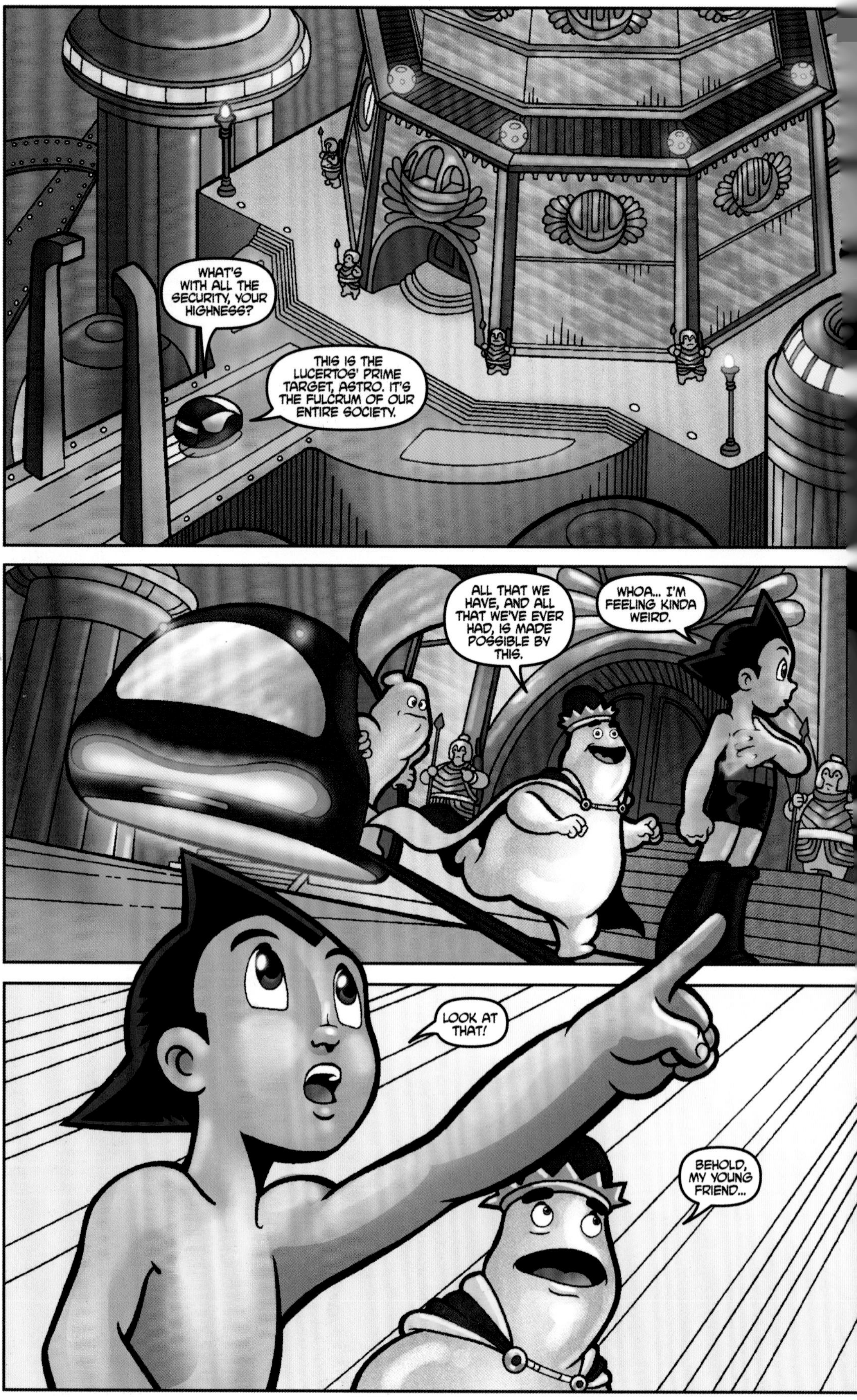
WHAT'S WITH ALL THE SECURITY, YOUR HIGHNESS?
THIS IS THE LUCERTOS' PRIME TARGET, ASTRO. IT'S THE FULCRUM OF OUR ENTIRE SOCIETY.
ALL THAT WE HAVE, AND ALL THAT WE'VE EVER HAD, IS MADE POSSIBLE BY THIS.
WHOA... I'M FEELING KINDA WEIRD.
LOOK AT THAT!
BEHOLD, MY YOUNG FRIEND...

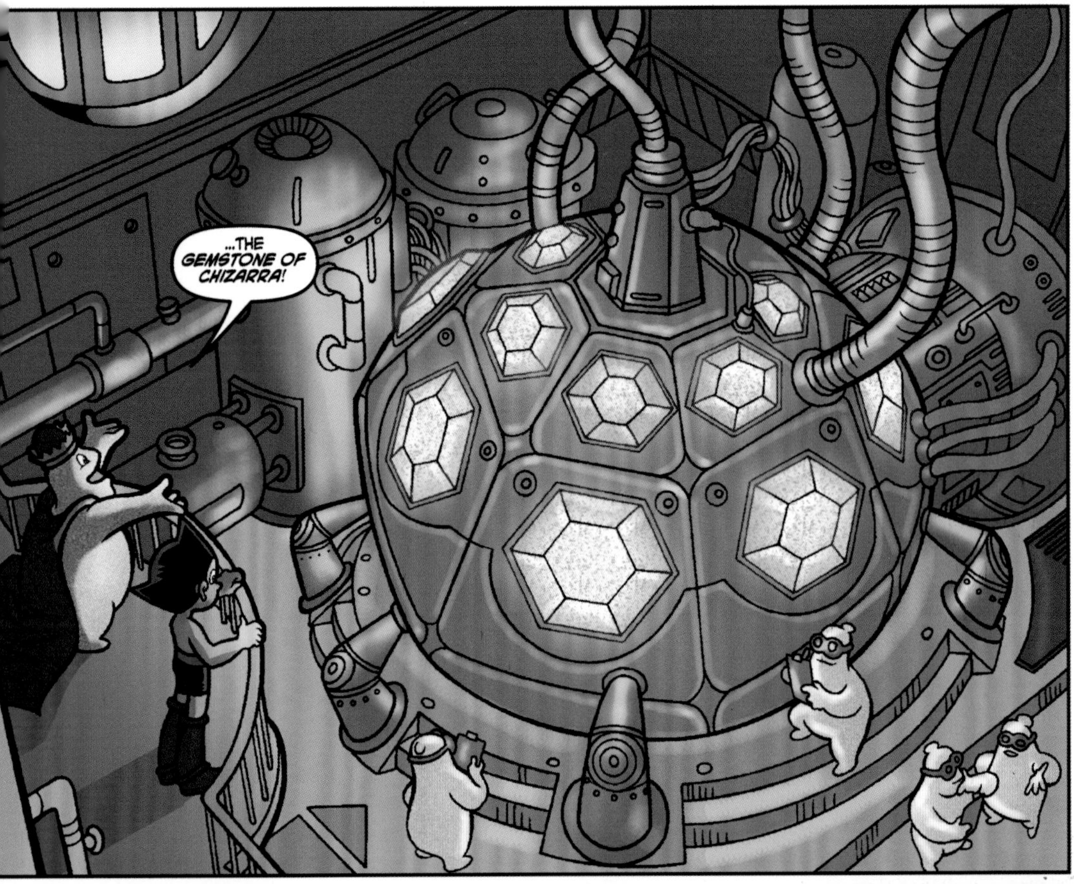
...THE GEMSTONE OF CHIZARRA!

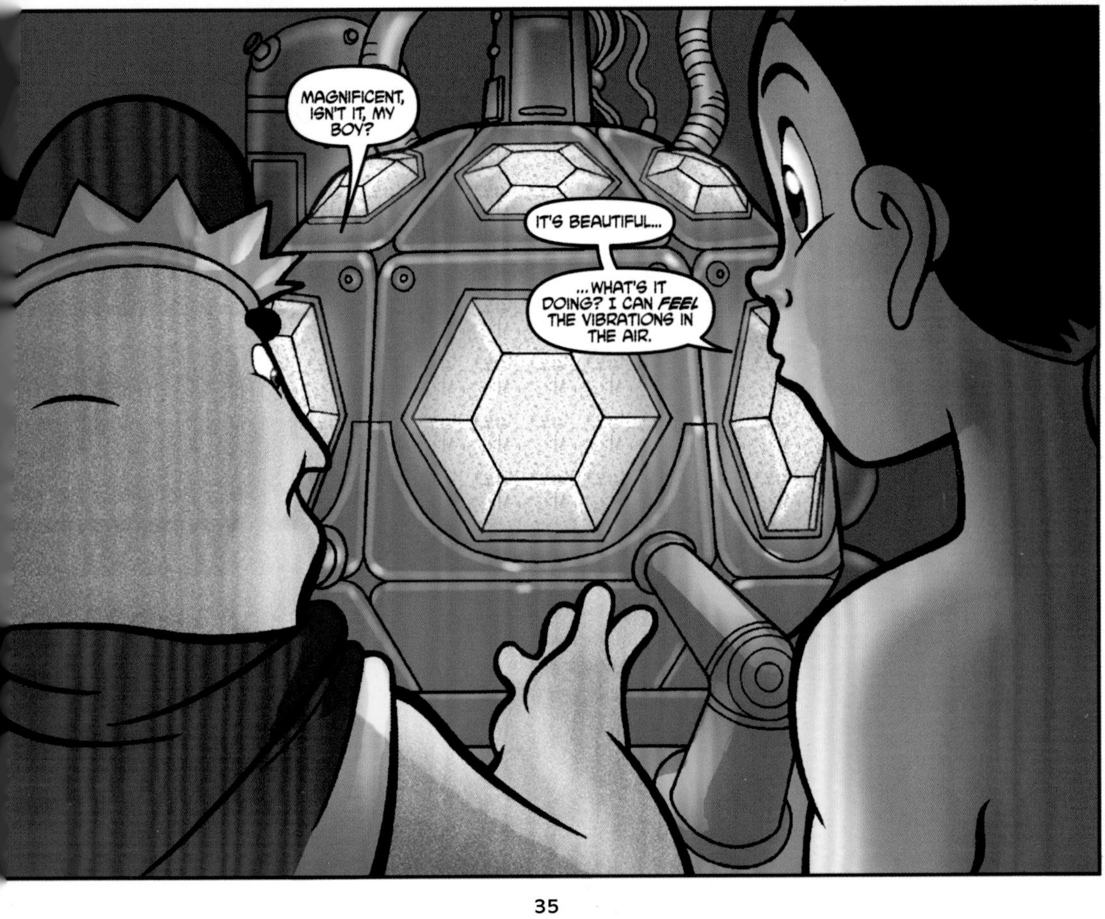
MAGNIFICENT, ISN'T IT, MY BOY?
IT'S BEAUTIFUL...
...WHAT'S IT DOING? I CAN FEEL THE VIBRATIONS IN THE AIR.

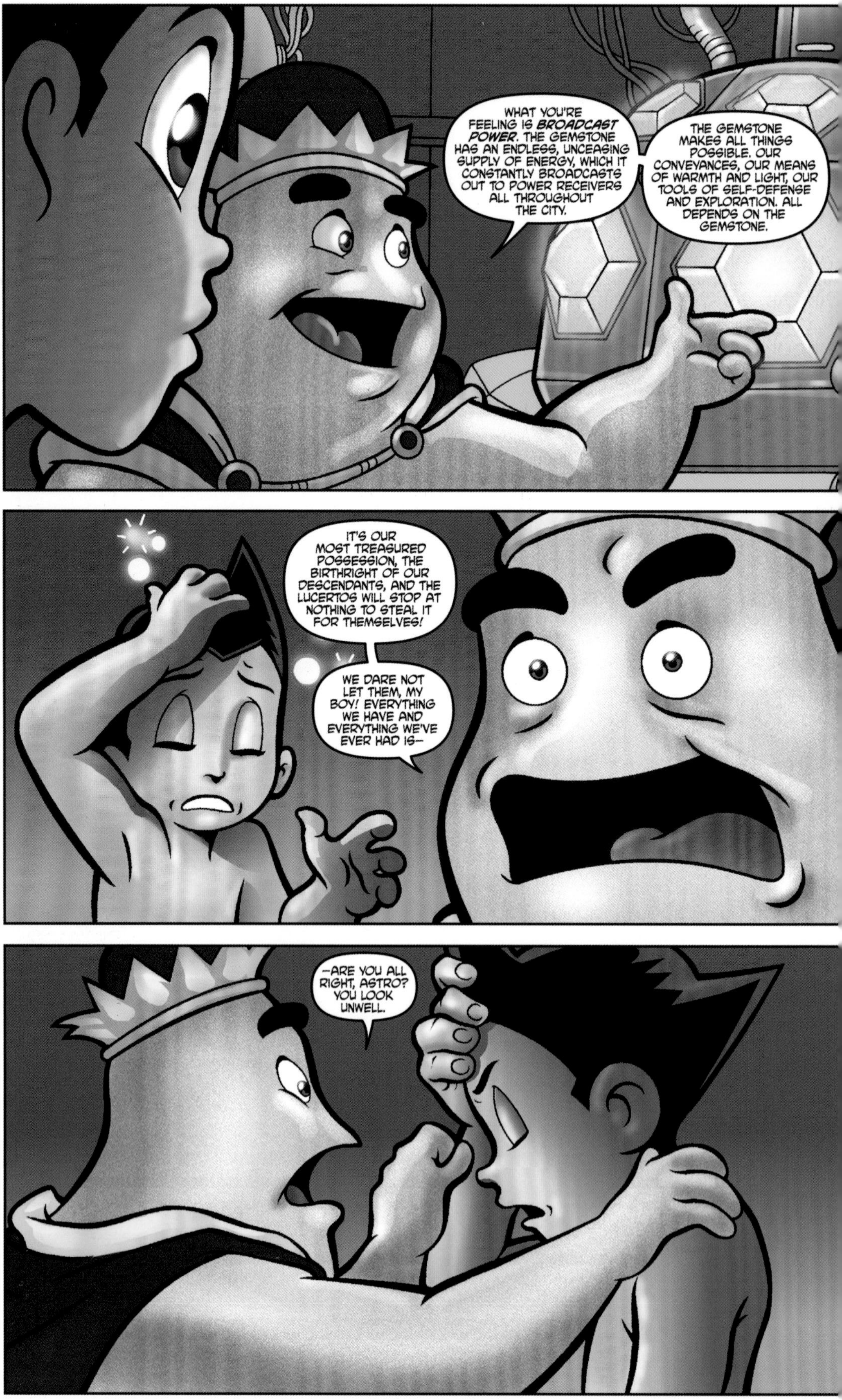
WHAT YOU'RE FEELING IS *BROADCAST POWER*. THE GEMSTONE HAS AN ENDLESS, UNCEASING SUPPLY OF ENERGY, WHICH IT CONSTANTLY BROADCASTS OUT TO POWER RECEIVERS ALL THROUGHOUT THE CITY.
THE GEMSTONE MAKES ALL THINGS POSSIBLE. OUR CONVEYANCES, OUR MEANS OF WARMTH AND LIGHT, OUR TOOLS OF SELF-DEFENSE AND EXPLORATION. ALL DEPENDS ON THE GEMSTONE.
IT'S OUR MOST TREASURED POSSESSION, THE BIRTHRIGHT OF OUR DESCENDANTS, AND THE LUCERTOS WILL STOP AT NOTHING TO STEAL IT FOR THEMSELVES!
WE DARE NOT LET THEM, MY BOY! EVERYTHING WE HAVE AND EVERYTHING WE'VE EVER HAD IS—
—ARE YOU ALL RIGHT, ASTRO? YOU LOOK UNWELL.

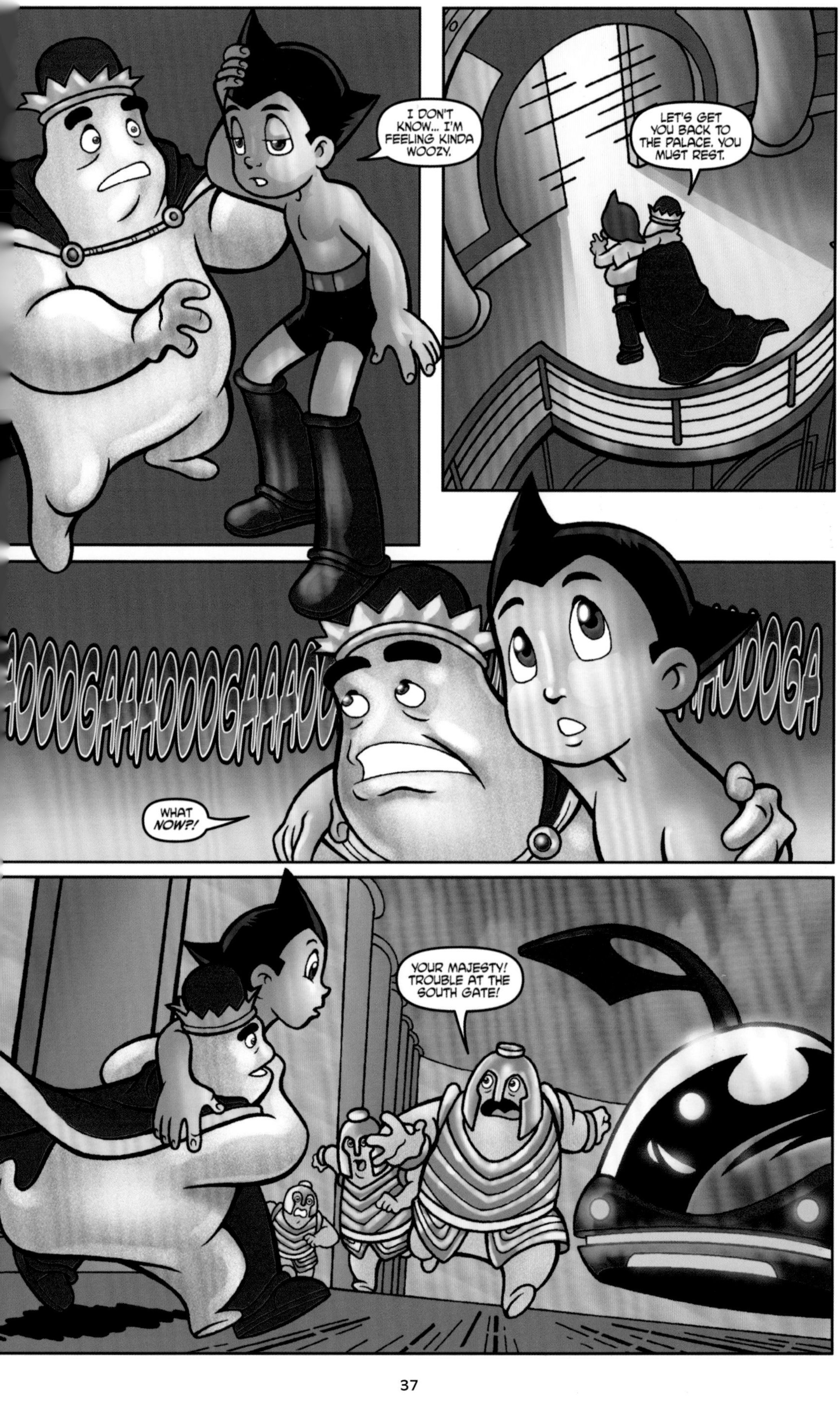
I DON'T KNOW... I'M FEELING KINDA WOOZY.
LET'S GET YOU BACK TO THE PALACE. YOU MUST REST.
AOOOGAAAOOOGAAAO
AOOOGA
WHAT NOW?!
YOUR MAJESTY! TROUBLE AT THE SOUTH GATE!

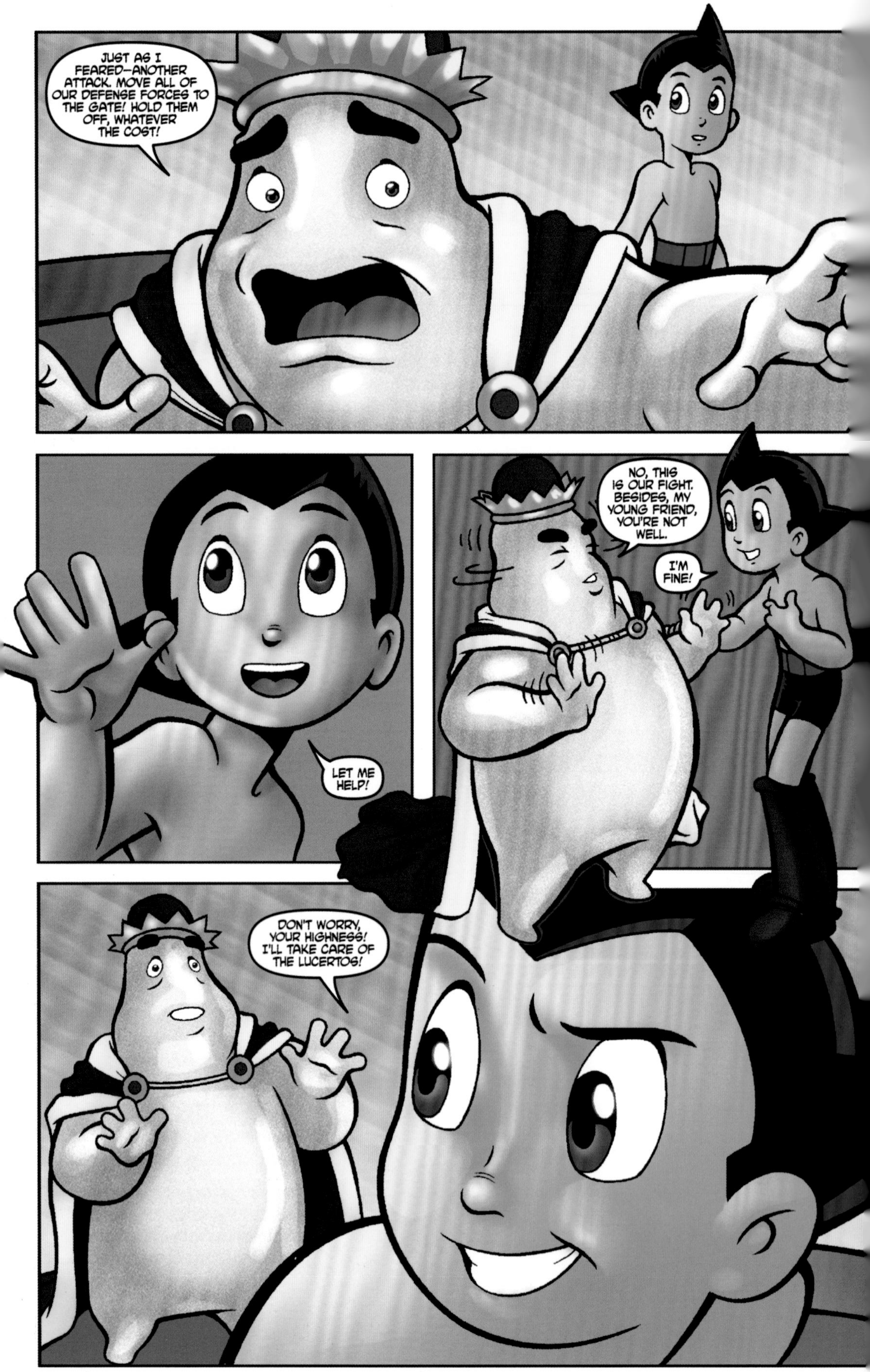
JUST AS I FEARED—ANOTHER ATTACK. MOVE ALL OF OUR DEFENSE FORCES TO THE GATE! HOLD THEM OFF, WHATEVER THE COST!
LET ME HELP!
NO, THIS IS OUR FIGHT. BESIDES, MY YOUNG FRIEND, YOU'RE NOT WELL.
I'M FINE!
DON'T WORRY, YOUR HIGHNESS! I'LL TAKE CARE OF THE LUCERTOS!

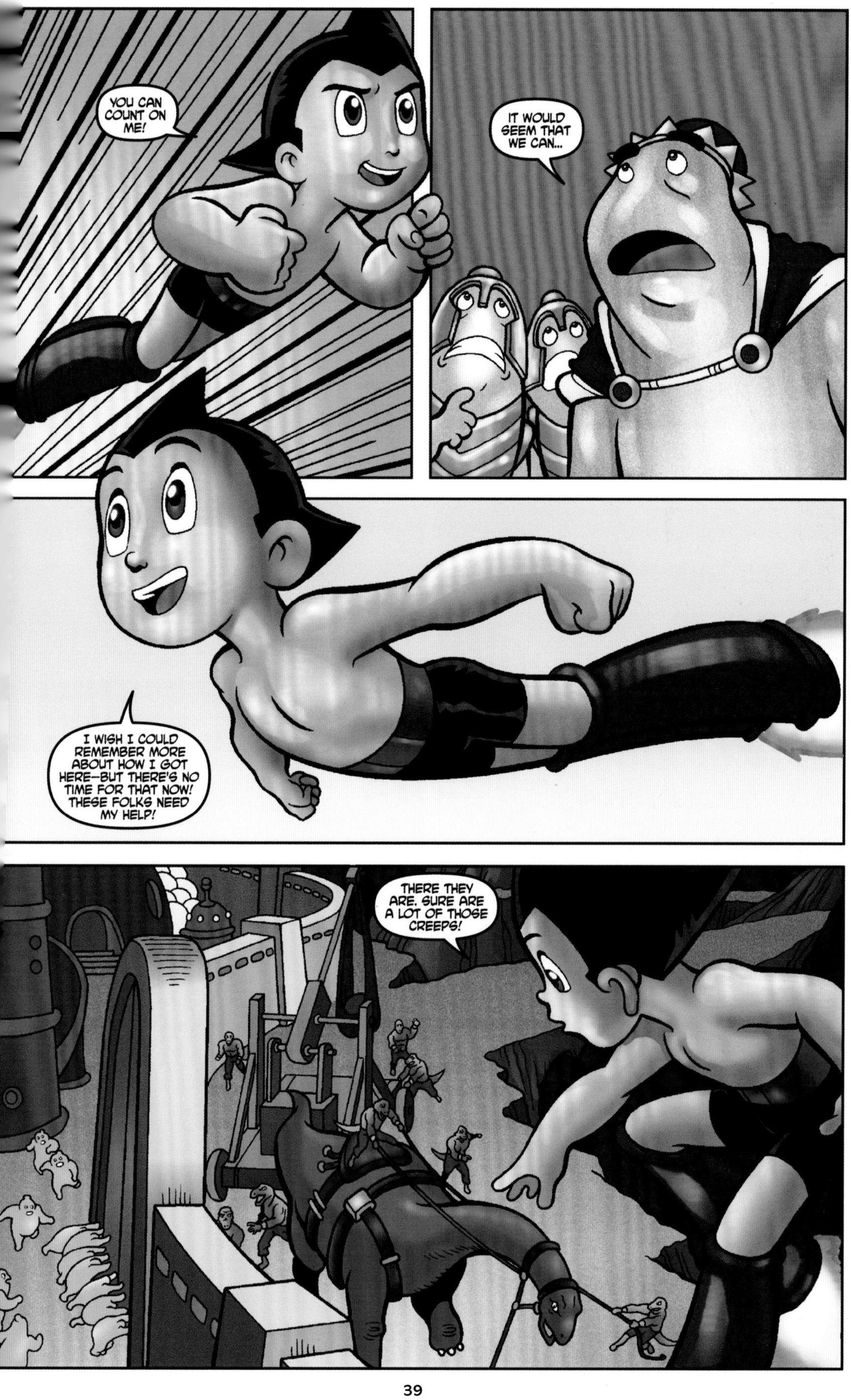
YOU CAN COUNT ON ME!
IT WOULD SEEM THAT WE CAN...
I WISH I COULD REMEMBER MORE ABOUT HOW I GOT HERE—BUT THERE'S NO TIME FOR THAT NOW! THESE FOLKS NEED MY HELP!
THERE THEY ARE. SURE ARE A LOT OF THOSE CREEPS!

"WHAT ARE THOSE THINGS?"

FIRE!

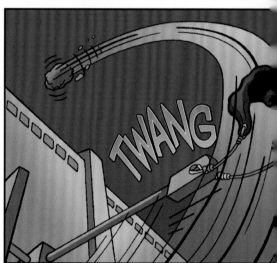

TWANG

SMASH

OH, NO! IT'S SOME KIND OF CATAPULT!

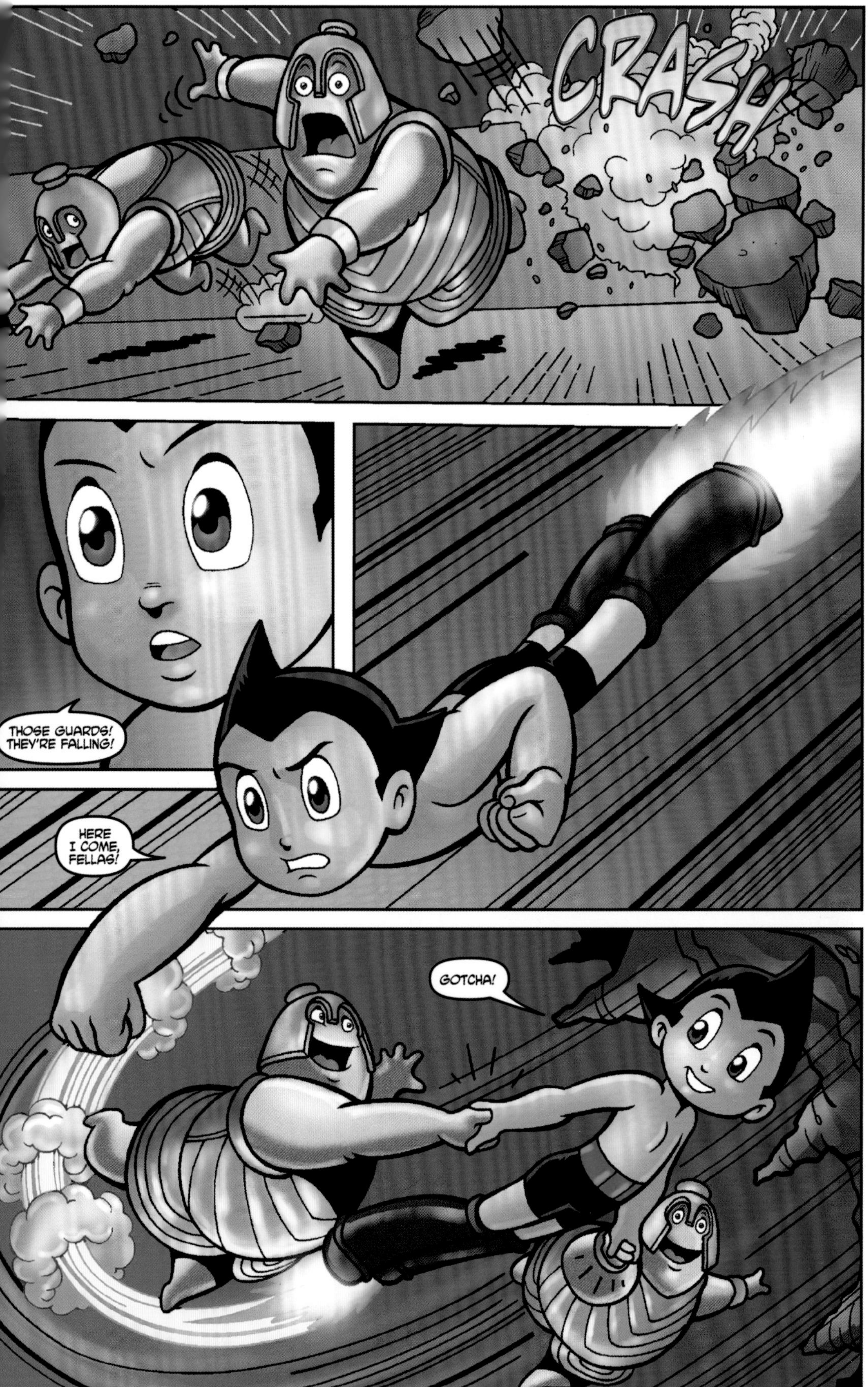
CRASH!
THOSE GUARDS! THEY'RE FALLING!
HERE I COME, FELLAS!
GOTCHA!

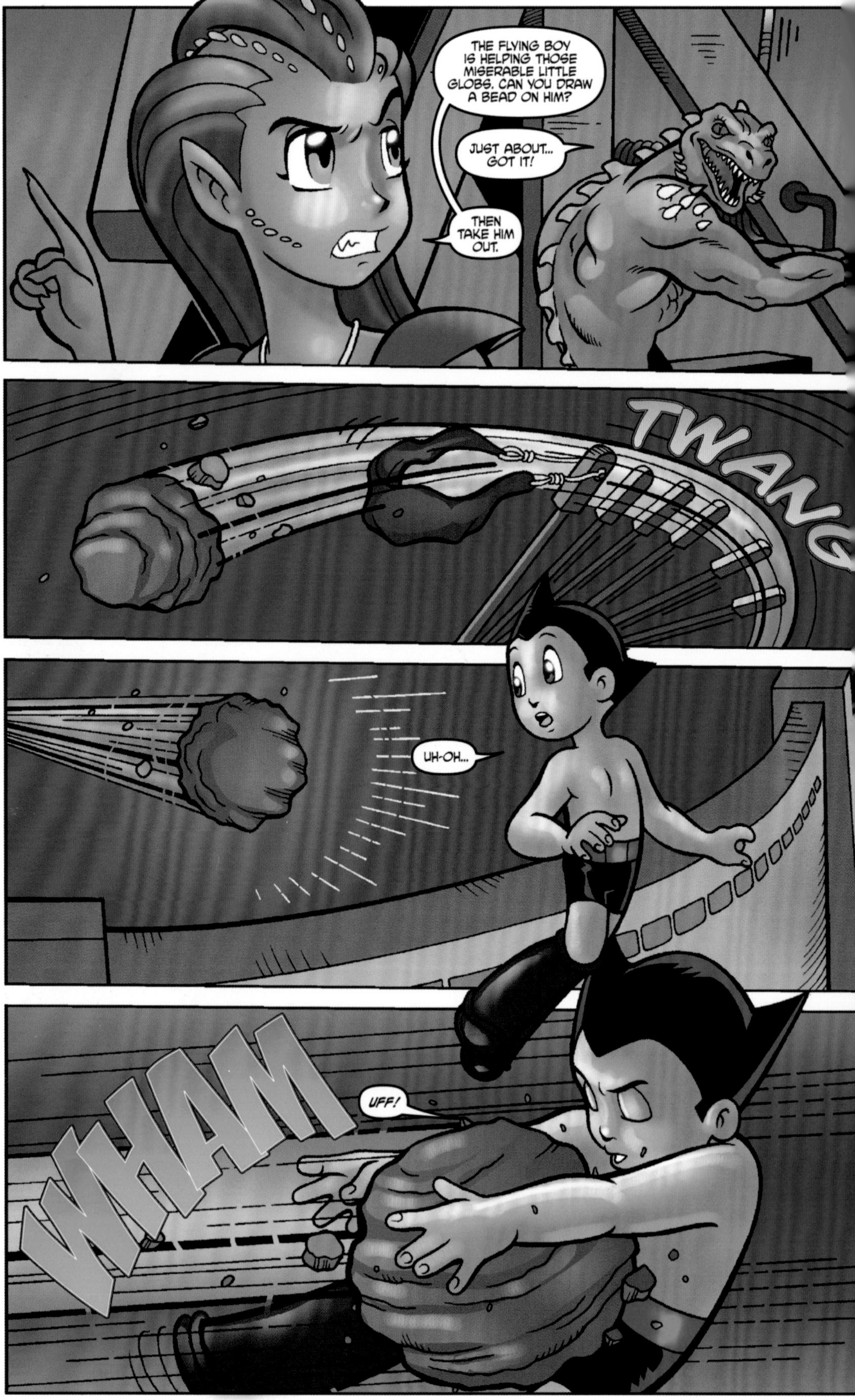
THE FLYING BOY IS HELPING THOSE MISERABLE LITTLE GLOBS. CAN YOU DRAW A BEAD ON HIM?
JUST ABOUT... GOT IT!
THEN TAKE HIM OUT.
TWANG
UH-OH...
WHAM
UFF!

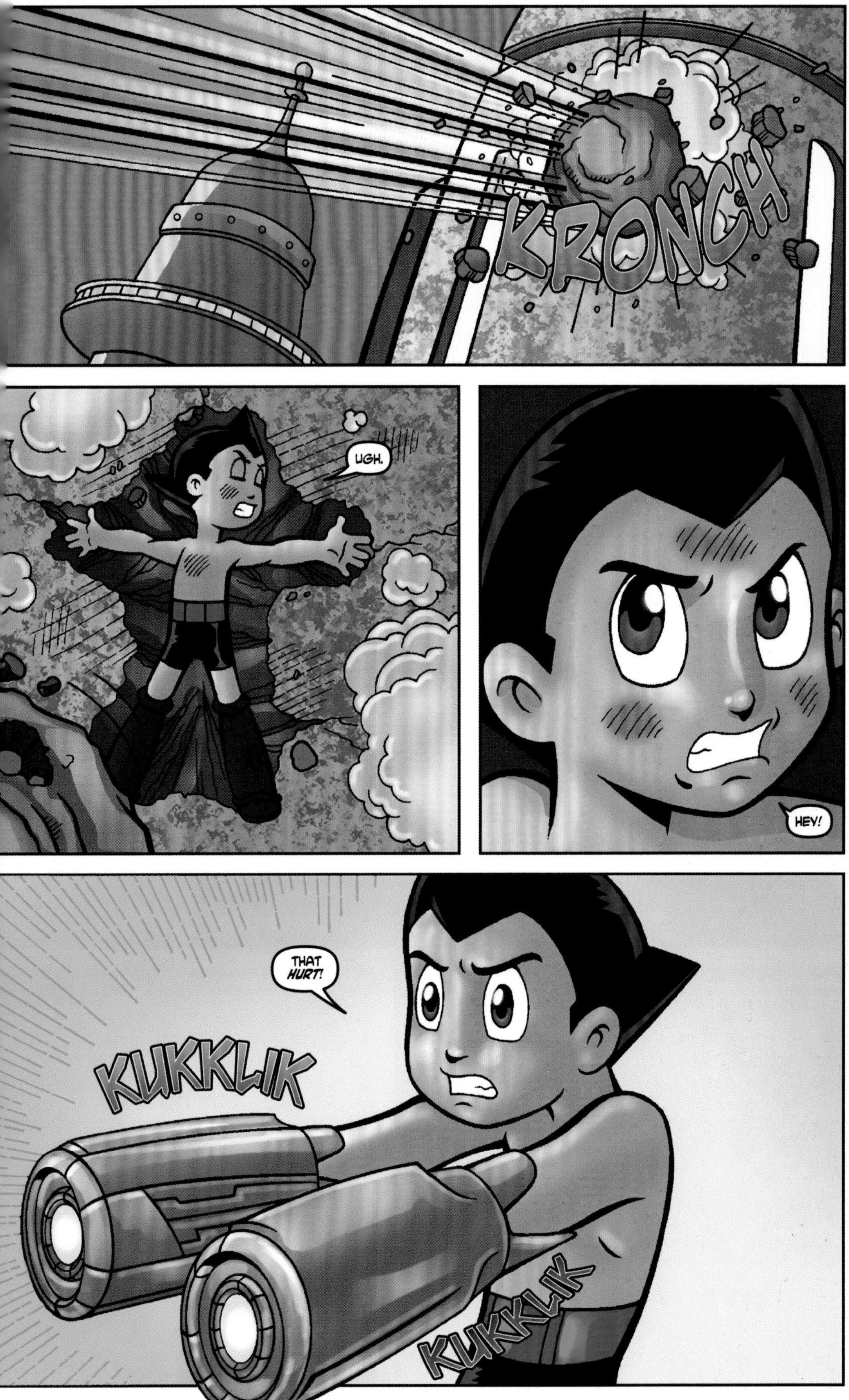
KRONCH
UGH.
HEY!
THAT HURT!
KUKKLIK
KUKKLIK

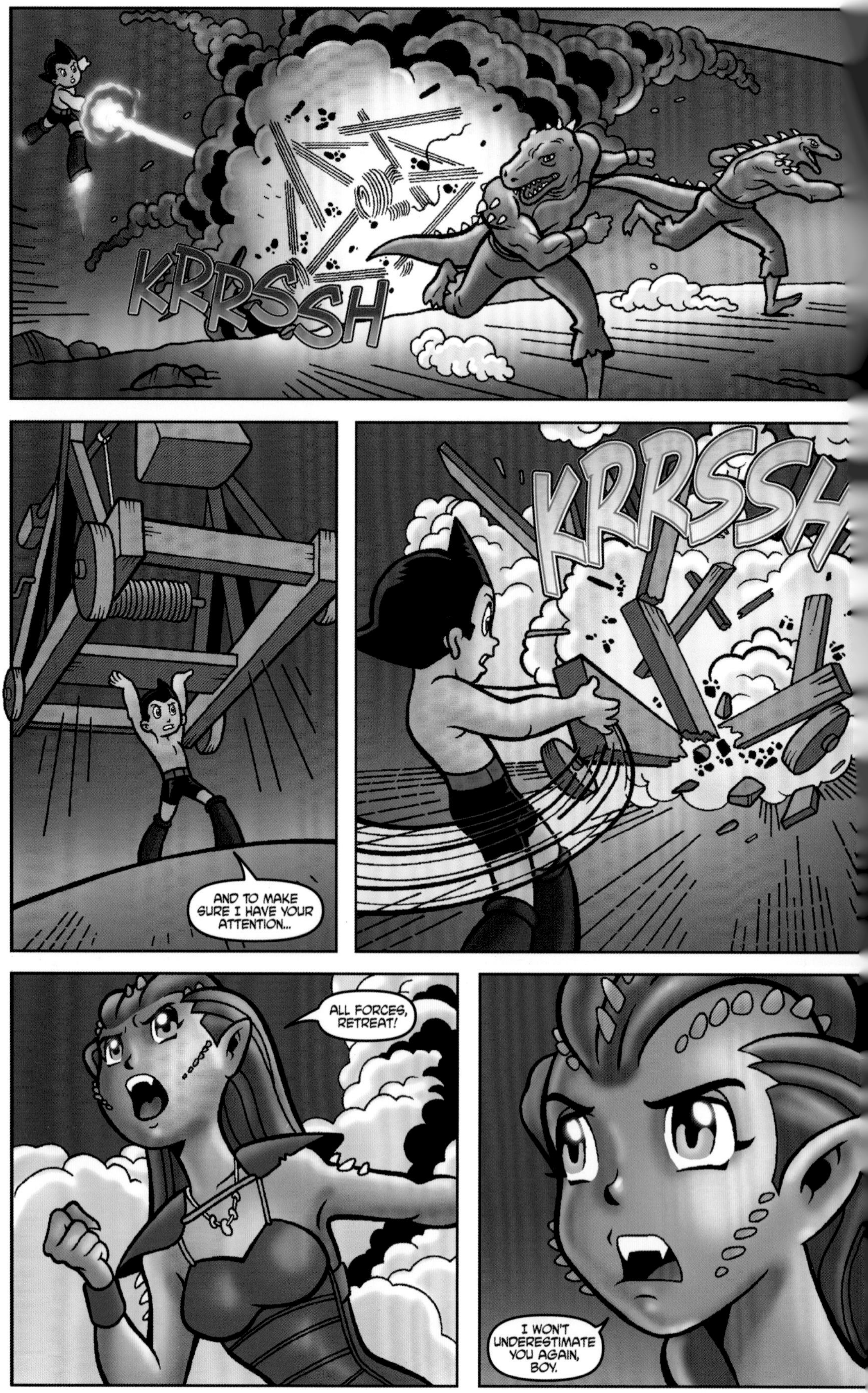
KRRSSH
AND TO MAKE SURE I HAVE YOUR ATTENTION...
KRRSSH
ALL FORCES, RETREAT!
I WON'T UNDERESTIMATE YOU AGAIN, BOY.

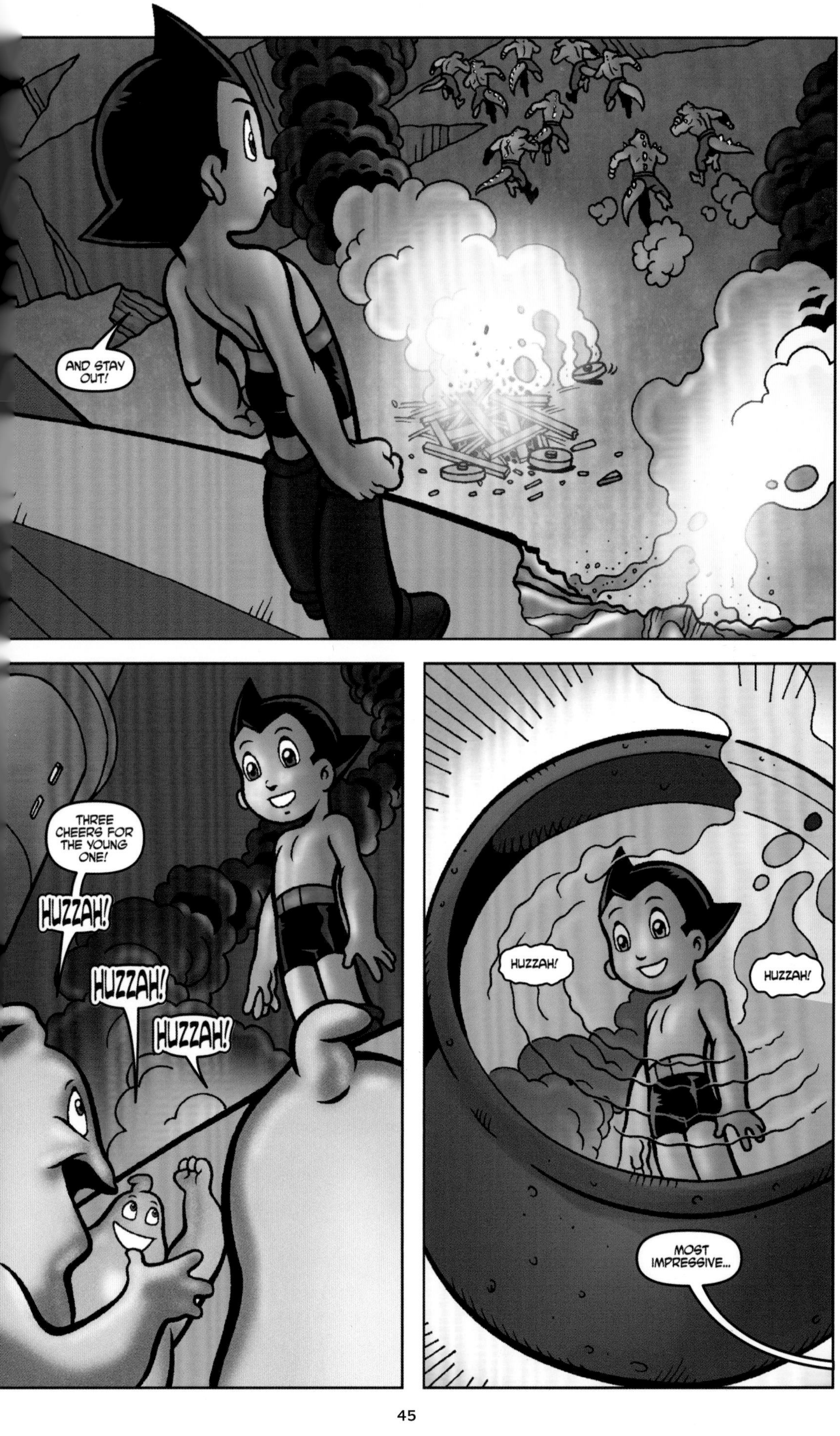
AND STAY OUT!
THREE CHEERS FOR THE YOUNG ONE!
HUZZAH!
HUZZAH!
HUZZAH!
HUZZAH!
HUZZAH!
MOST IMPRESSIVE...

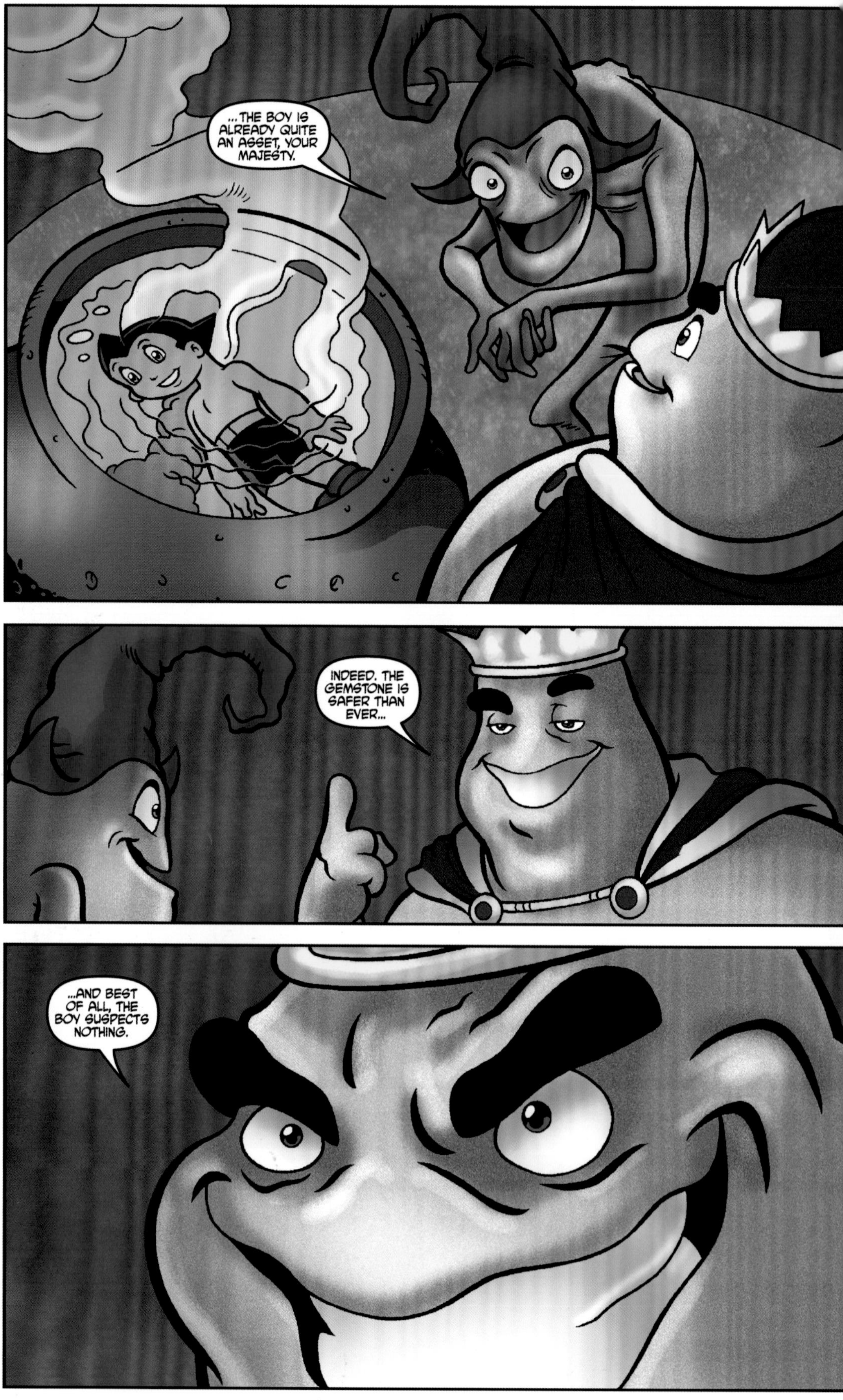
...THE BOY IS ALREADY QUITE AN ASSET, YOUR MAJESTY.
INDEED. THE GEMSTONE IS SAFER THAN EVER...
...AND BEST OF ALL, THE BOY SUSPECTS NOTHING.

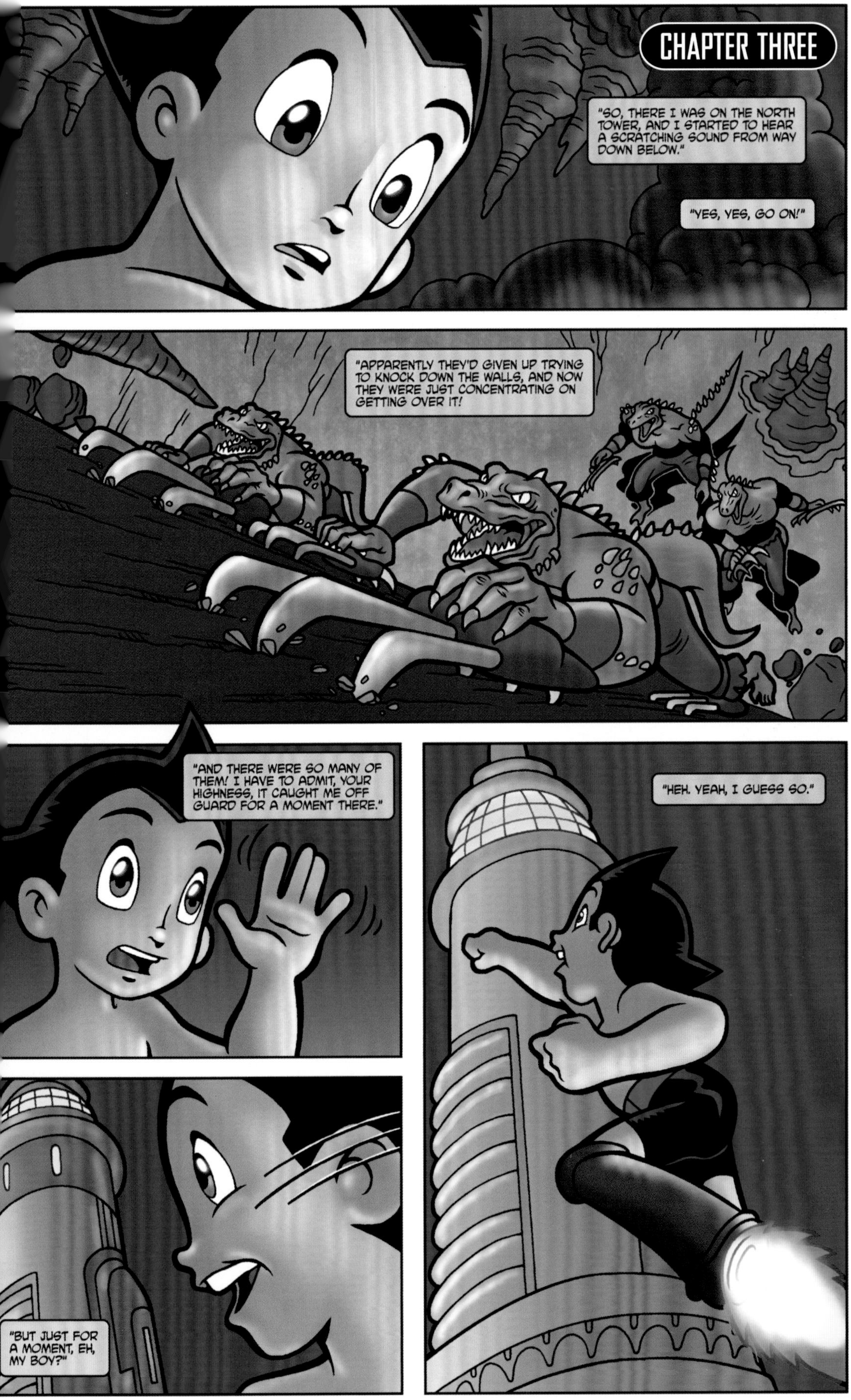
CHAPTER THREE
"SO, THERE I WAS ON THE NORTH TOWER, AND I STARTED TO HEAR A SCRATCHING SOUND FROM WAY DOWN BELOW."
"YES, YES, GO ON!"
"APPARENTLY THEY'D GIVEN UP TRYING TO KNOCK DOWN THE WALLS, AND NOW THEY WERE JUST CONCENTRATING ON GETTING OVER IT!
"AND THERE WERE SO MANY OF THEM! I HAVE TO ADMIT, YOUR HIGHNESS, IT CAUGHT ME OFF GUARD FOR A MOMENT THERE."
"BUT JUST FOR A MOMENT, EH, MY BOY?"
"HEH. YEAH, I GUESS SO."

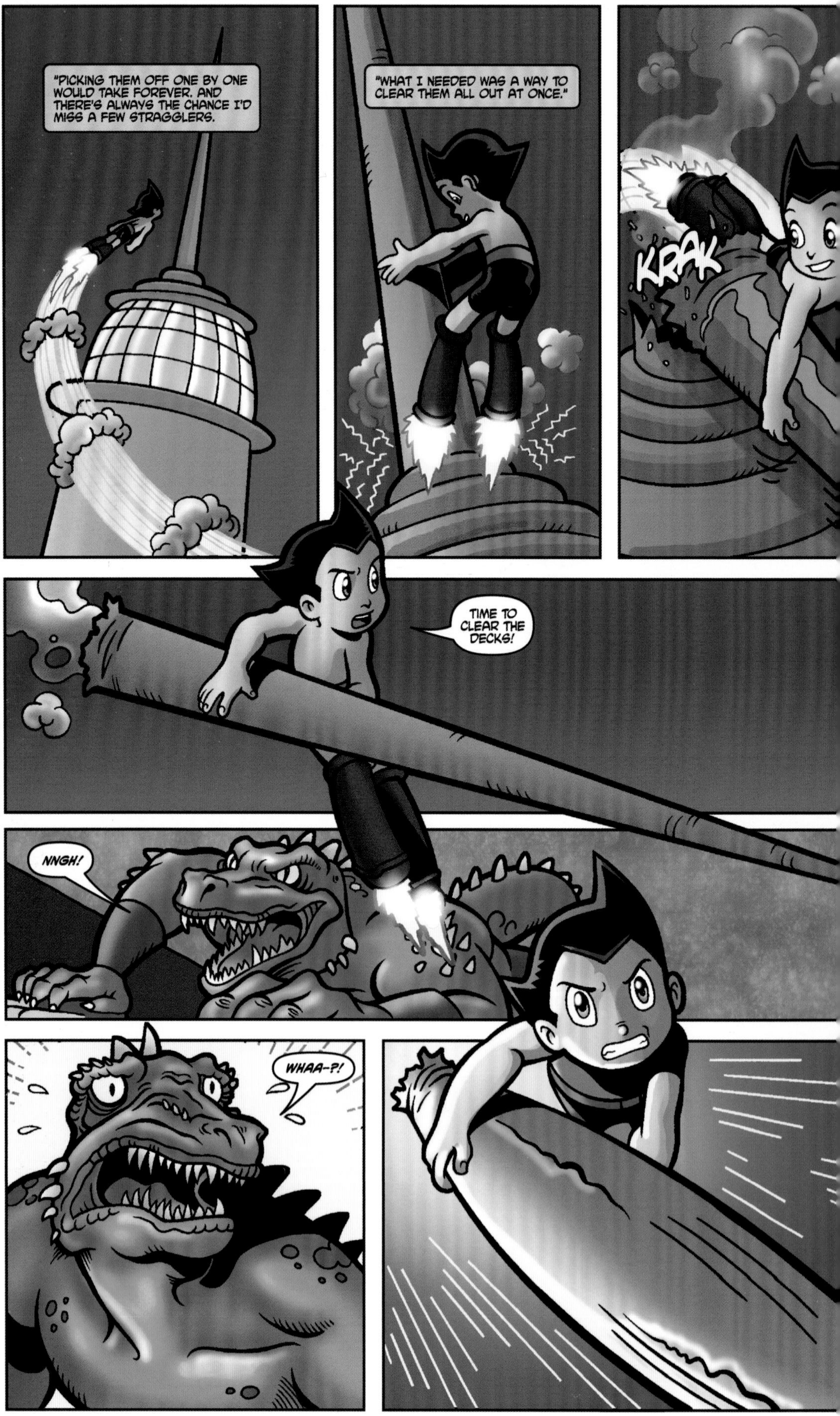
"PICKING THEM OFF ONE BY ONE WOULD TAKE FOREVER. AND THERE'S ALWAYS THE CHANCE I'D MISS A FEW STRAGGLERS.
"WHAT I NEEDED WAS A WAY TO CLEAR THEM ALL OUT AT ONCE."
KRAK
TIME TO CLEAR THE DECKS!
NNGH!
WHAA--?!

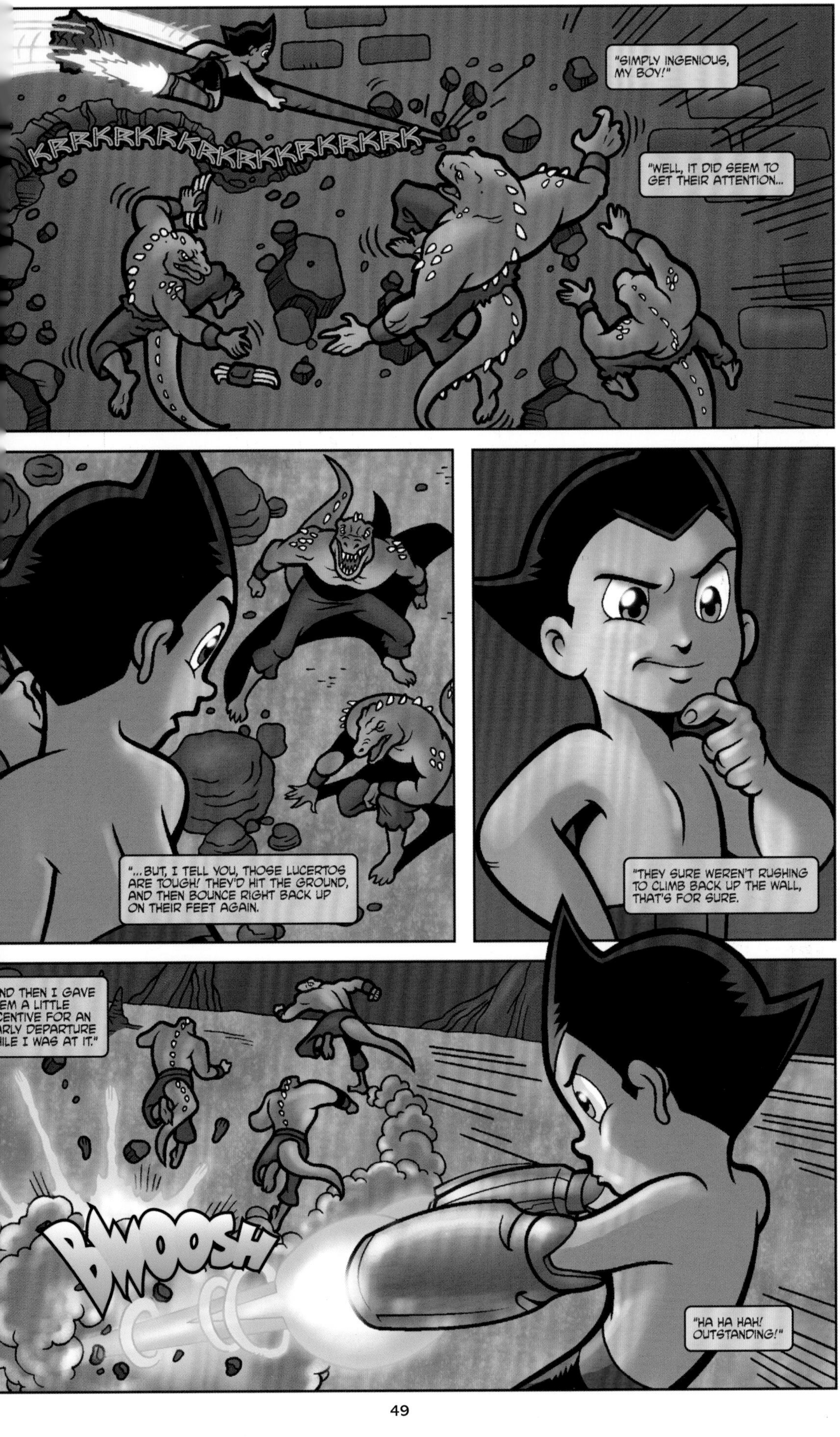
"SIMPLY INGENIOUS, MY BOY!"
KRRKRKRKRKRKRKKRKRKRK
"WELL, IT DID SEEM TO GET THEIR ATTENTION...
"...BUT, I TELL YOU, THOSE LUCERTOS ARE TOUGH! THEY'D HIT THE GROUND, AND THEN BOUNCE RIGHT BACK UP ON THEIR FEET AGAIN.
"THEY SURE WEREN'T RUSHING TO CLIMB BACK UP THE WALL, THAT'S FOR SURE.
AND THEN I GAVE HEM A LITTLE CENTIVE FOR AN ARLY DEPARTURE HILE I WAS AT IT."
BWOOSH
"HA HA HAH! OUTSTANDING!"

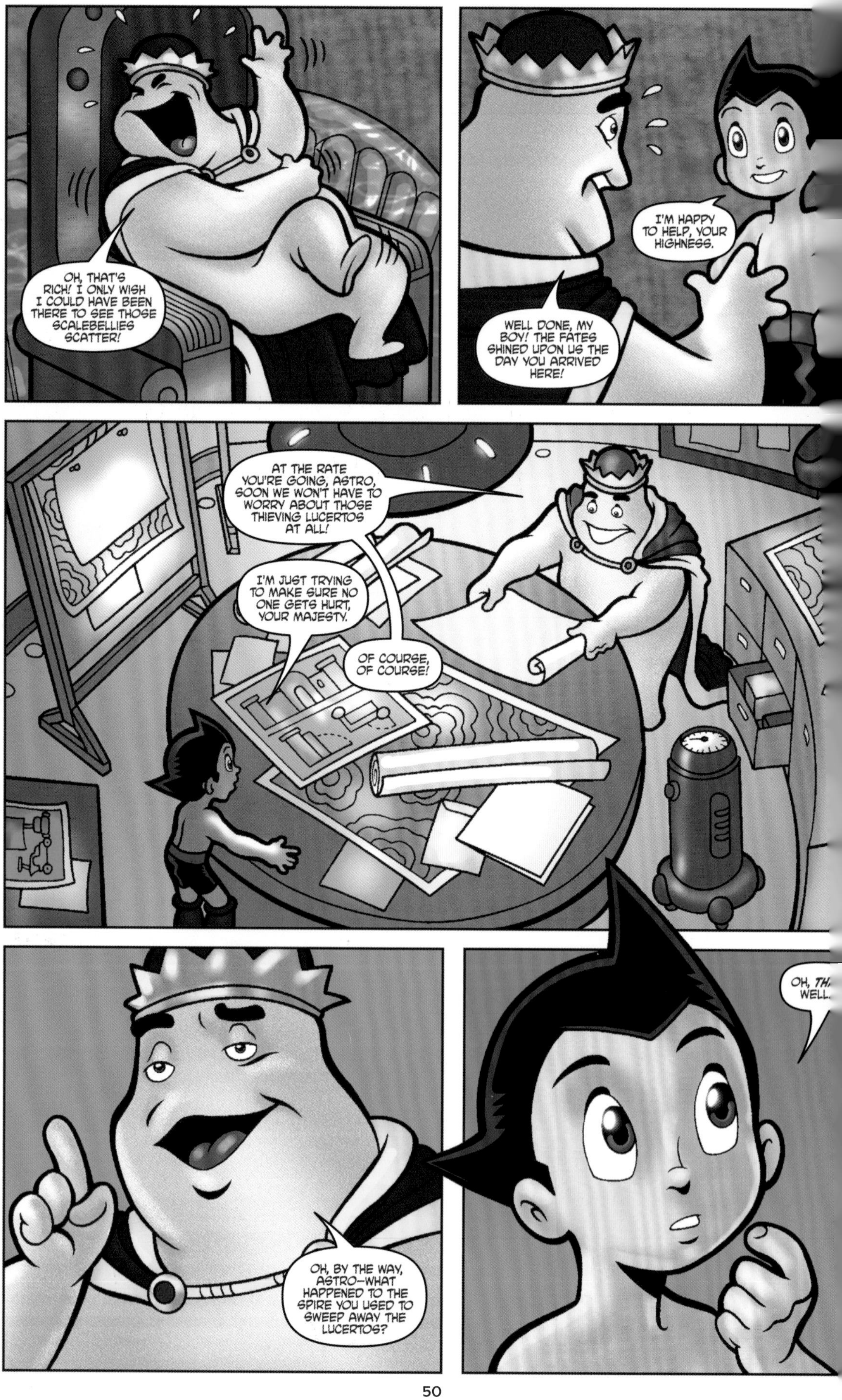
OH, THAT'S RICH! I ONLY WISH I COULD HAVE BEEN THERE TO SEE THOSE SCALEBELLIES SCATTER!
WELL DONE, MY BOY! THE FATES SHINED UPON US THE DAY YOU ARRIVED HERE!
I'M HAPPY TO HELP, YOUR HIGHNESS.
AT THE RATE YOU'RE GOING, ASTRO, SOON WE WON'T HAVE TO WORRY ABOUT THOSE THIEVING LUCERTOS AT ALL!
I'M JUST TRYING TO MAKE SURE NO ONE GETS HURT, YOUR MAJESTY.
OF COURSE, OF COURSE!
OH, BY THE WAY, ASTRO—WHAT HAPPENED TO THE SPIRE YOU USED TO SWEEP AWAY THE LUCERTOS?
OH, TH
WELL.

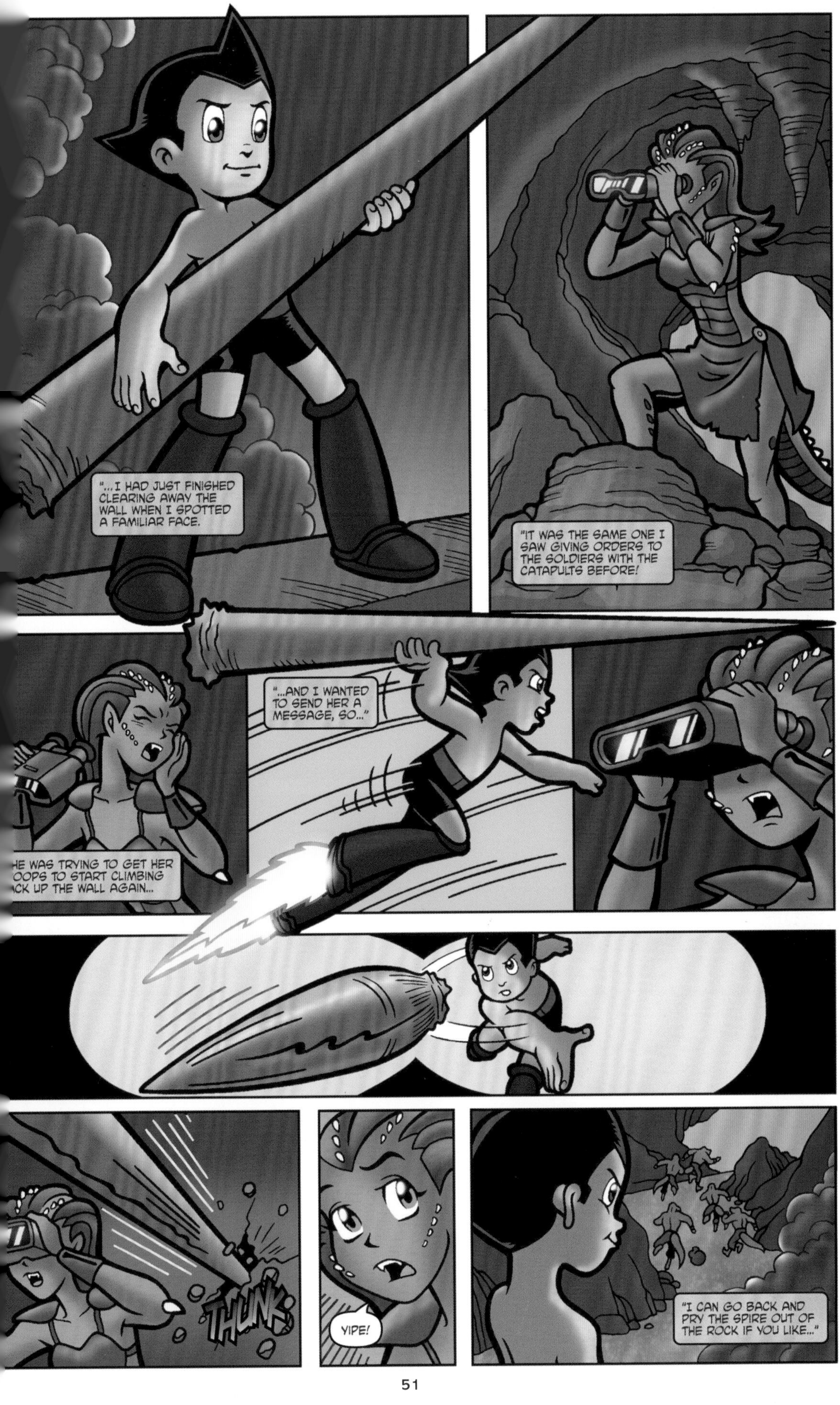

"...I HAD JUST FINISHED CLEARING AWAY THE WALL WHEN I SPOTTED A FAMILIAR FACE.
"IT WAS THE SAME ONE I SAW GIVING ORDERS TO THE SOLDIERS WITH THE CATAPULTS BEFORE!
HE WAS TRYING TO GET HER OOPS TO START CLIMBING CK UP THE WALL AGAIN...
"...AND I WANTED TO SEND HER A MESSAGE, SO..."
THUNK
YIPE!
"I CAN GO BACK AND PRY THE SPIRE OUT OF THE ROCK IF YOU LIKE..."

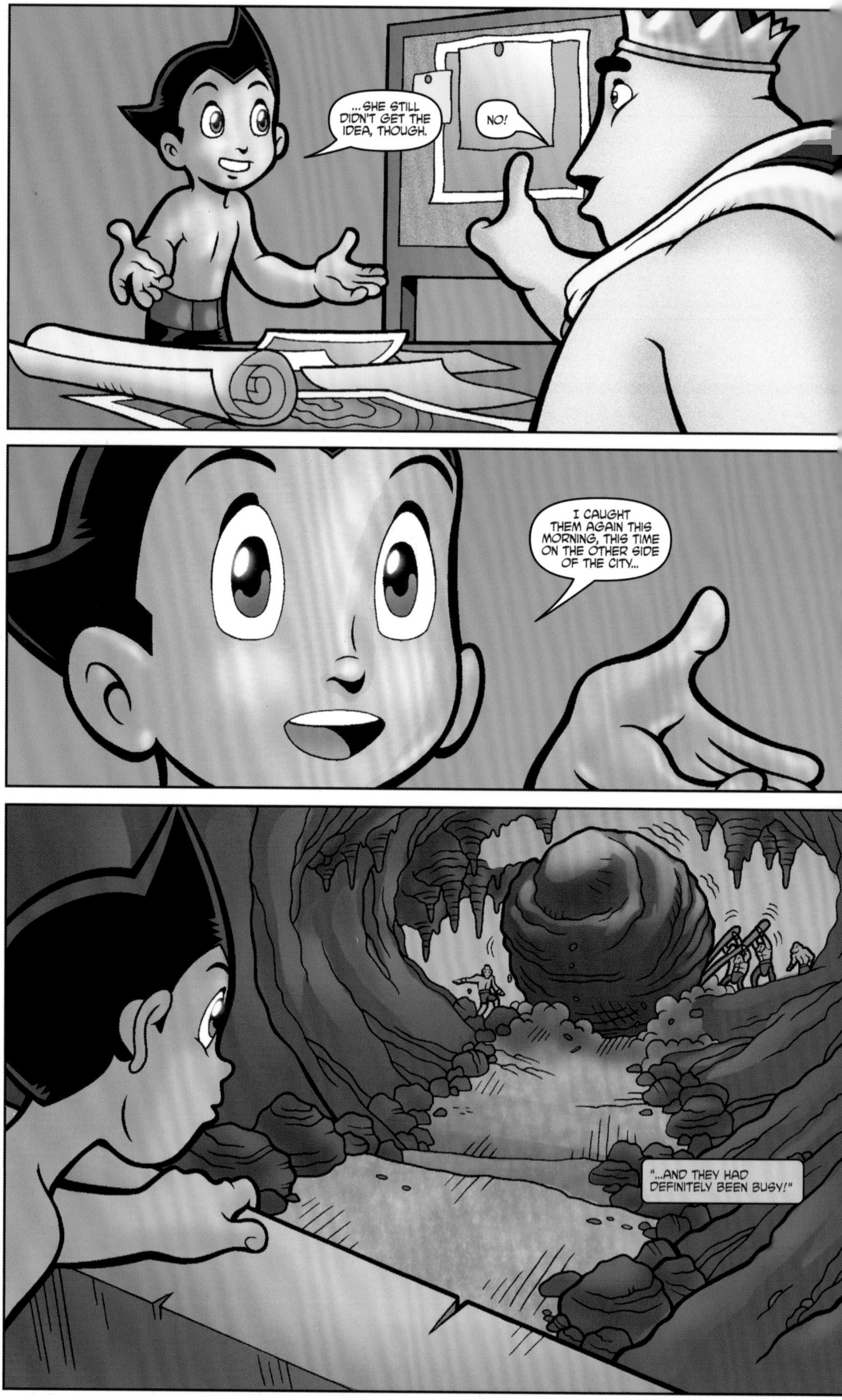
...SHE STILL DIDN'T GET THE IDEA, THOUGH.
NO!
I CAUGHT THEM AGAIN THIS MORNING, THIS TIME ON THE OTHER SIDE OF THE CITY...
"...AND THEY HAD DEFINITELY BEEN BUSY!"

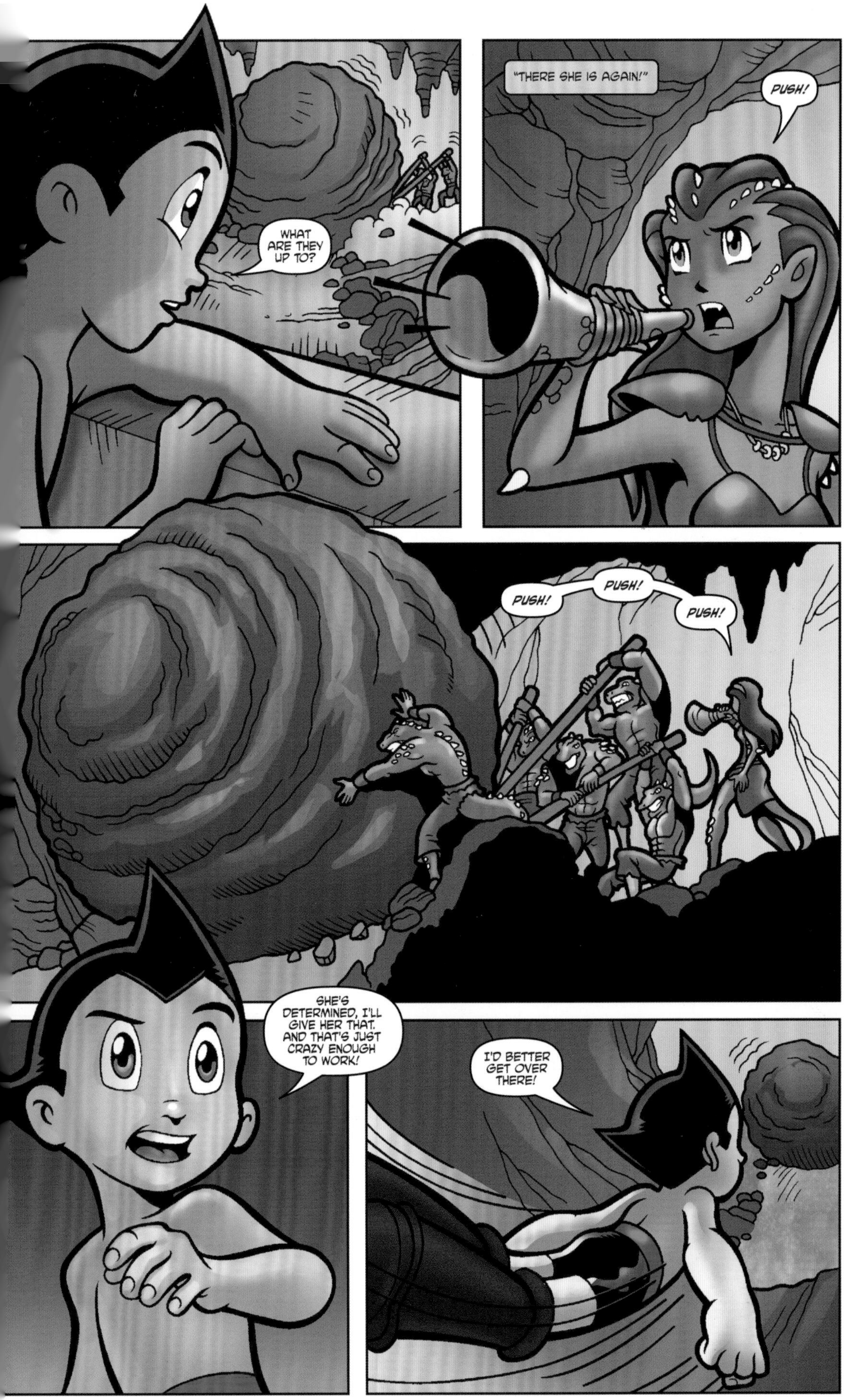
WHAT ARE THEY UP TO?
"THERE SHE IS AGAIN!"
PUSH!
PUSH!
PUSH!
PUSH!
SHE'S DETERMINED, I'LL GIVE HER THAT. AND THAT'S JUST CRAZY ENOUGH TO WORK!
I'D BETTER GET OVER THERE!

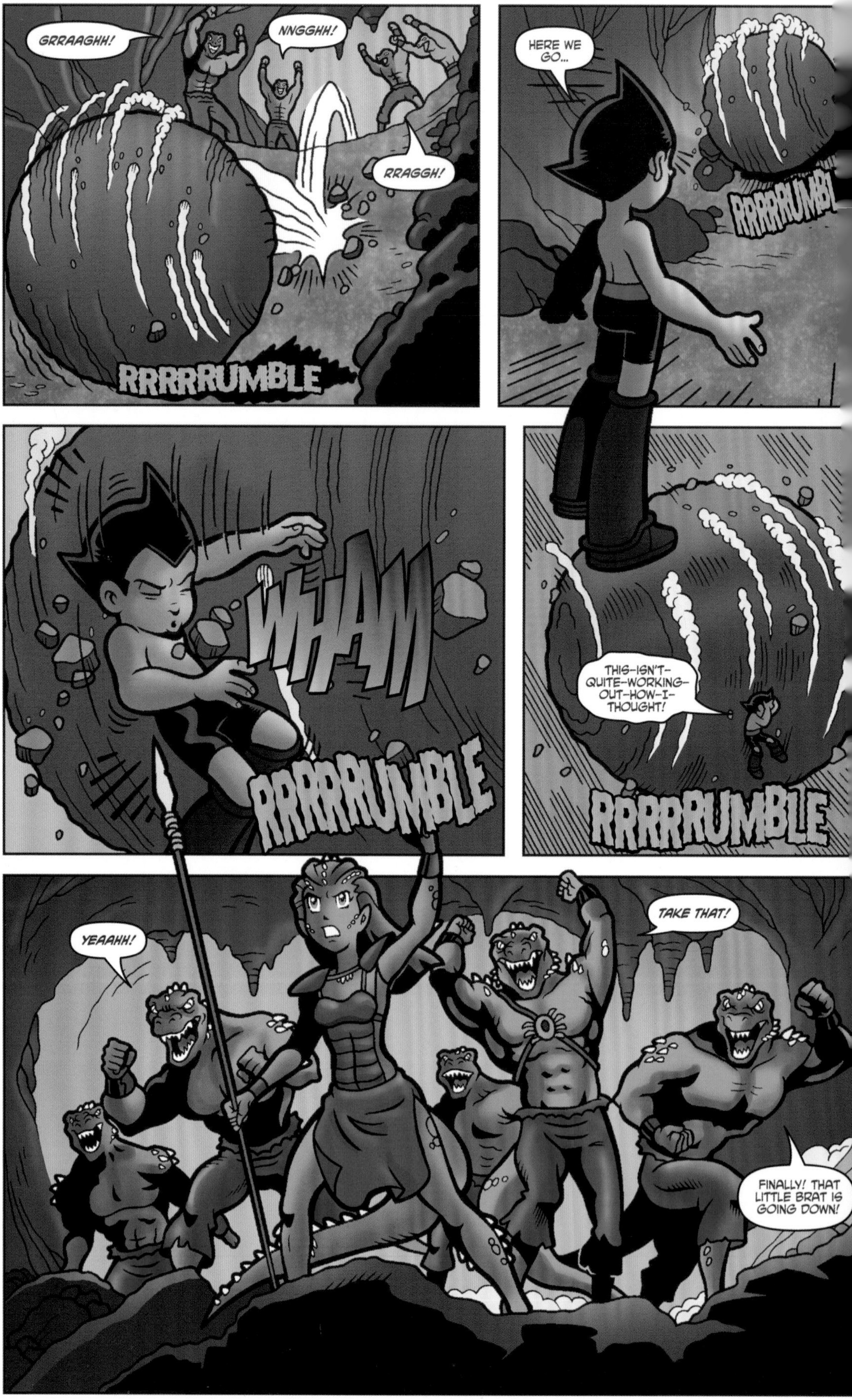
GRRAAGHH!
NNGGHH!
RRAGGH!
RRRRRUMBLE
HERE WE GO...
RRRRRUMBLE
WHAM
RRRRRUMBLE
THIS-ISN'T-QUITE-WORKING-OUT-HOW-I-THOUGHT!
RRRRRUMBLE
YEAAHH!
TAKE THAT!
FINALLY! THAT LITTLE BRAT IS GOING DOWN!

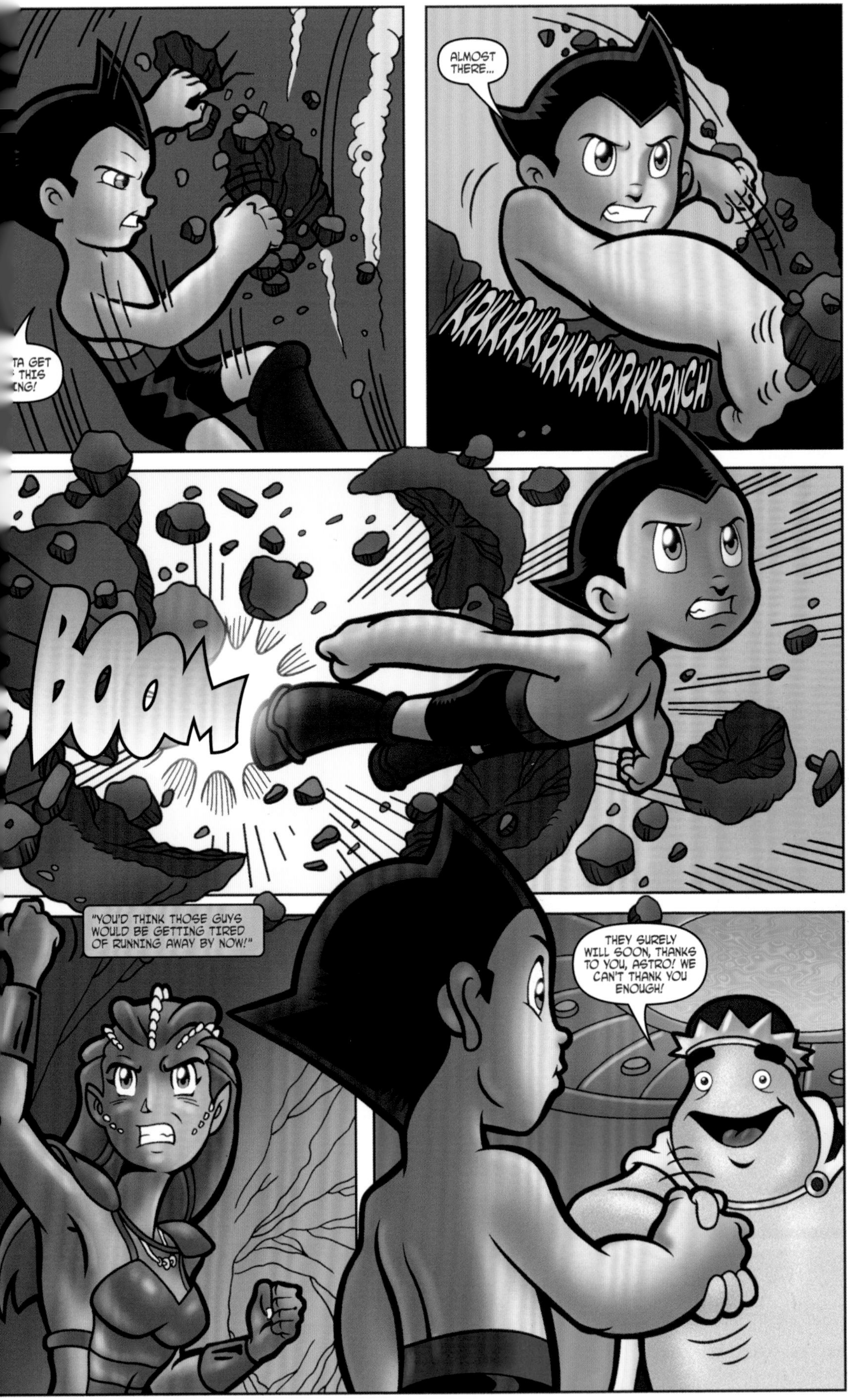

TA GET
THIS
NG!
ALMOST THERE...
KRKKRKKRKKRKKRKKRKKRNCH
BOOM
"YOU'D THINK THOSE GUYS WOULD BE GETTING TIRED OF RUNNING AWAY BY NOW!"
THEY SURELY WILL SOON, THANKS TO YOU, ASTRO! WE CAN'T THANK YOU ENOUGH!

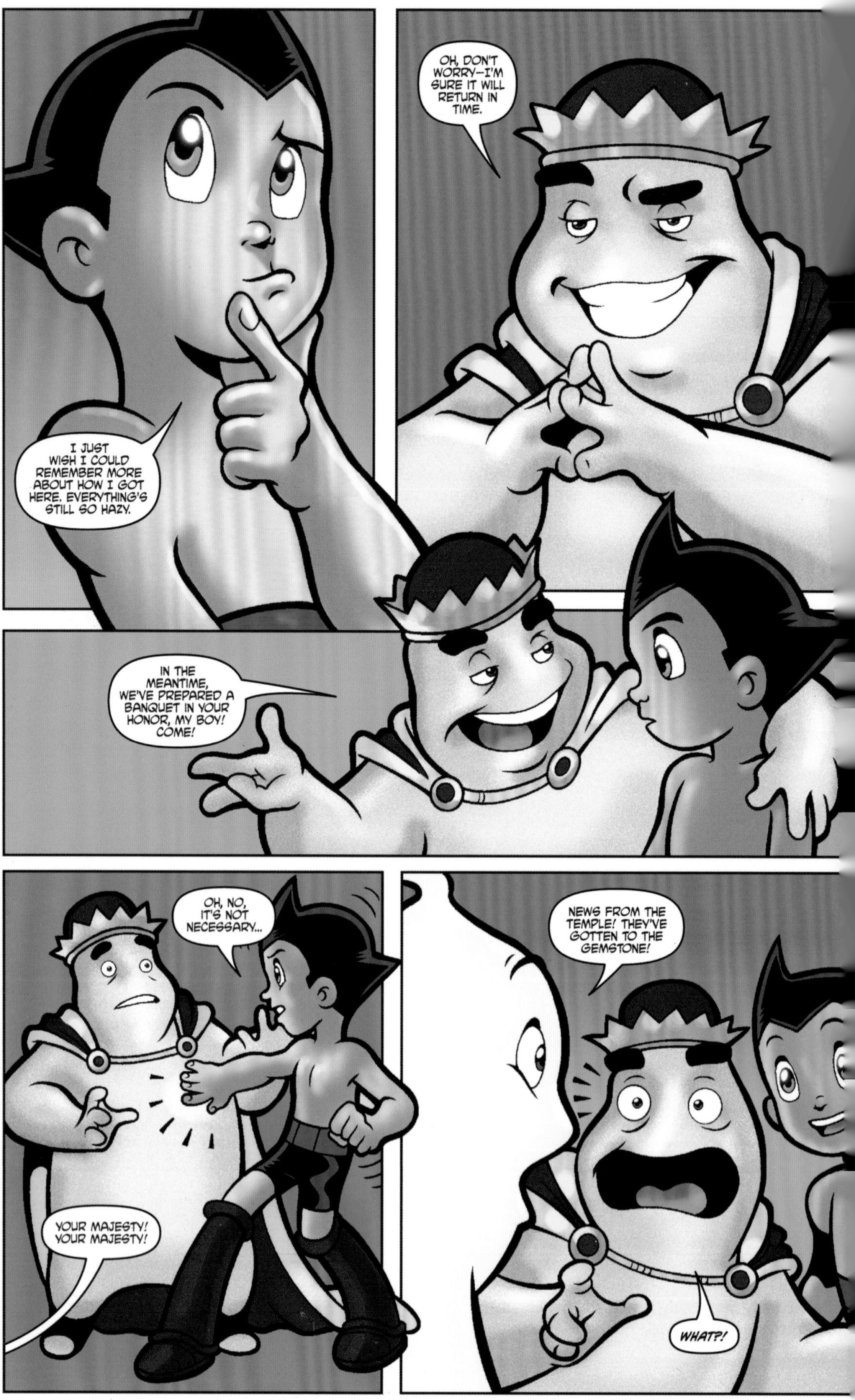
I JUST WISH I COULD REMEMBER MORE ABOUT HOW I GOT HERE. EVERYTHING'S STILL SO HAZY.
OH, DON'T WORRY—I'M SURE IT WILL RETURN IN TIME.
IN THE MEANTIME, WE'VE PREPARED A BANQUET IN YOUR HONOR, MY BOY! COME!
OH, NO, IT'S NOT NECESSARY...
YOUR MAJESTY! YOUR MAJESTY!
NEWS FROM THE TEMPLE! THEY'VE GOTTEN TO THE GEMSTONE!
WHAT?!

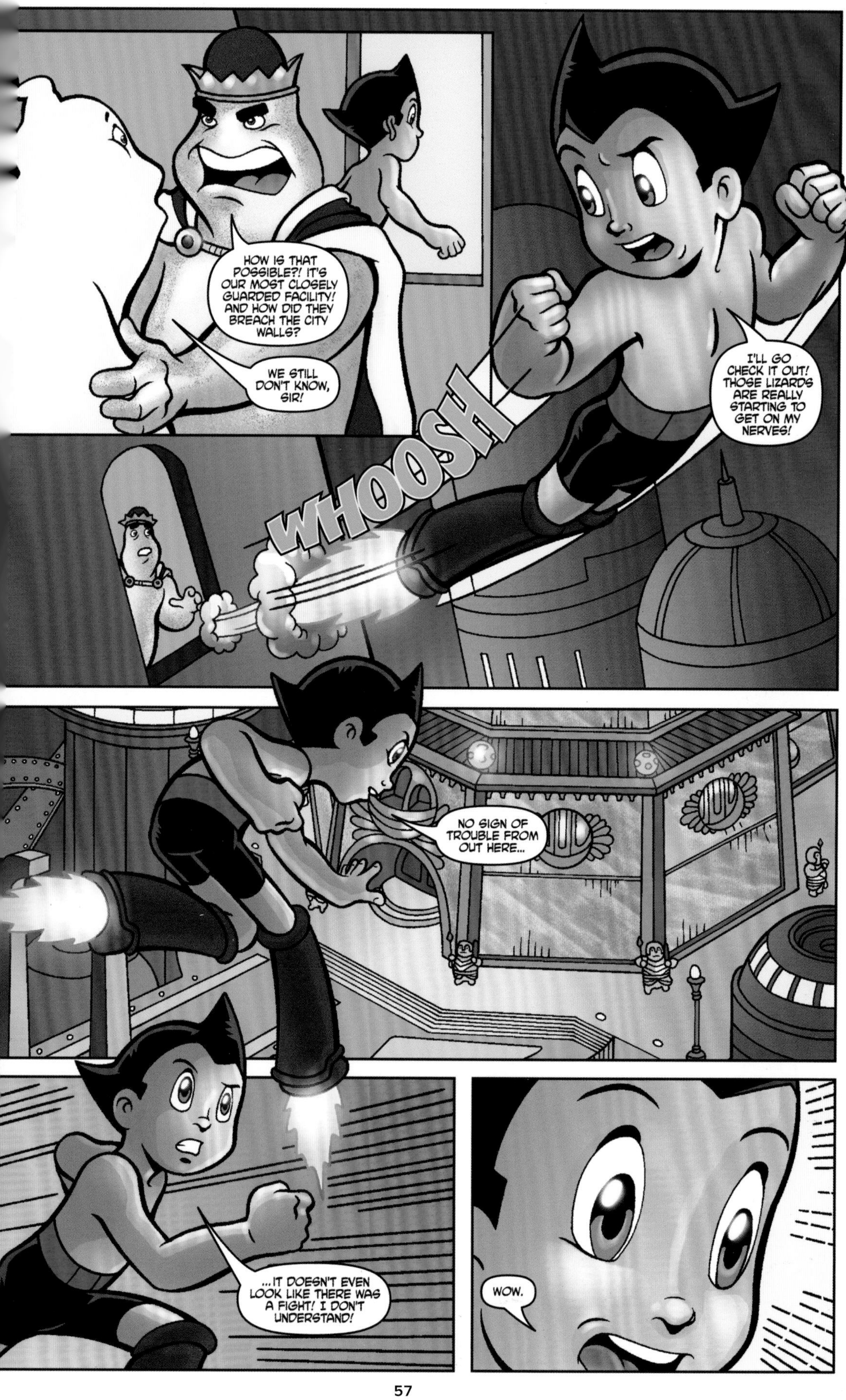
HOW IS THAT POSSIBLE?! IT'S OUR MOST CLOSELY GUARDED FACILITY! AND HOW DID THEY BREACH THE CITY WALLS?
WE STILL DON'T KNOW, SIR!
I'LL GO CHECK IT OUT! THOSE LIZARDS ARE REALLY STARTING TO GET ON MY NERVES!
WHOOSH
NO SIGN OF TROUBLE FROM OUT HERE...
...IT DOESN'T EVEN LOOK LIKE THERE WAS A FIGHT! I DON'T UNDERSTAND!
WOW.

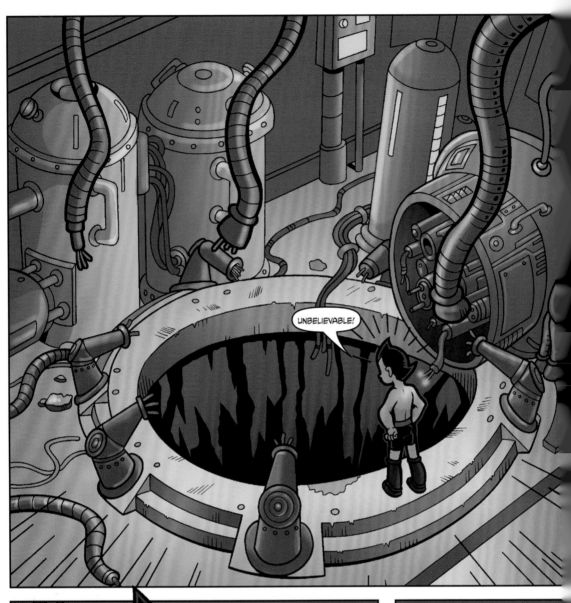

UNBELIEVABLE!

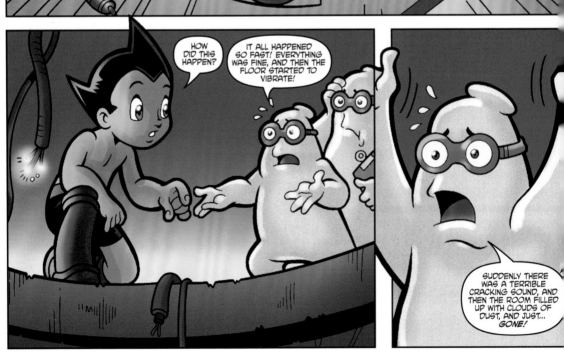

HOW DID THIS HAPPEN?

IT ALL HAPPENED SO FAST! EVERYTHING WAS FINE, AND THEN THE FLOOR STARTED TO VIBRATE!

SUDDENLY THERE WAS A TERRIBLE CRACKING SOUND, AND THEN THE ROOM FILLED UP WITH CLOUDS OF DUST, AND JUST... GONE!

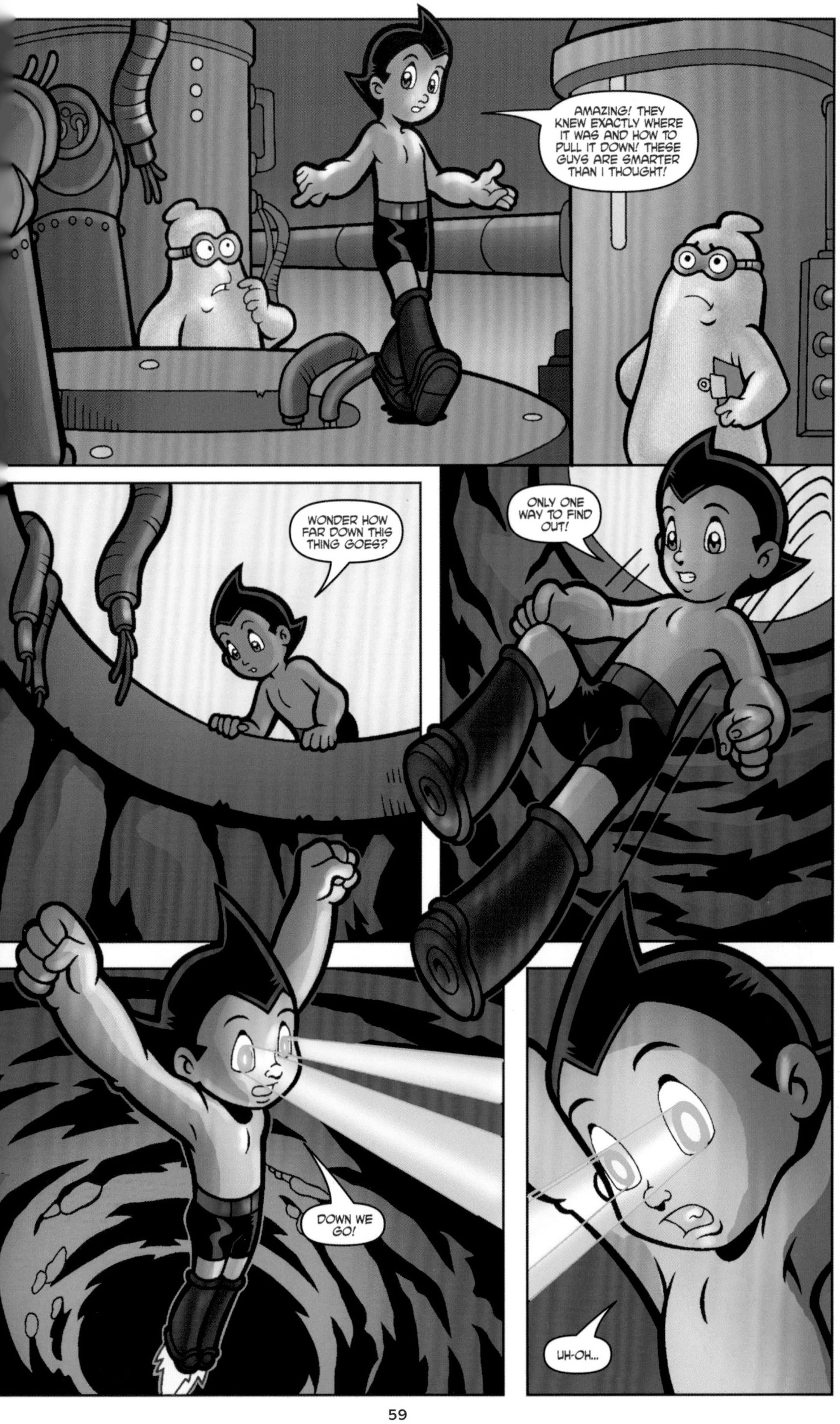
AMAZING! THEY KNEW EXACTLY WHERE IT WAS AND HOW TO PULL IT DOWN! THESE GUYS ARE SMARTER THAN I THOUGHT!
WONDER HOW FAR DOWN THIS THING GOES?
ONLY ONE WAY TO FIND OUT!
DOWN WE GO!
UH-OH...

...A TRAP! I SHOULDA EXPECTED THIS!

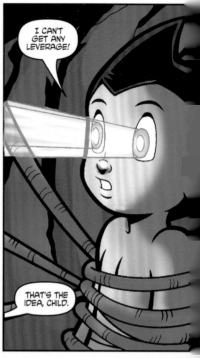

I CAN'T GET ANY LEVERAGE!

THAT'S THE IDEA, CHILD.

IT'S YOU!

INDEED, LITTLE ONE. AND YOU HAVE GROWN INTO QUITE A NUISANCE.

HOW APPROPRIATE TO SEE YOU HANGING THERE LIKE THAT, MY LITTLE FRIEND. YOU REALLY HAVE BEEN NOTHING MORE THAN A PUPPET ON A STRING.

YOU'RE ON THE WRONG SIDE OF THIS, BOY. BELIEVE ME.

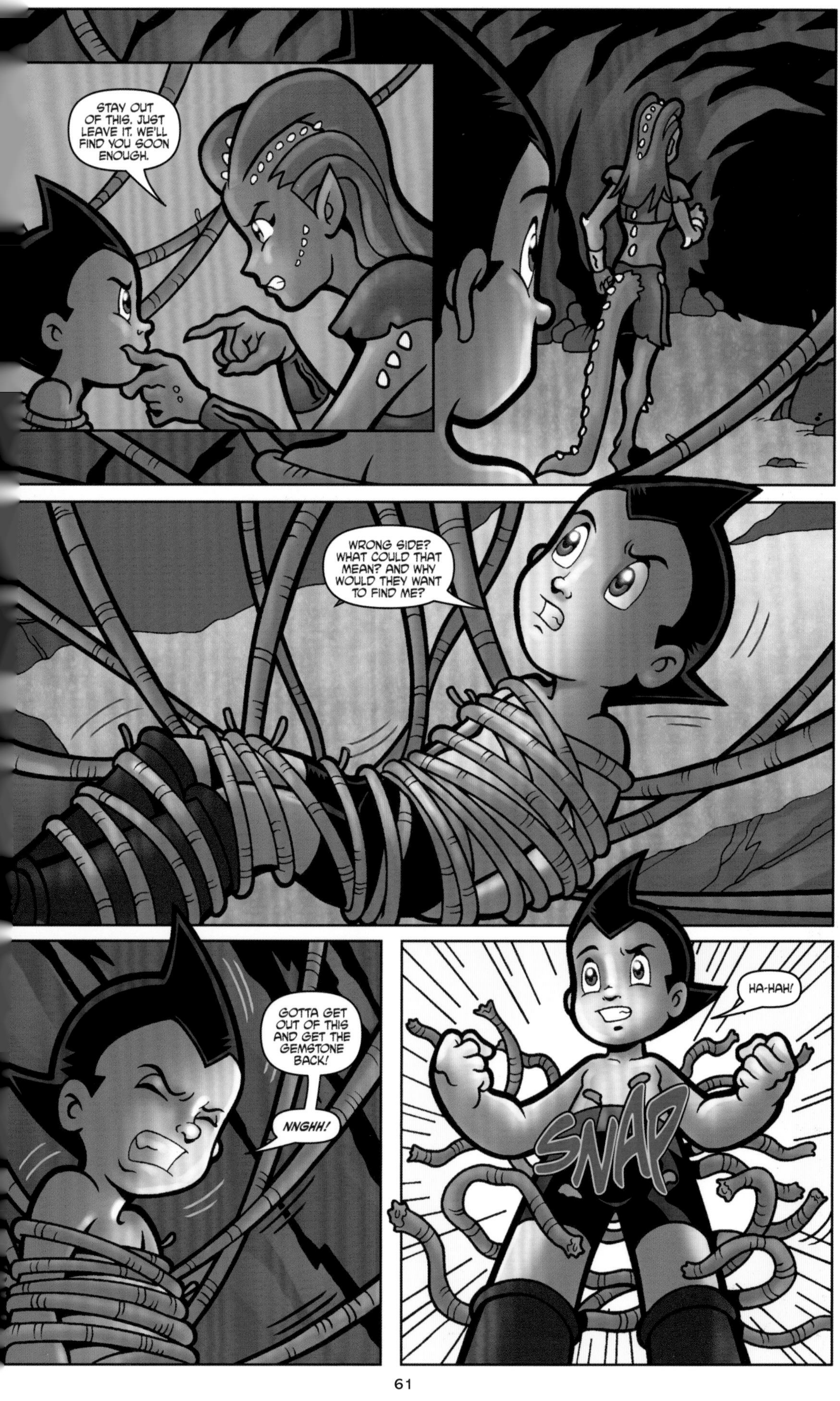
STAY OUT OF THIS. JUST LEAVE IT. WE'LL FIND YOU SOON ENOUGH.
WRONG SIDE? WHAT COULD THAT MEAN? AND WHY WOULD THEY WANT TO FIND ME?
GOTTA GET OUT OF THIS AND GET THE GEMSTONE BACK!
NNGHH!
HA-HAH!
SNAP

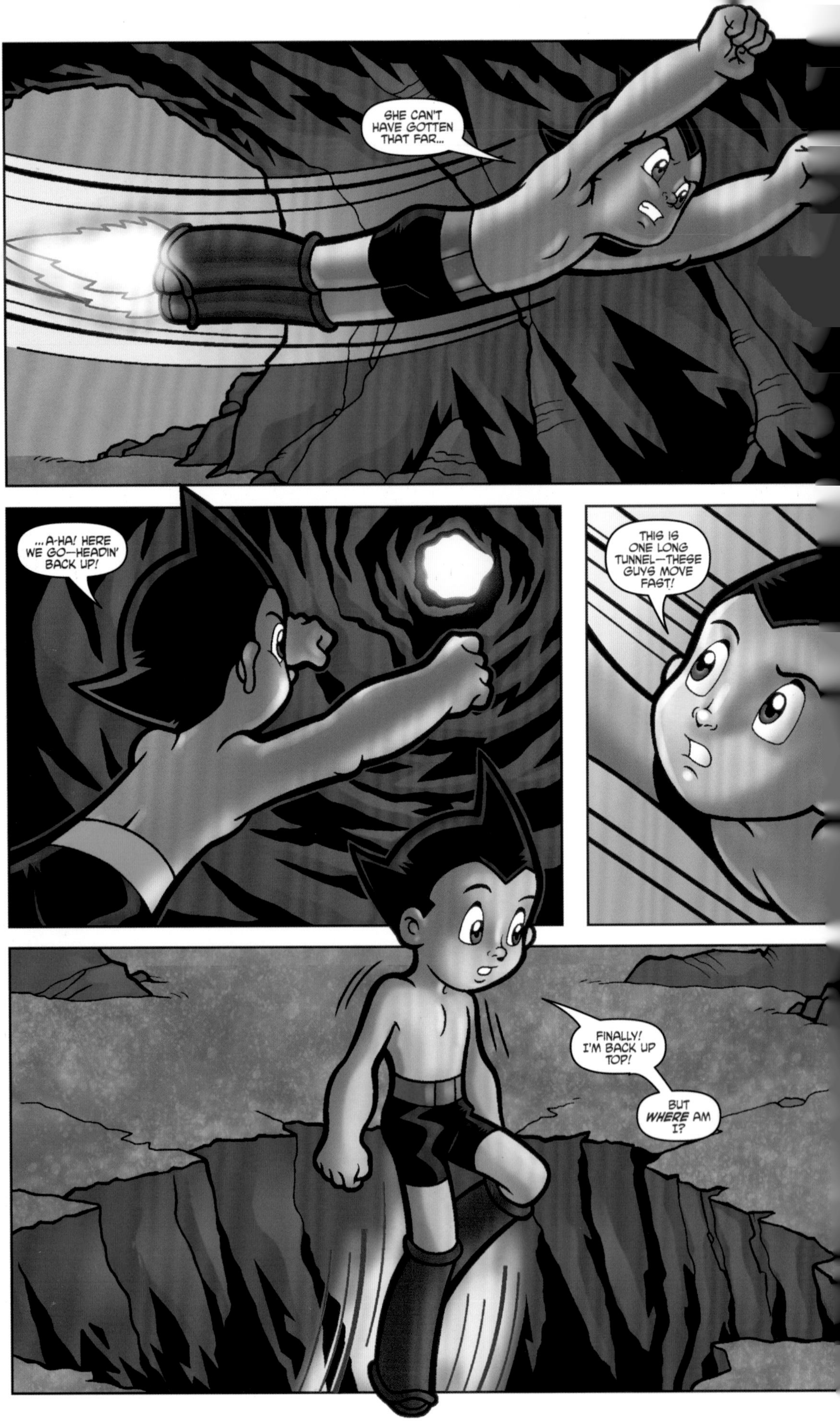
SHE CAN'T HAVE GOTTEN THAT FAR...
...A-HA! HERE WE GO—HEADIN' BACK UP!
THIS IS ONE LONG TUNNEL—THESE GUYS MOVE FAST!
FINALLY! I'M BACK UP TOP!
BUT *WHERE* AM I?

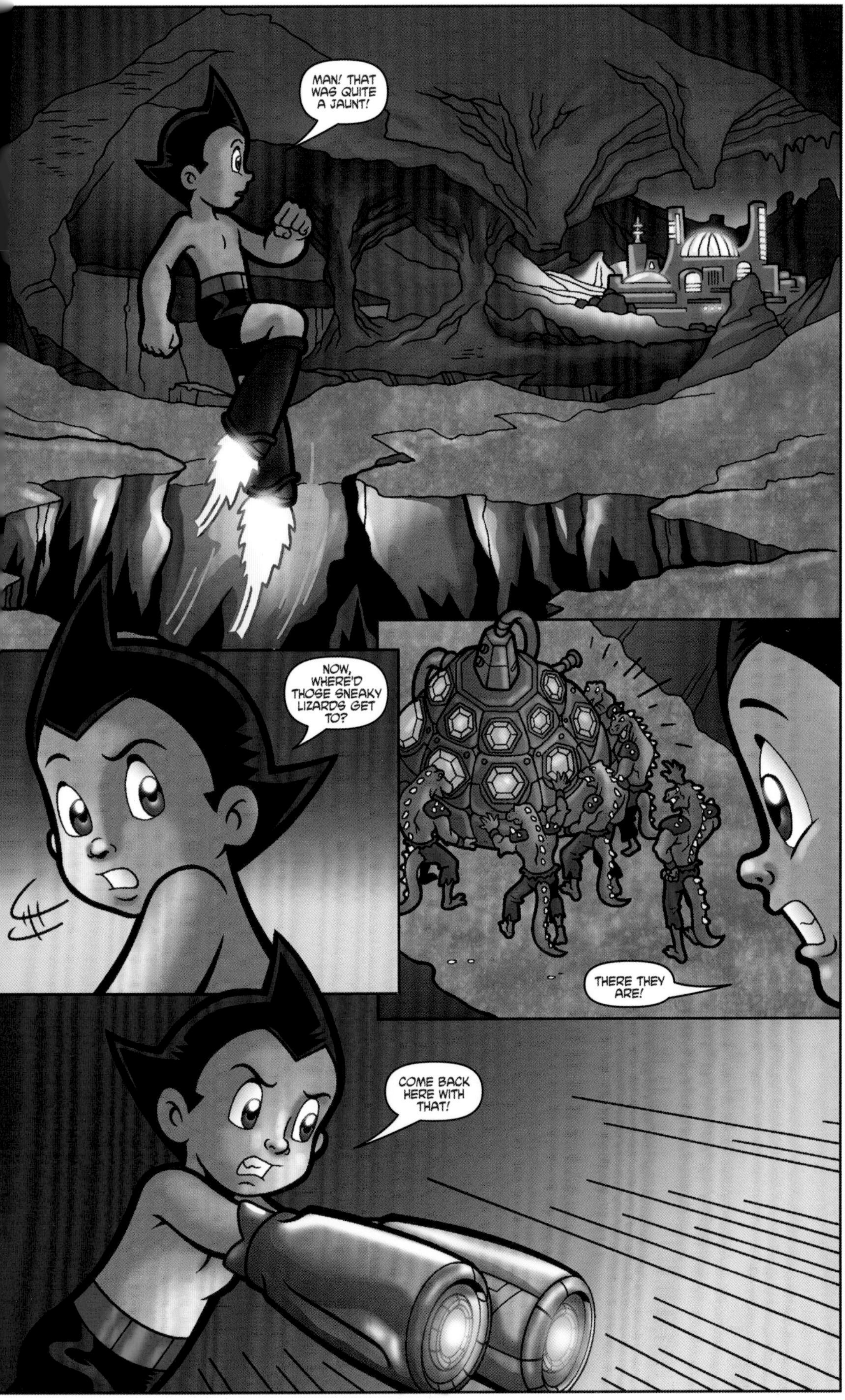
MAN! THAT WAS QUITE A JAUNT!
NOW, WHERE'D THOSE SNEAKY LIZARDS GET TO?
THERE THEY ARE!
COME BACK HERE WITH THAT!

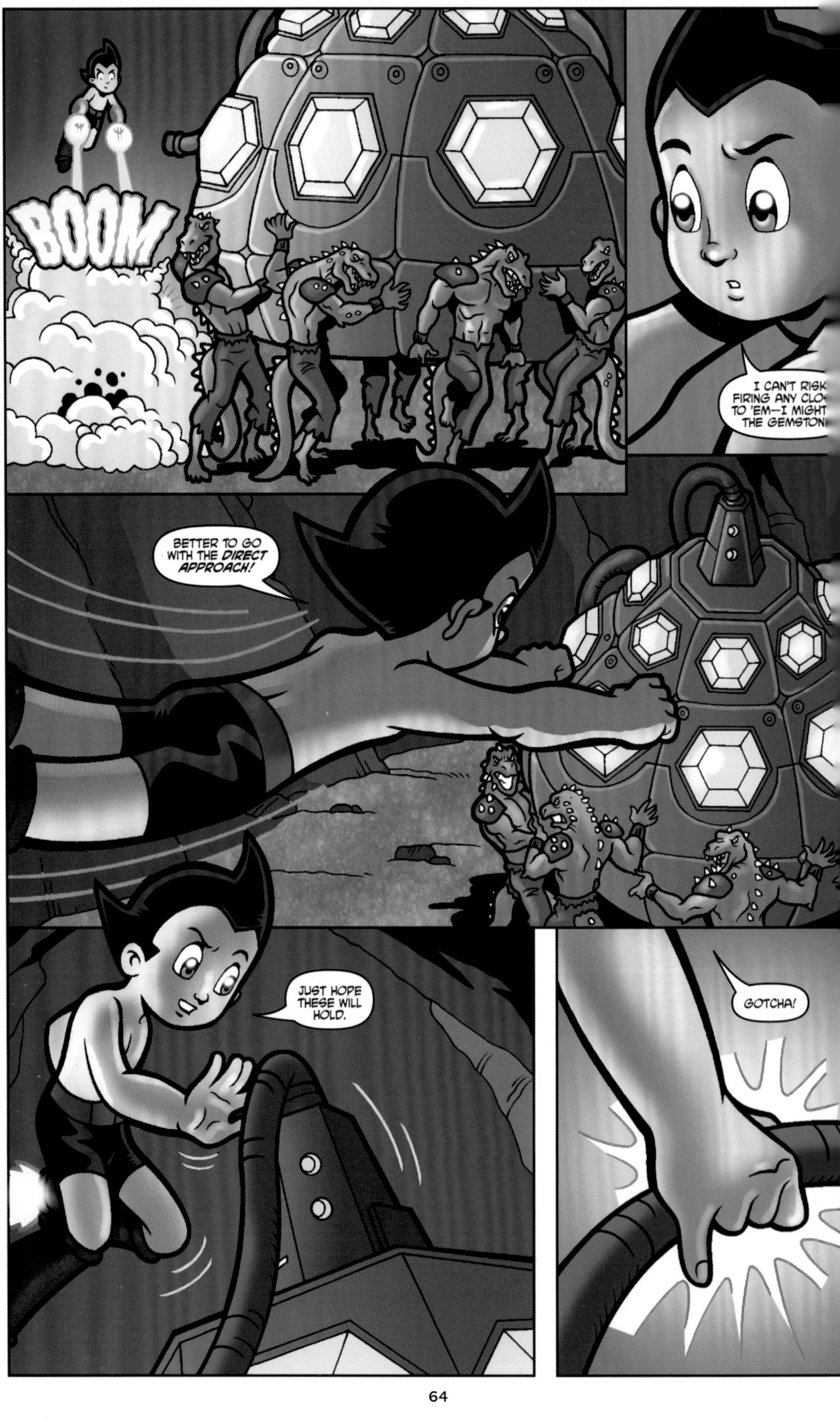
BOOM
I CAN'T RISK FIRING ANY CLO TO 'EM—I MIGHT THE GEMSTON
BETTER TO GO WITH THE *DIRECT APPROACH!*
JUST HOPE THESE WILL HOLD.
GOTCHA!

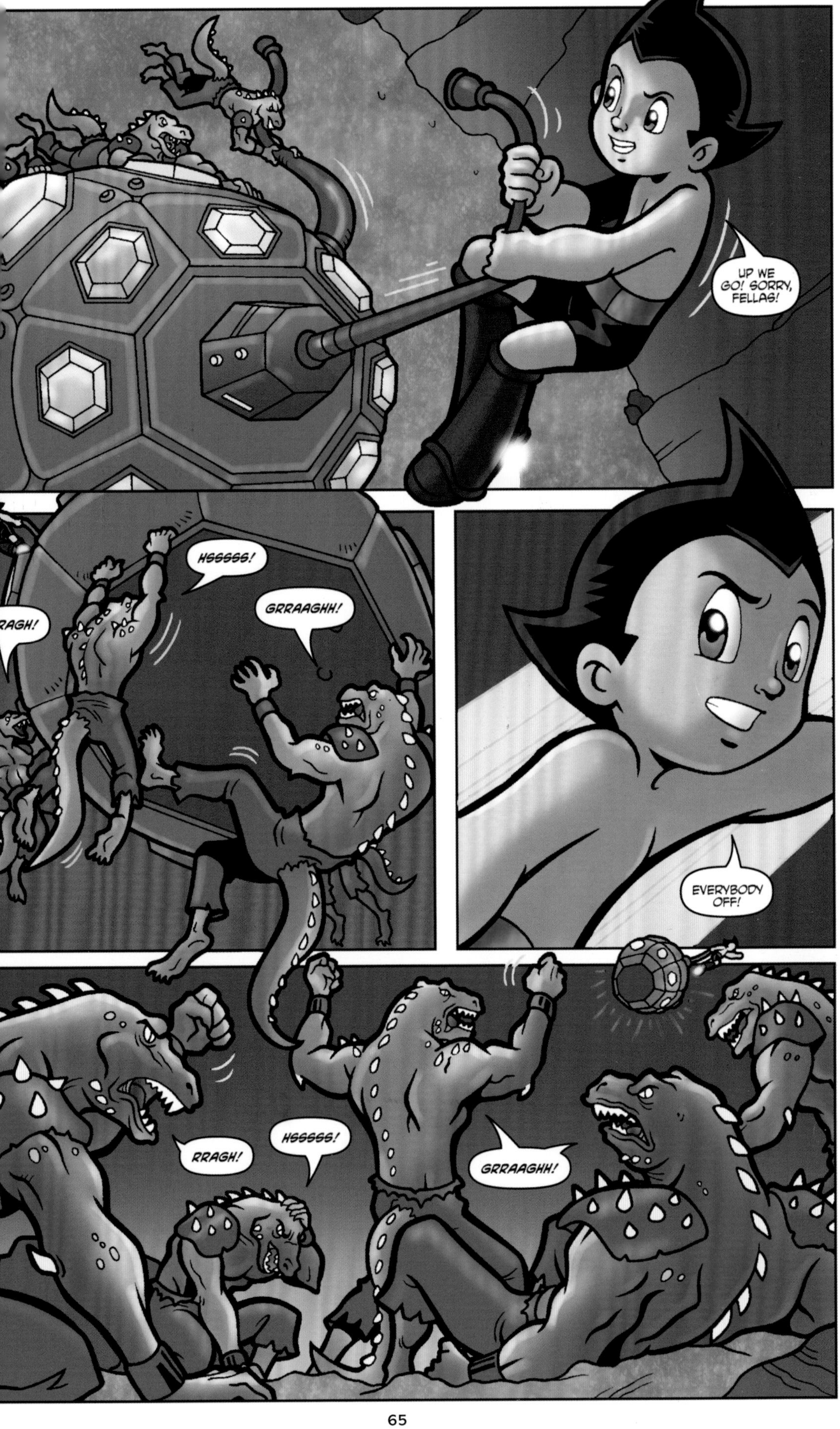
UP WE GO! SORRY, FELLAS!
HSSSSS!
GRRAAGHH!
RAGH!
EVERYBODY OFF!
RRAGH!
HSSSSS!
GRRAAGHH!

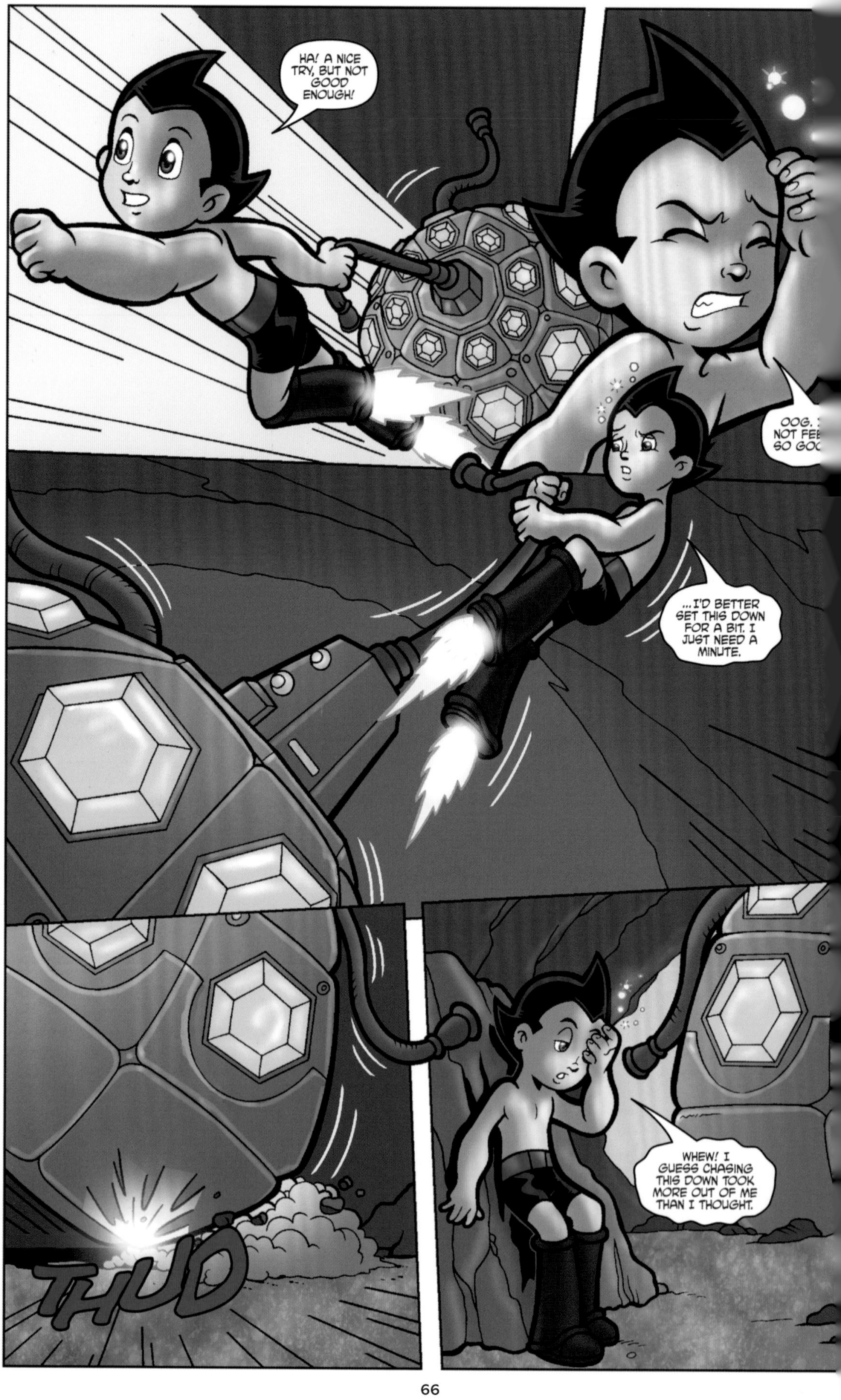
HA! A NICE TRY, BUT NOT GOOD ENOUGH!
OOG. I'M NOT FEELING SO GOOD...
...I'D BETTER SET THIS DOWN FOR A BIT. I JUST NEED A MINUTE.
THUD
WHEW! I GUESS CHASING THIS DOWN TOOK MORE OUT OF ME THAN I THOUGHT.

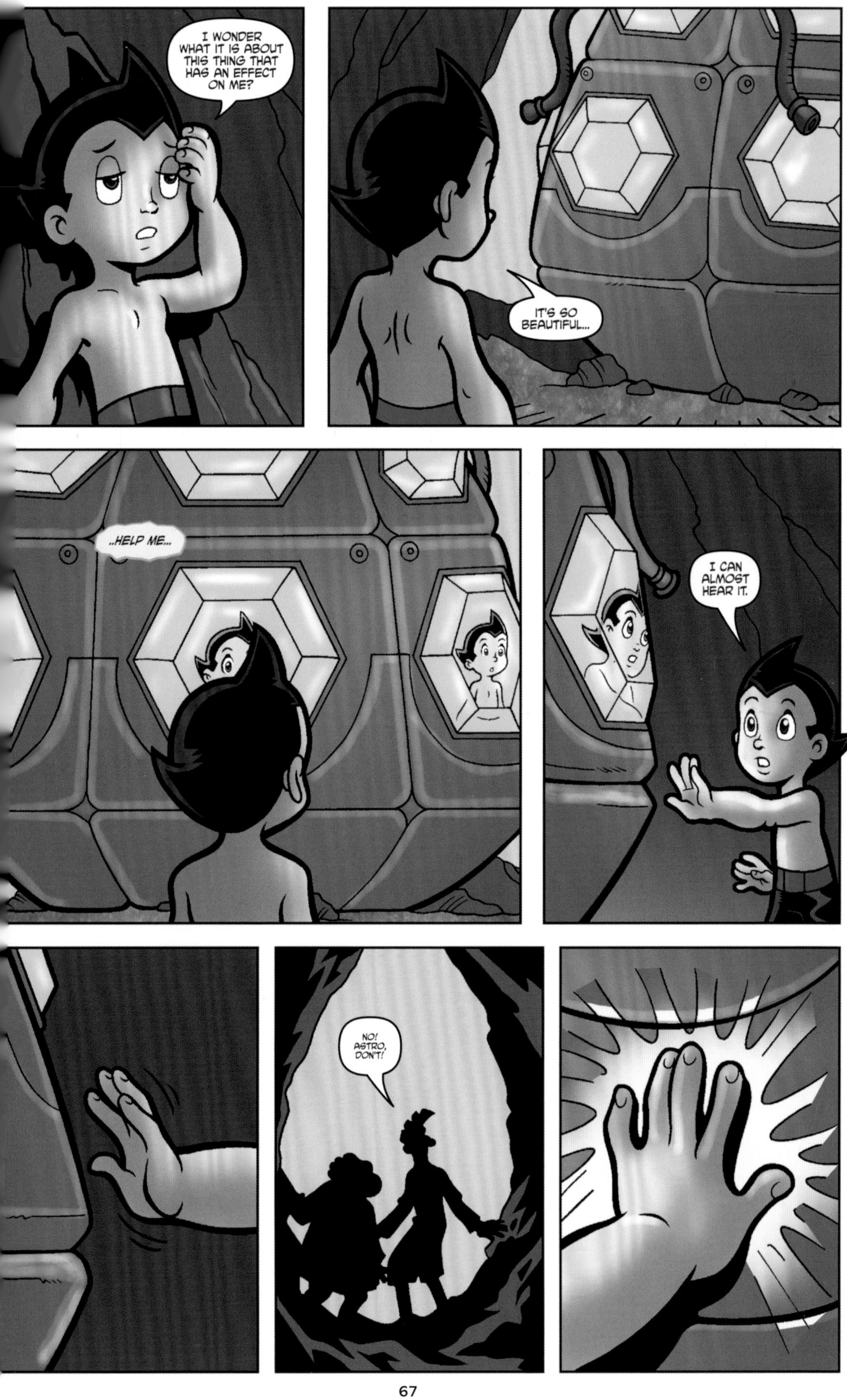
I WONDER WHAT IT IS ABOUT THIS THING THAT HAS AN EFFECT ON ME?
IT'S SO BEAUTIFUL...
..HELP ME...
I CAN ALMOST HEAR IT.
NO! ASTRO, DON'T!

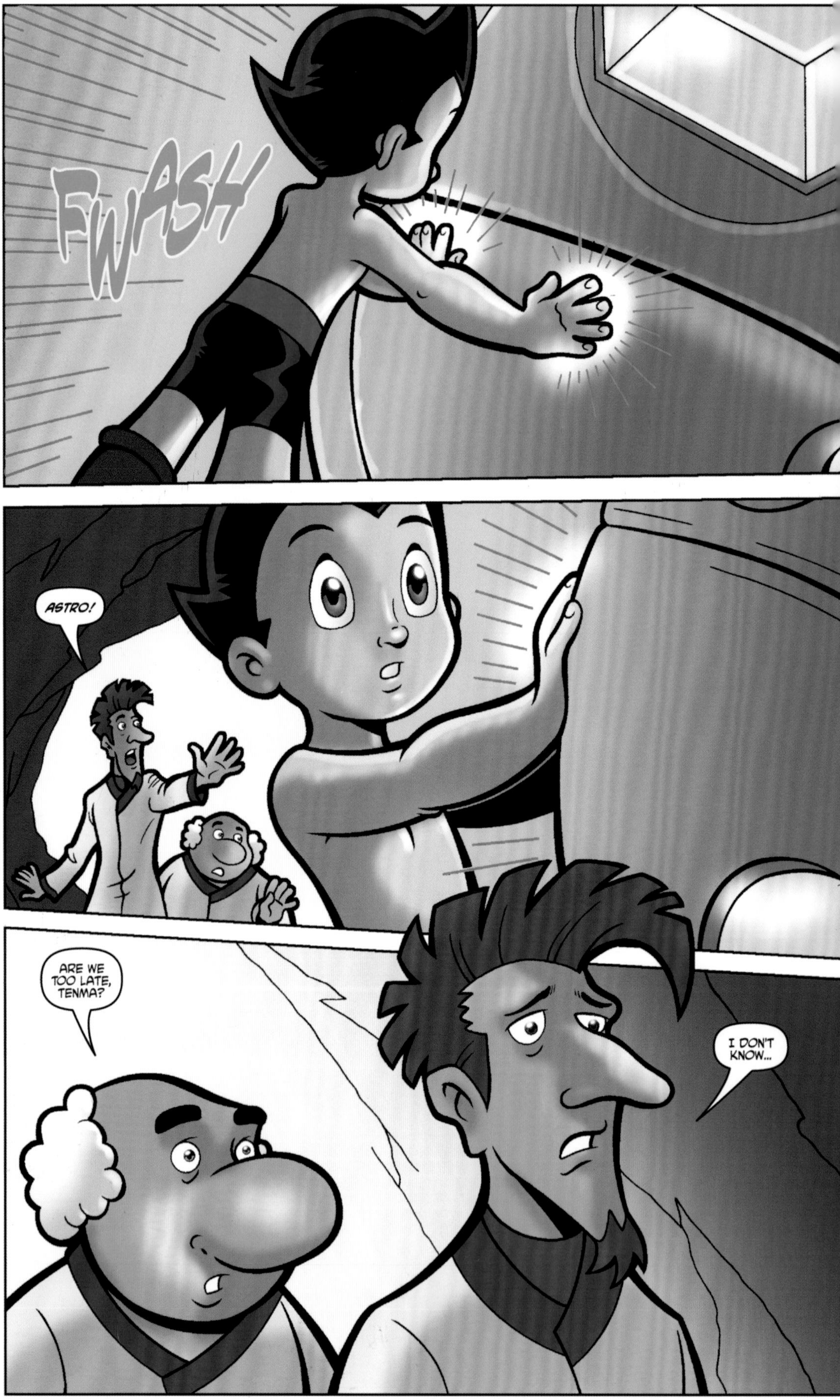
FWASH
ASTRO!
ARE WE TOO LATE, TENMA?
I DON'T KNOW...

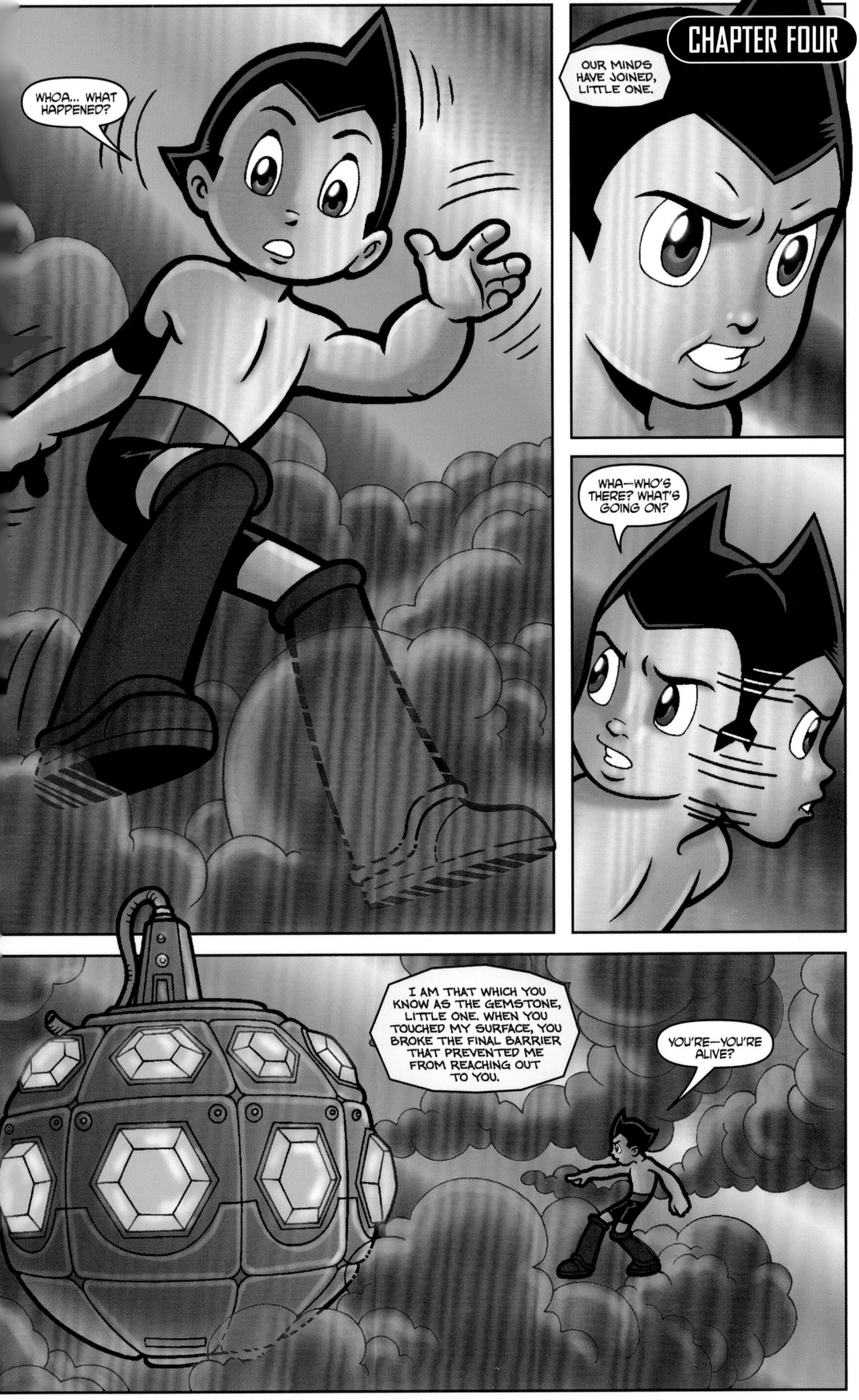
CHAPTER FOUR
WHOA... WHAT HAPPENED?
OUR MINDS HAVE JOINED, LITTLE ONE.
WHA—WHO'S THERE? WHAT'S GOING ON?
I AM THAT WHICH YOU KNOW AS THE GEMSTONE, LITTLE ONE. WHEN YOU TOUCHED MY SURFACE, YOU BROKE THE FINAL BARRIER THAT PREVENTED ME FROM REACHING OUT TO YOU.
YOU'RE—YOU'RE ALIVE?

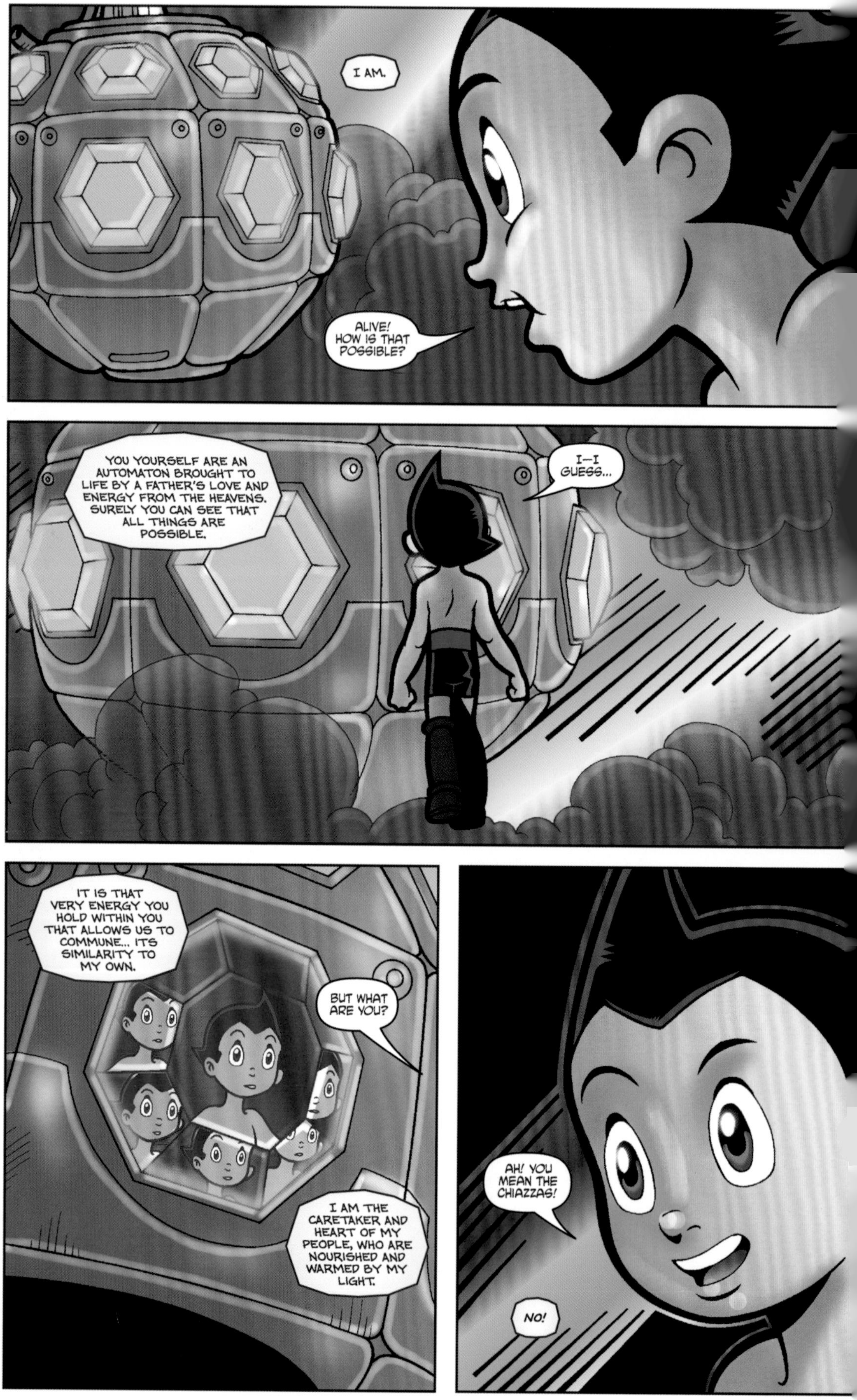
I AM.
ALIVE! HOW IS THAT POSSIBLE?
YOU YOURSELF ARE AN AUTOMATON BROUGHT TO LIFE BY A FATHER'S LOVE AND ENERGY FROM THE HEAVENS. SURELY YOU CAN SEE THAT ALL THINGS ARE POSSIBLE.
I—I GUESS...
IT IS THAT VERY ENERGY YOU HOLD WITHIN YOU THAT ALLOWS US TO COMMUNE... ITS SIMILARITY TO MY OWN.
BUT WHAT ARE YOU?
I AM THE CARETAKER AND HEART OF MY PEOPLE, WHO ARE NOURISHED AND WARMED BY MY LIGHT.
AH! YOU MEAN THE CHIAZZAS!
NO!

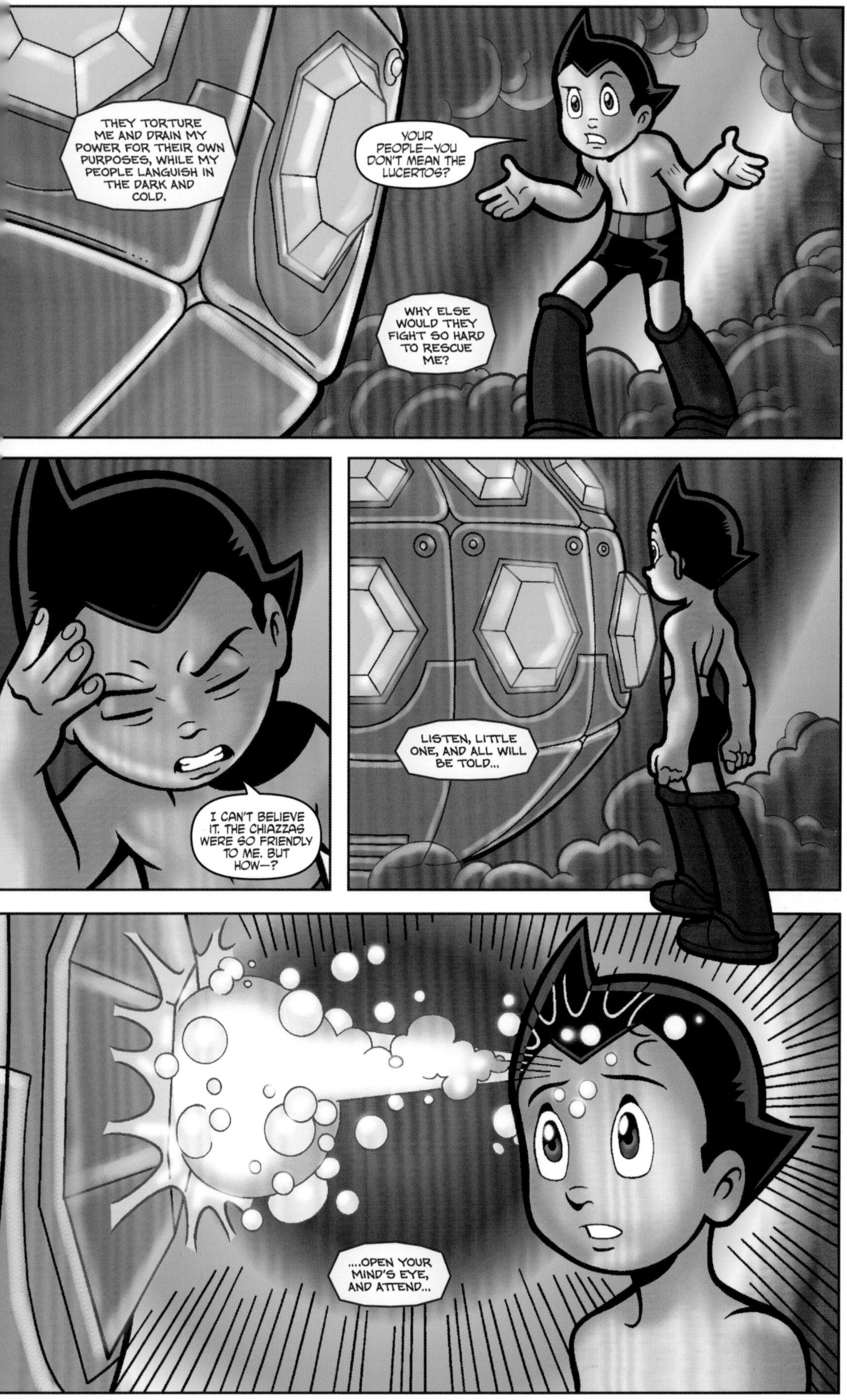
THEY TORTURE ME AND DRAIN MY POWER FOR THEIR OWN PURPOSES, WHILE MY PEOPLE LANGUISH IN THE DARK AND COLD.
YOUR PEOPLE—YOU DON'T MEAN THE LUCERTOS?
WHY ELSE WOULD THEY FIGHT SO HARD TO RESCUE ME?
I CAN'T BELIEVE IT. THE CHIAZZAS WERE SO FRIENDLY TO ME. BUT HOW--?
LISTEN, LITTLE ONE, AND ALL WILL BE TOLD...
....OPEN YOUR MIND'S EYE, AND ATTEND...

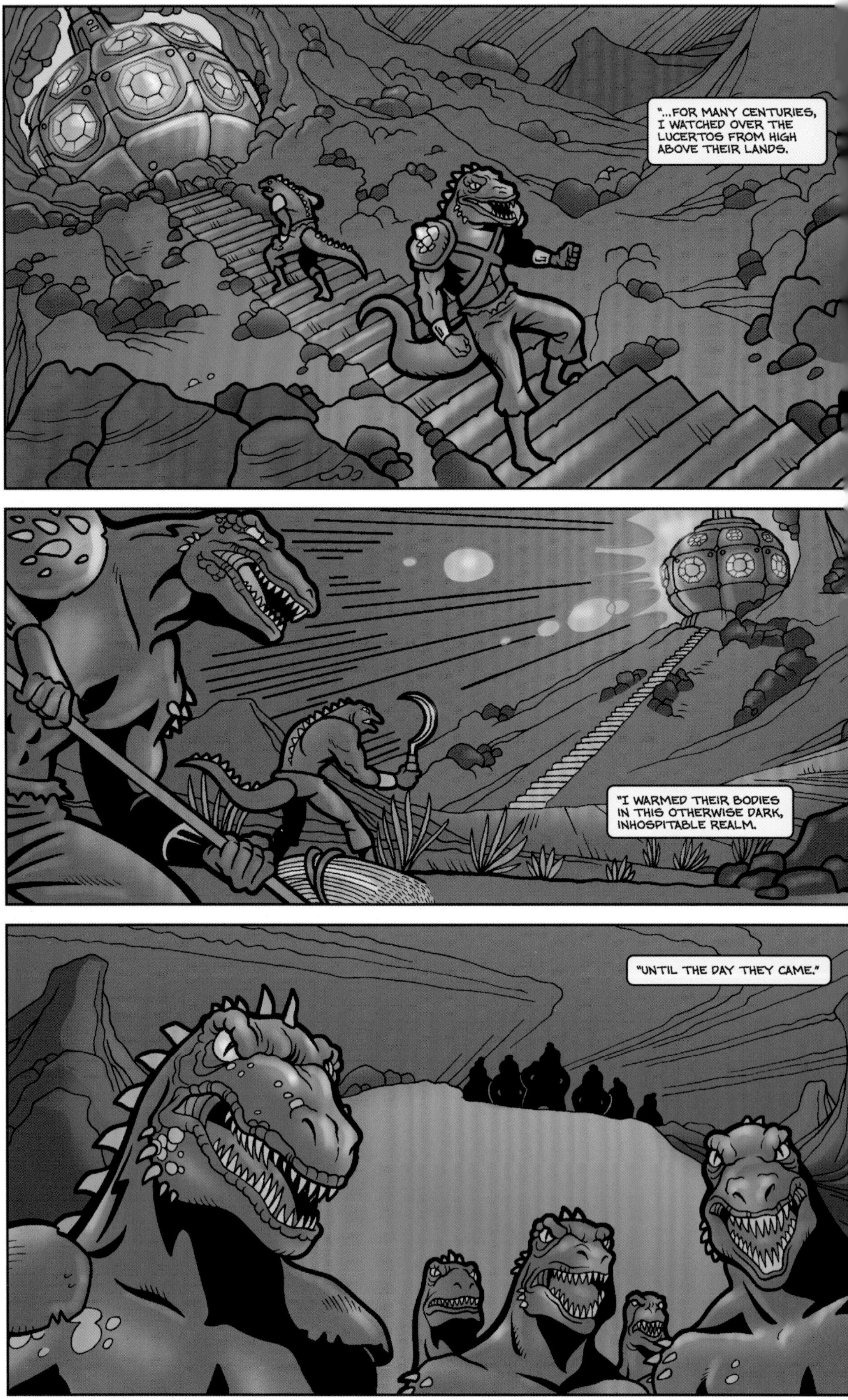
"...FOR MANY CENTURIES, I WATCHED OVER THE LUCERTOS FROM HIGH ABOVE THEIR LANDS.
"I WARMED THEIR BODIES IN THIS OTHERWISE DARK, INHOSPITABLE REALM.
"UNTIL THE DAY THEY CAME."

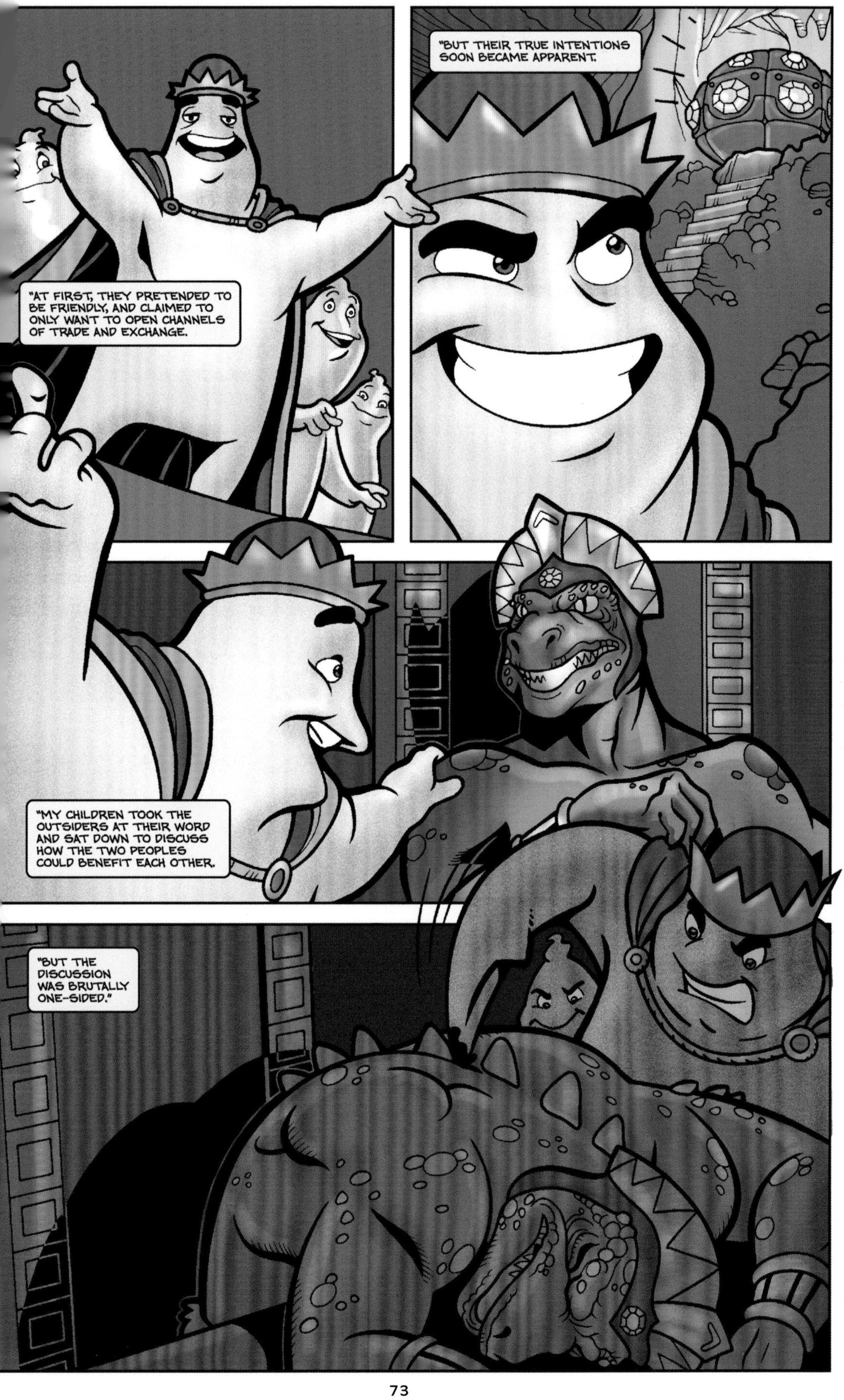
"AT FIRST, THEY PRETENDED TO BE FRIENDLY, AND CLAIMED TO ONLY WANT TO OPEN CHANNELS OF TRADE AND EXCHANGE.
"BUT THEIR TRUE INTENTIONS SOON BECAME APPARENT.
"MY CHILDREN TOOK THE OUTSIDERS AT THEIR WORD AND SAT DOWN TO DISCUSS HOW THE TWO PEOPLES COULD BENEFIT EACH OTHER.
"BUT THE DISCUSSION WAS BRUTALLY ONE-SIDED."

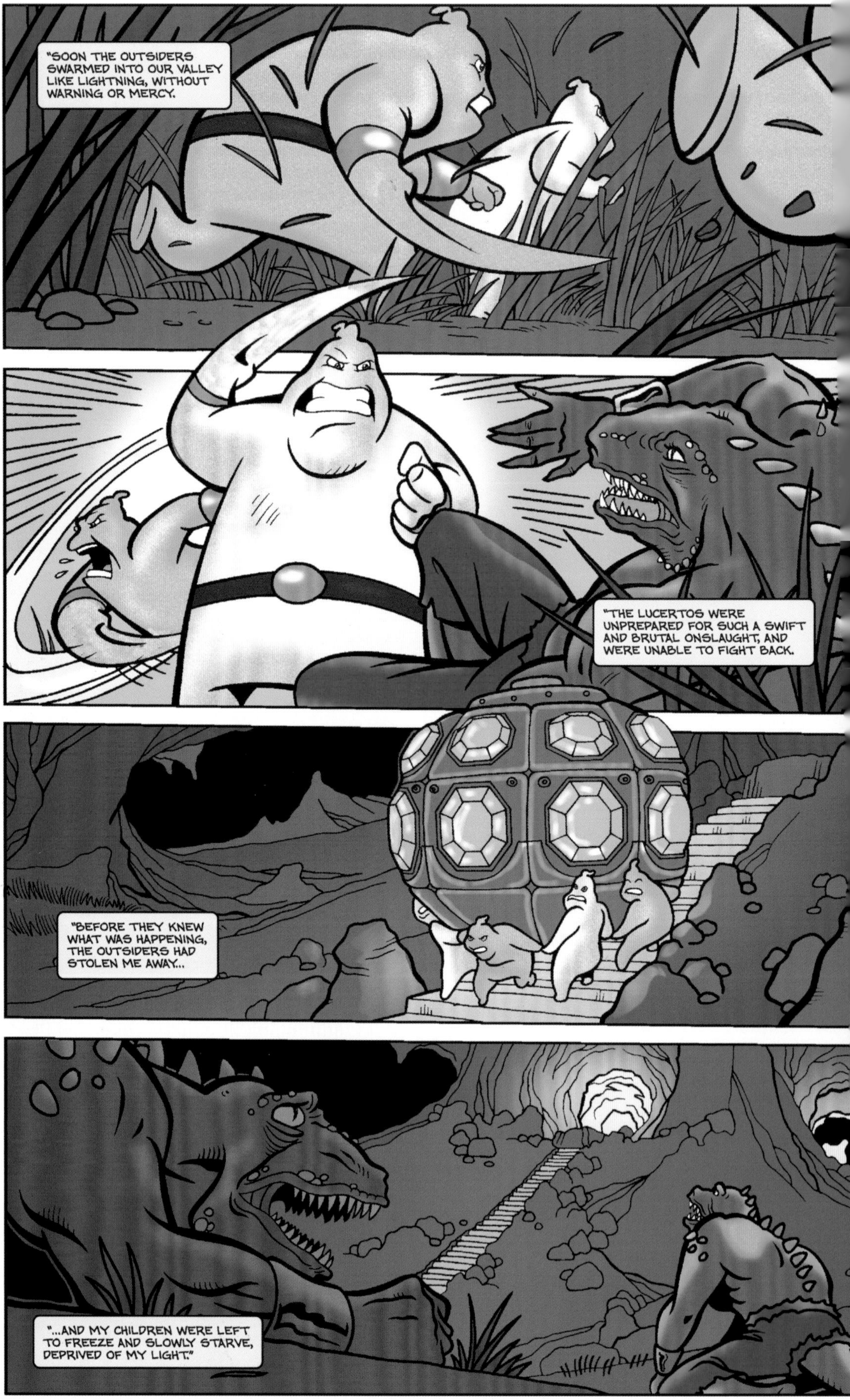
"SOON THE OUTSIDERS SWARMED INTO OUR VALLEY LIKE LIGHTNING, WITHOUT WARNING OR MERCY.
"THE LUCERTOS WERE UNPREPARED FOR SUCH A SWIFT AND BRUTAL ONSLAUGHT, AND WERE UNABLE TO FIGHT BACK.
"BEFORE THEY KNEW WHAT WAS HAPPENING, THE OUTSIDERS HAD STOLEN ME AWAY...
"...AND MY CHILDREN WERE LEFT TO FREEZE AND SLOWLY STARVE, DEPRIVED OF MY LIGHT."

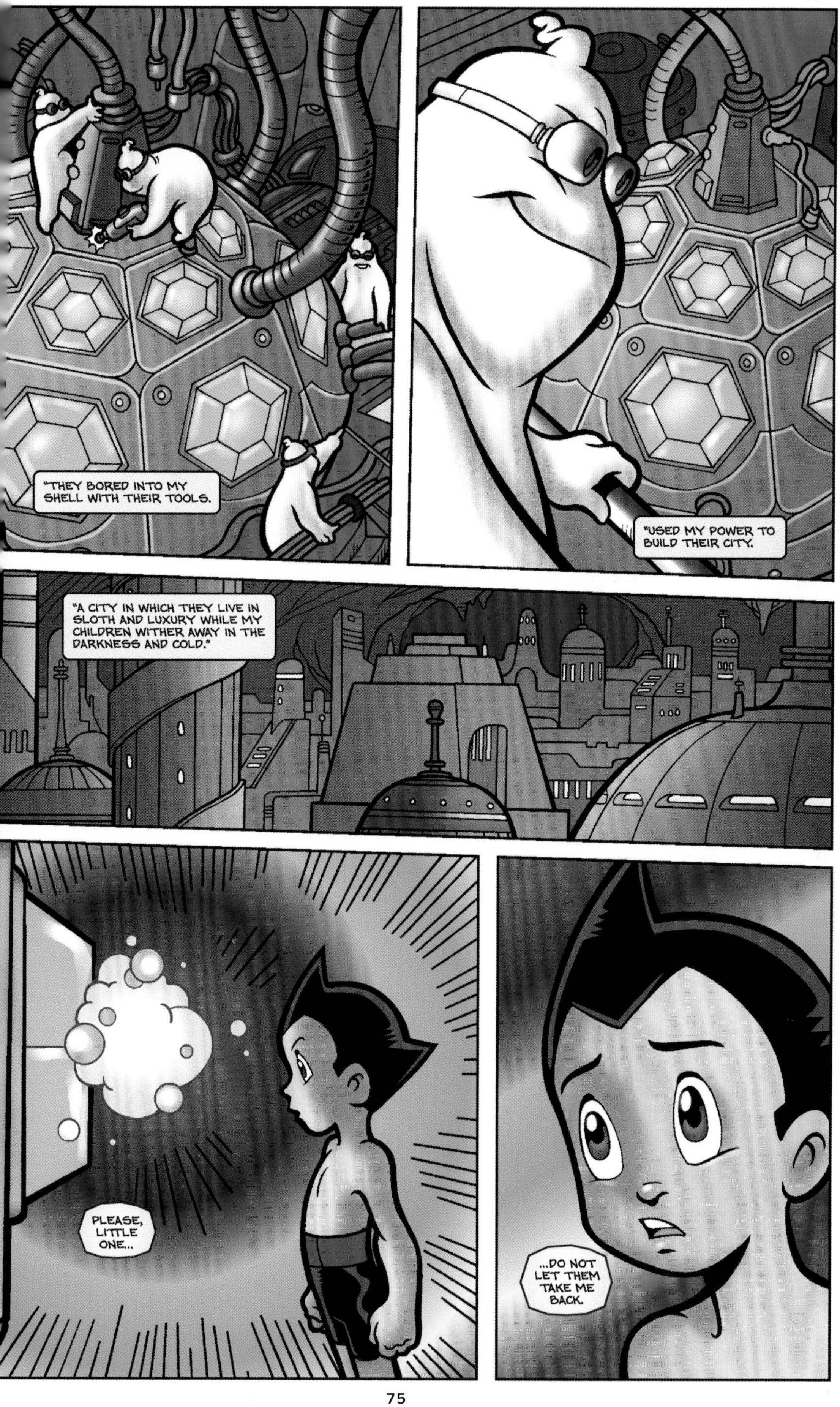
"THEY BORED INTO MY SHELL WITH THEIR TOOLS.
"USED MY POWER TO BUILD THEIR CITY.
"A CITY IN WHICH THEY LIVE IN SLOTH AND LUXURY WHILE MY CHILDREN WITHER AWAY IN THE DARKNESS AND COLD."
PLEASE, LITTLE ONE...
...DO NOT LET THEM TAKE ME BACK.

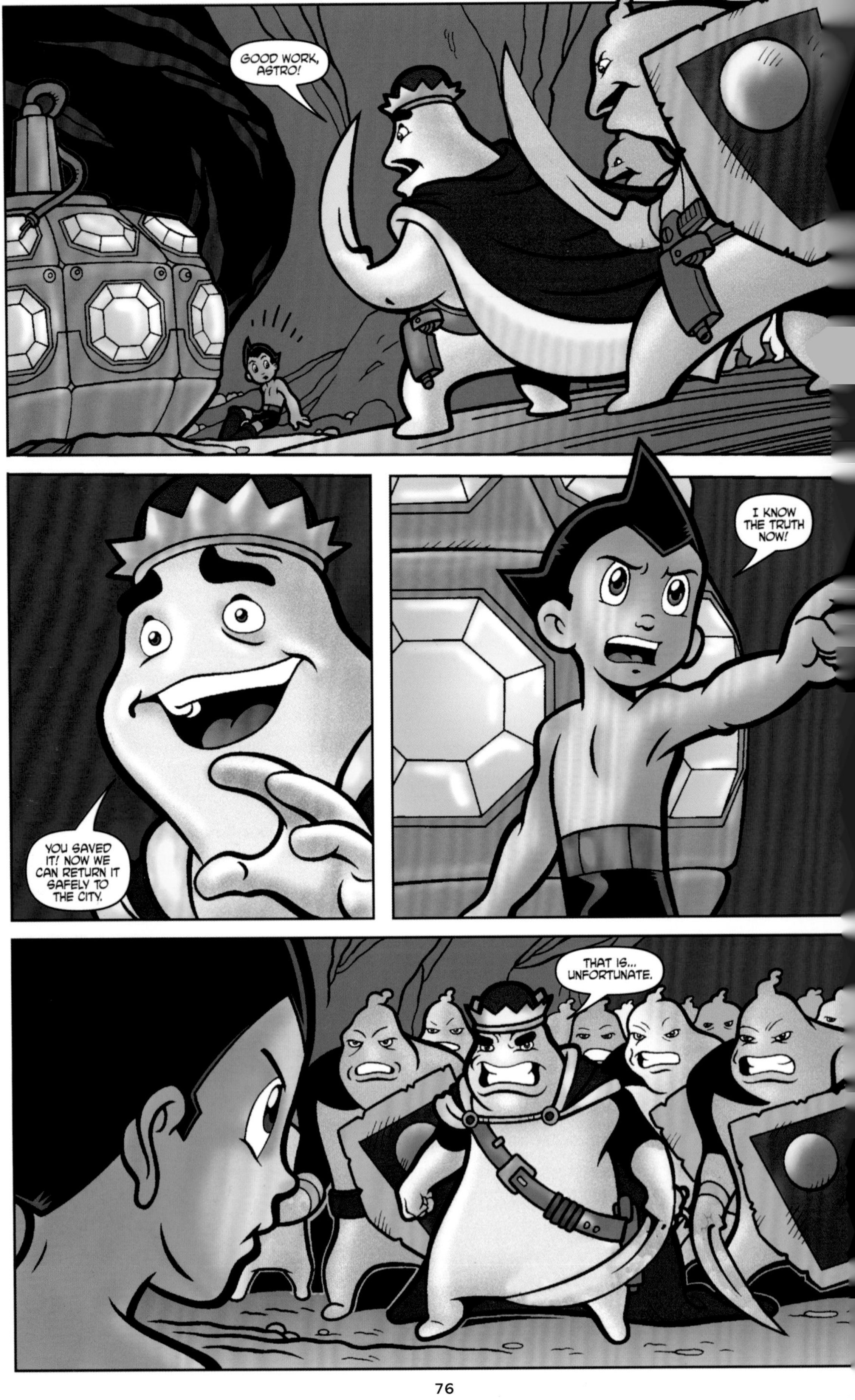
GOOD WORK, ASTRO!
YOU SAVED IT! NOW WE CAN RETURN IT SAFELY TO THE CITY.
I KNOW THE TRUTH NOW!
THAT IS... UNFORTUNATE.

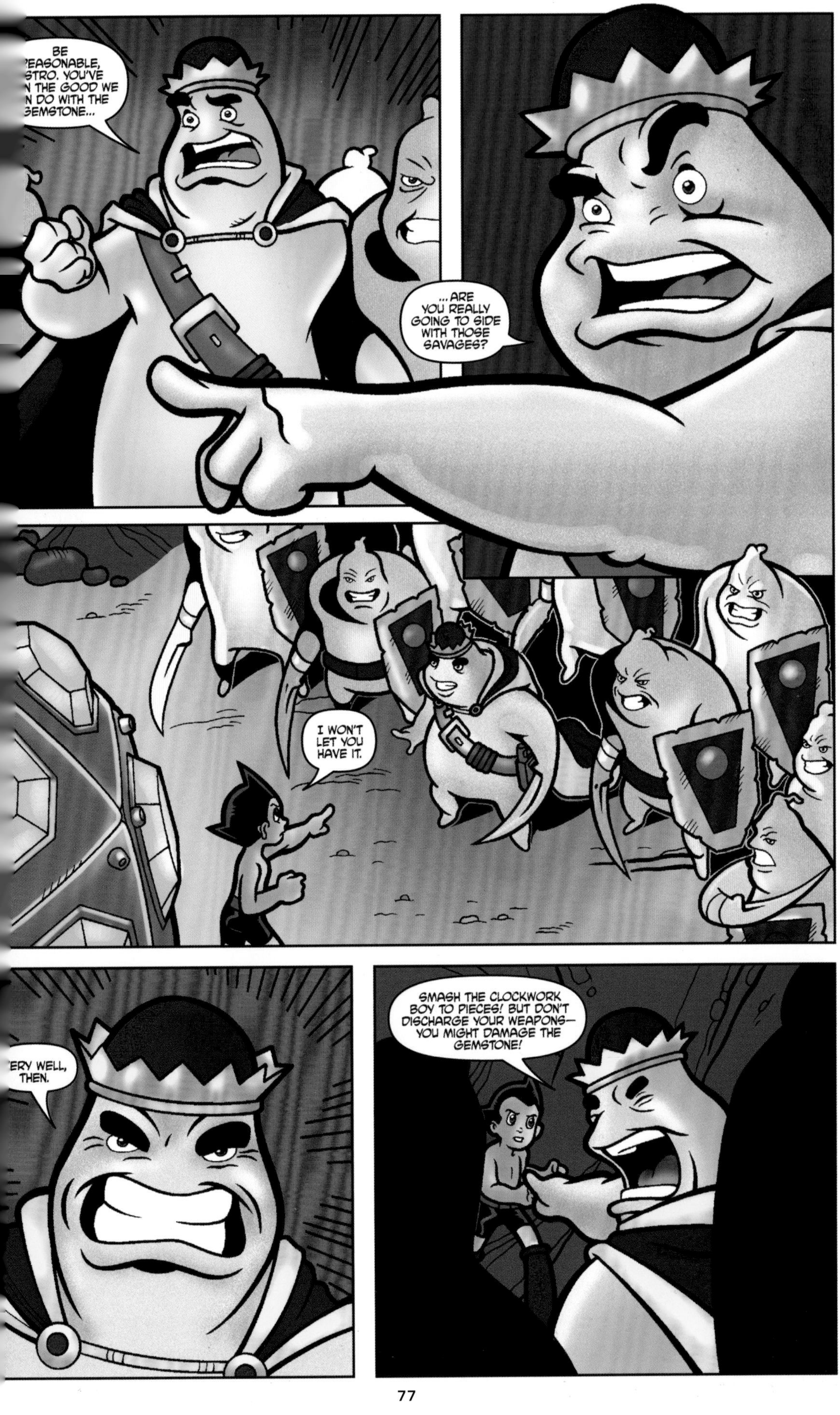
BE REASONABLE, ASTRO. YOU'VE SEEN THE GOOD WE CAN DO WITH THE GEMSTONE...
...ARE YOU REALLY GOING TO SIDE WITH THOSE SAVAGES?
I WON'T LET YOU HAVE IT.
VERY WELL, THEN.
SMASH THE CLOCKWORK BOY TO PIECES! BUT DON'T DISCHARGE YOUR WEAPONS— YOU MIGHT DAMAGE THE GEMSTONE!

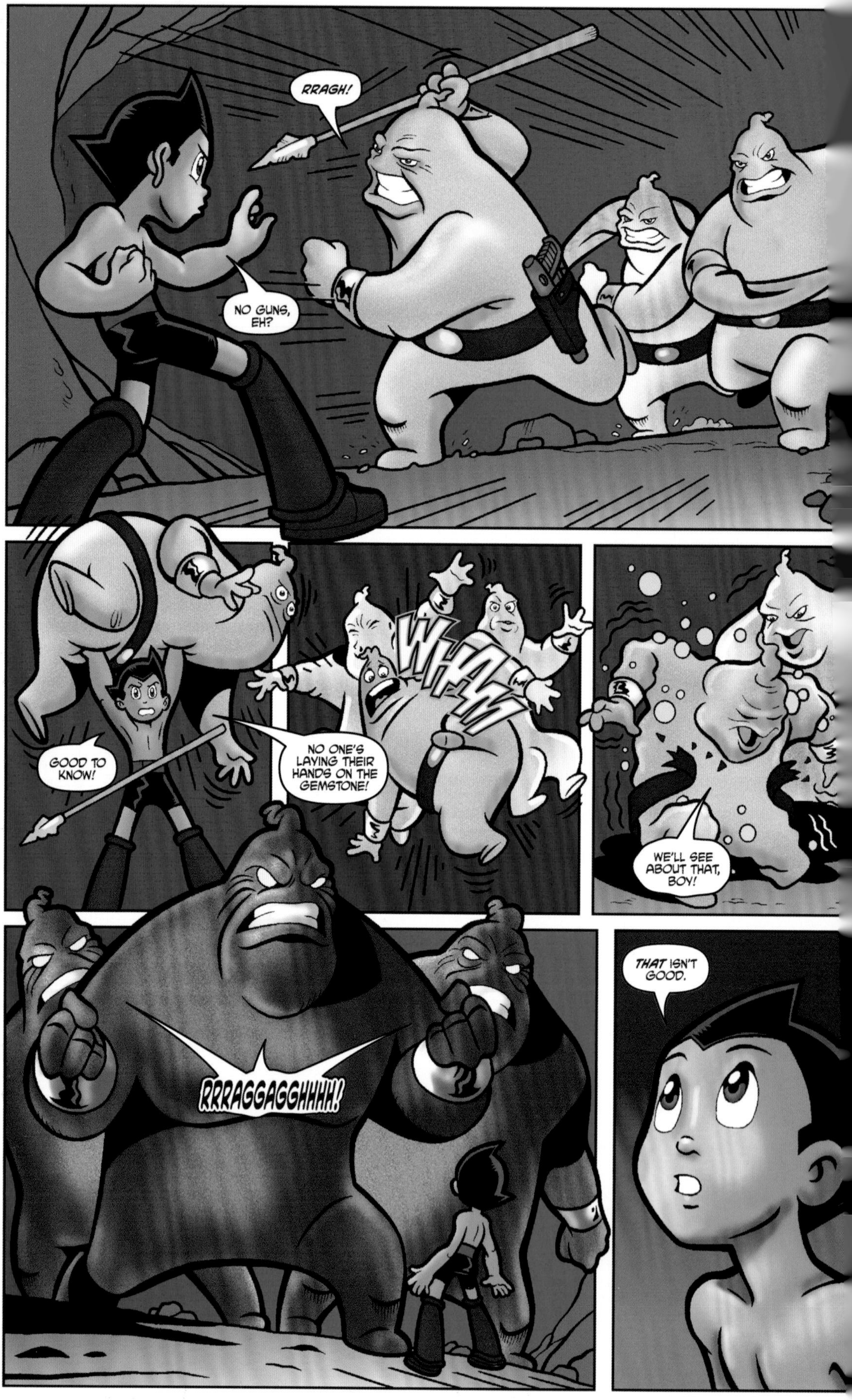
RRAGH!
NO GUNS, EH?
GOOD TO KNOW!
NO ONE'S LAYING THEIR HANDS ON THE GEMSTONE!
WHAM
WE'LL SEE ABOUT THAT, BOY!
RRRAGGAGGHHHH!
THAT ISN'T GOOD.

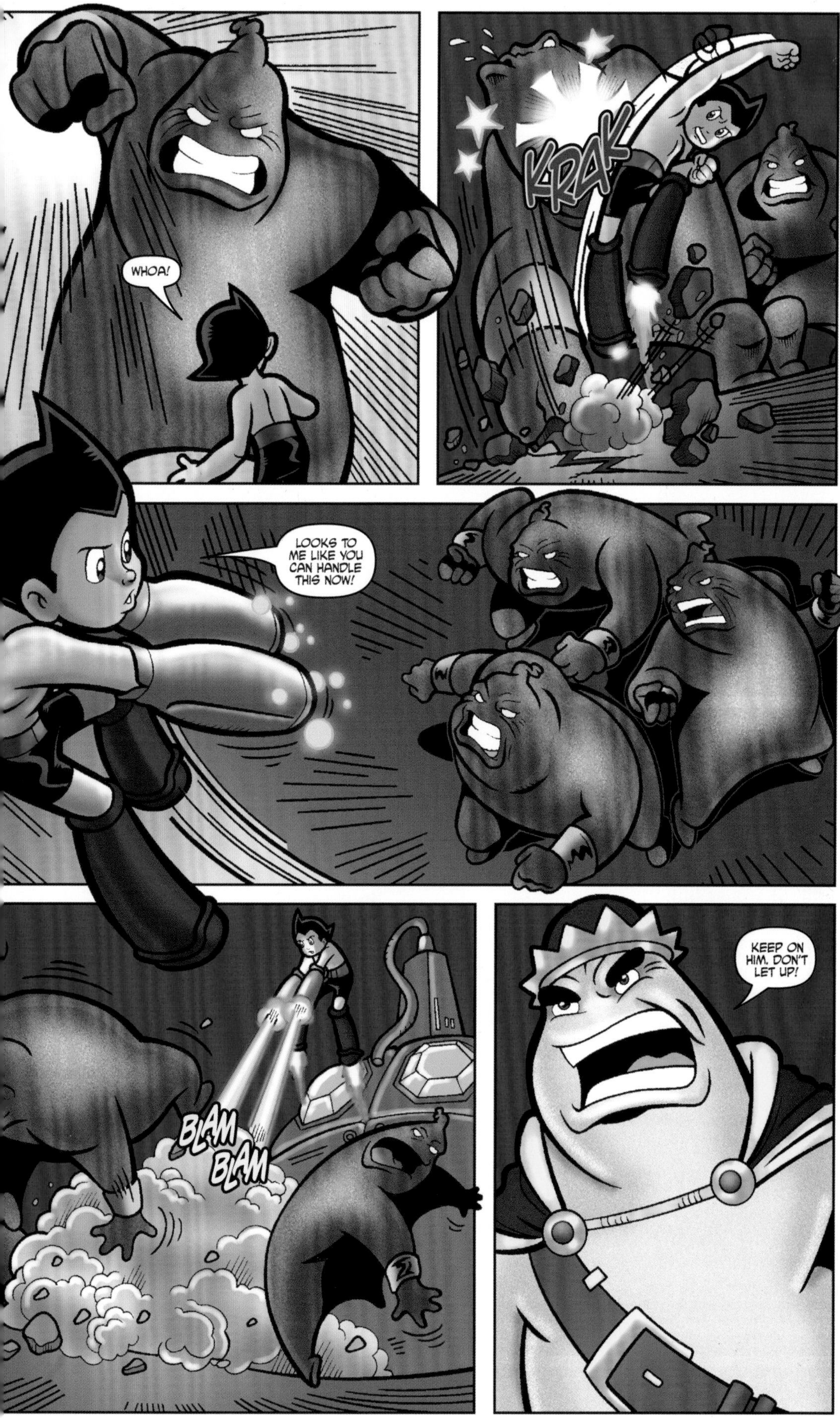
WHOA!
KRAK
LOOKS TO ME LIKE YOU CAN HANDLE THIS NOW!
BLAM
BLAM
KEEP ON HIM. DON'T LET UP!

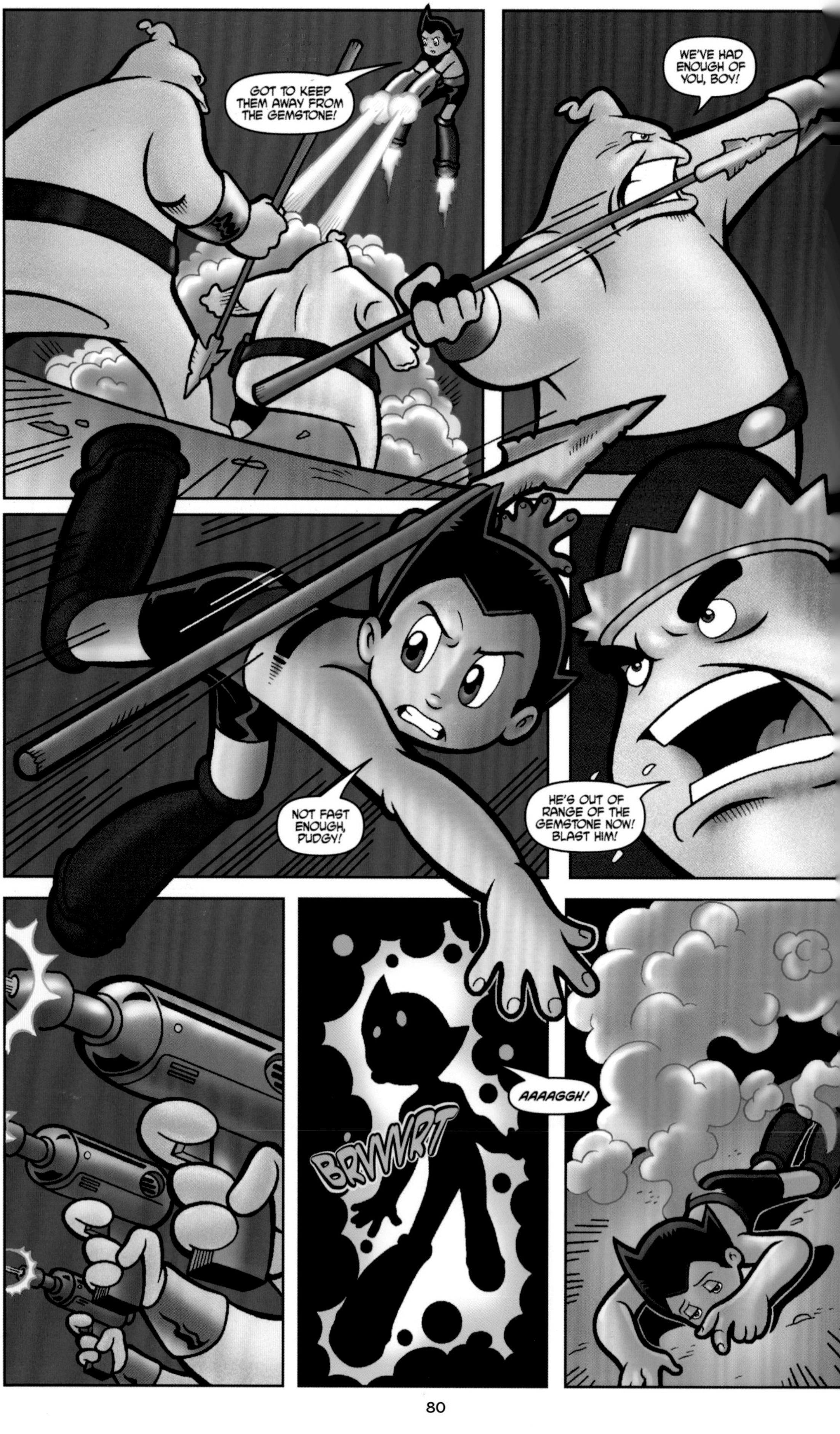
GOT TO KEEP THEM AWAY FROM THE GEMSTONE!
WE'VE HAD ENOUGH OF YOU, BOY!
NOT FAST ENOUGH, PUDGY!
HE'S OUT OF RANGE OF THE GEMSTONE NOW! BLAST HIM!
AAAAGGH!
BRVVVRT

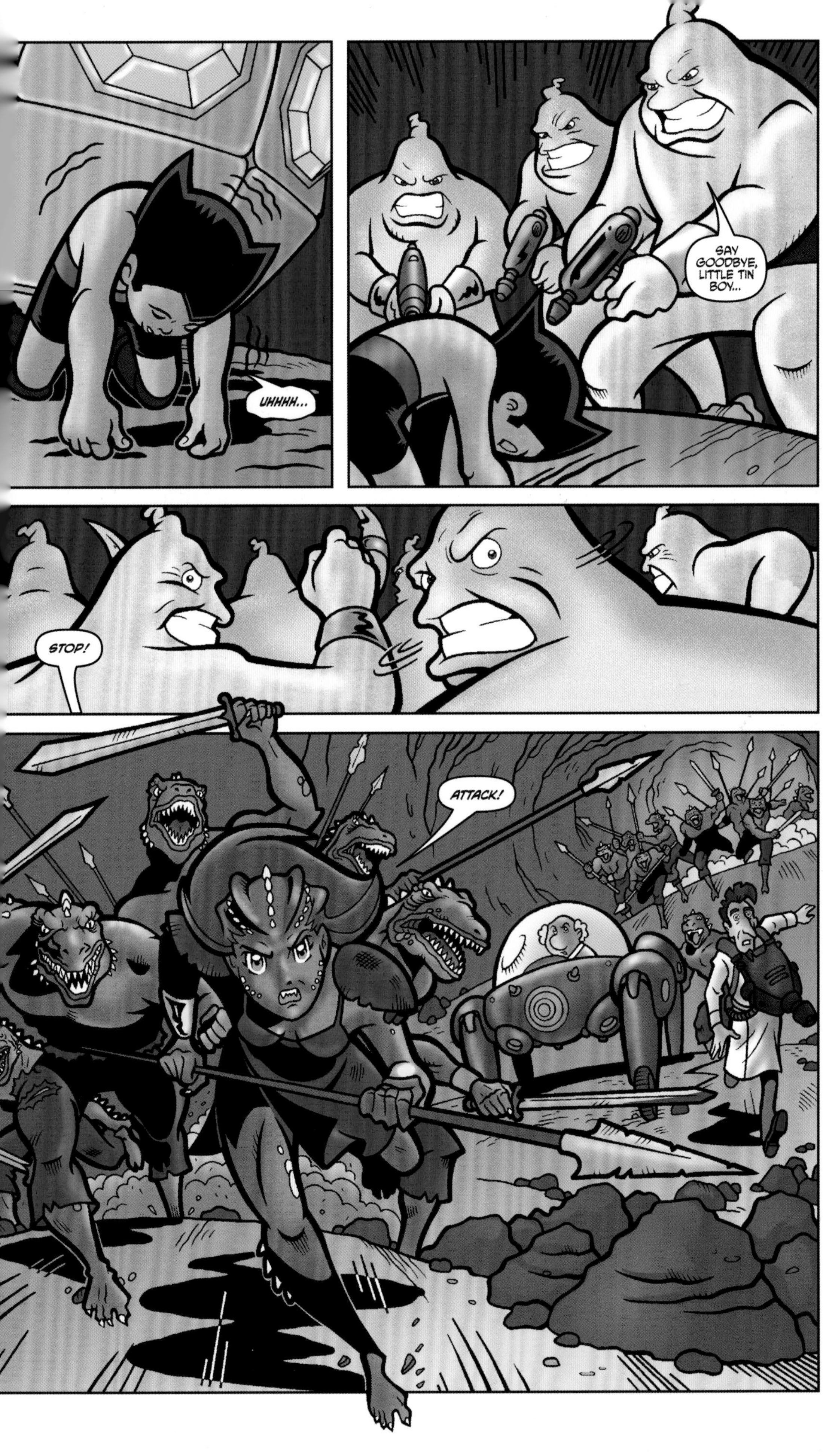
UHHHH...
SAY GOODBYE, LITTLE TIN BOY...
STOP!
ATTACK!

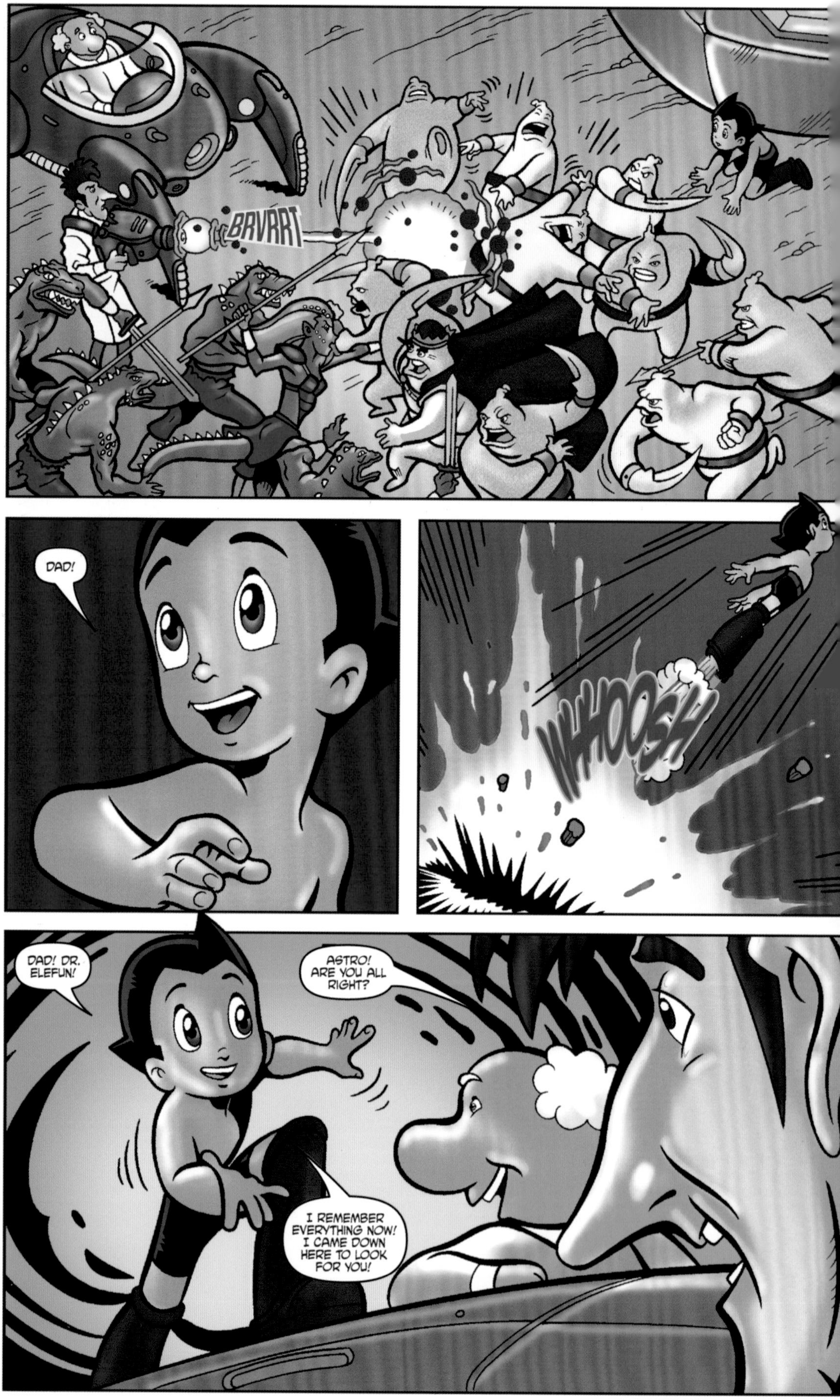
BRVRRT
DAD!
WHOOSH
DAD! DR. ELEFUN!
ASTRO! ARE YOU ALL RIGHT?
I REMEMBER EVERYTHING NOW! I CAME DOWN HERE TO LOOK FOR YOU!

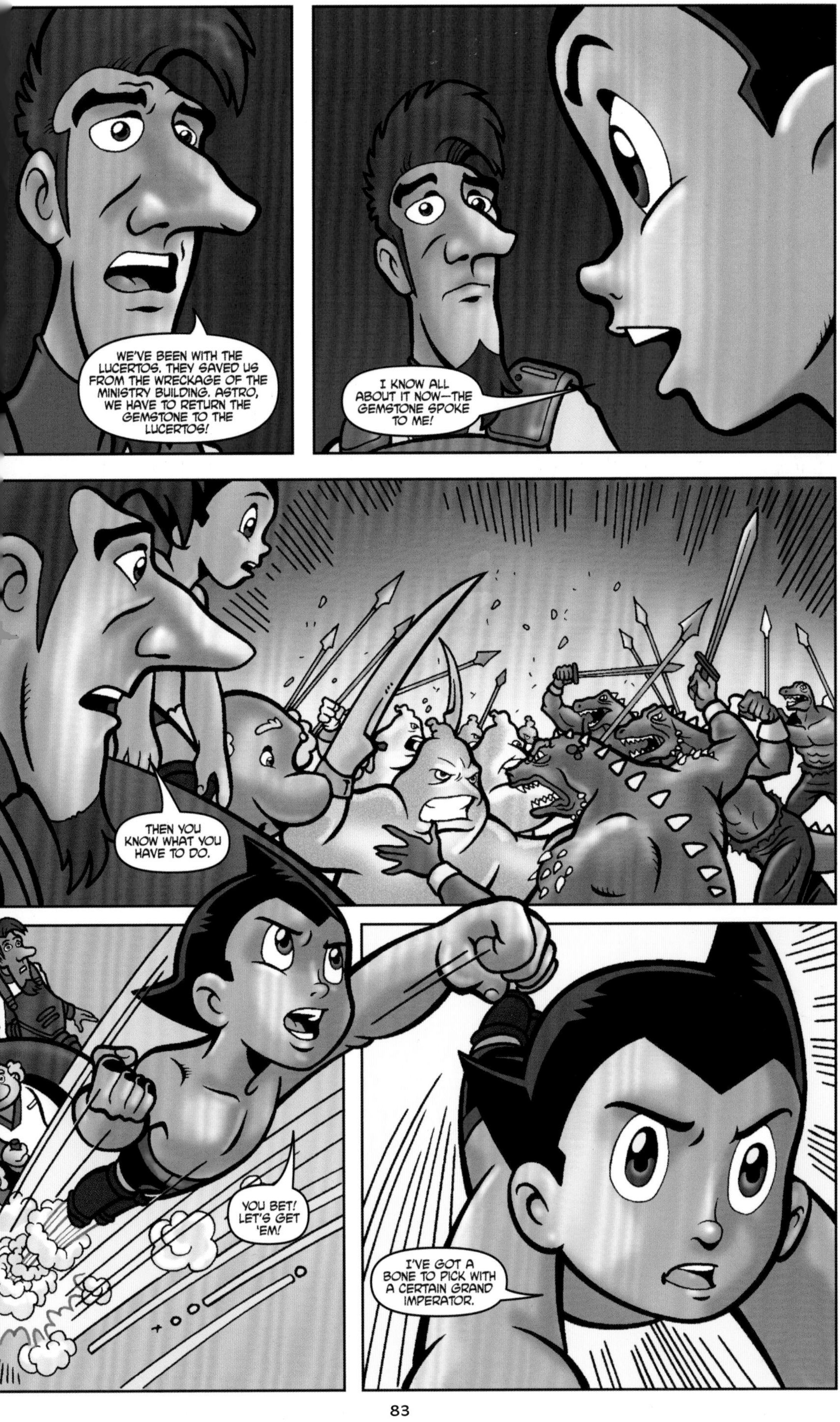
WE'VE BEEN WITH THE LUCERTOS. THEY SAVED US FROM THE WRECKAGE OF THE MINISTRY BUILDING. ASTRO, WE HAVE TO RETURN THE GEMSTONE TO THE LUCERTOS!
I KNOW ALL ABOUT IT NOW—THE GEMSTONE SPOKE TO ME!
THEN YOU KNOW WHAT YOU HAVE TO DO.
YOU BET! LET'S GET 'EM!
I'VE GOT A BONE TO PICK WITH A CERTAIN GRAND IMPERATOR.

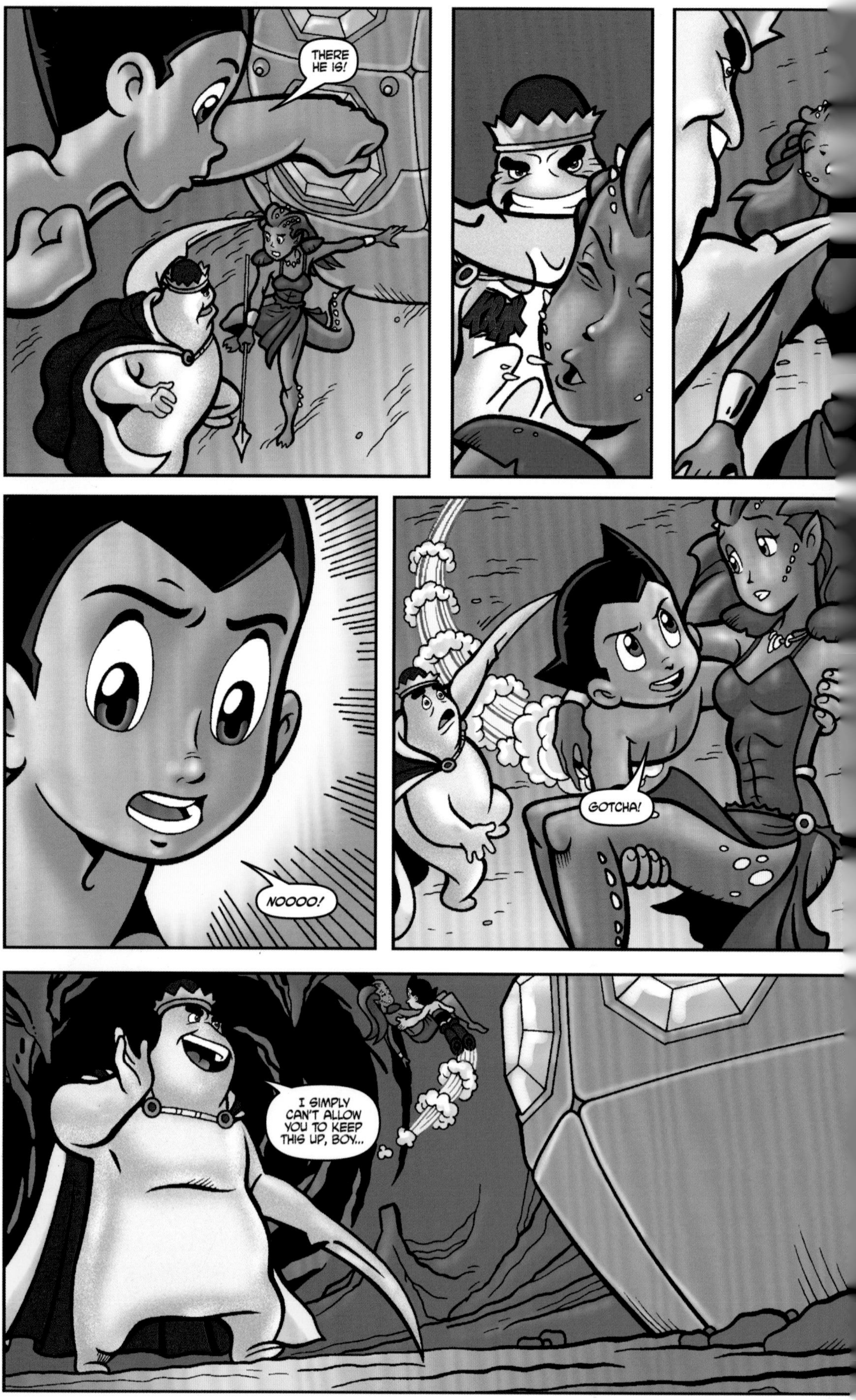
THERE HE IS!
NOOOO!
GOTCHA!
I SIMPLY CAN'T ALLOW YOU TO KEEP THIS UP, BOY...

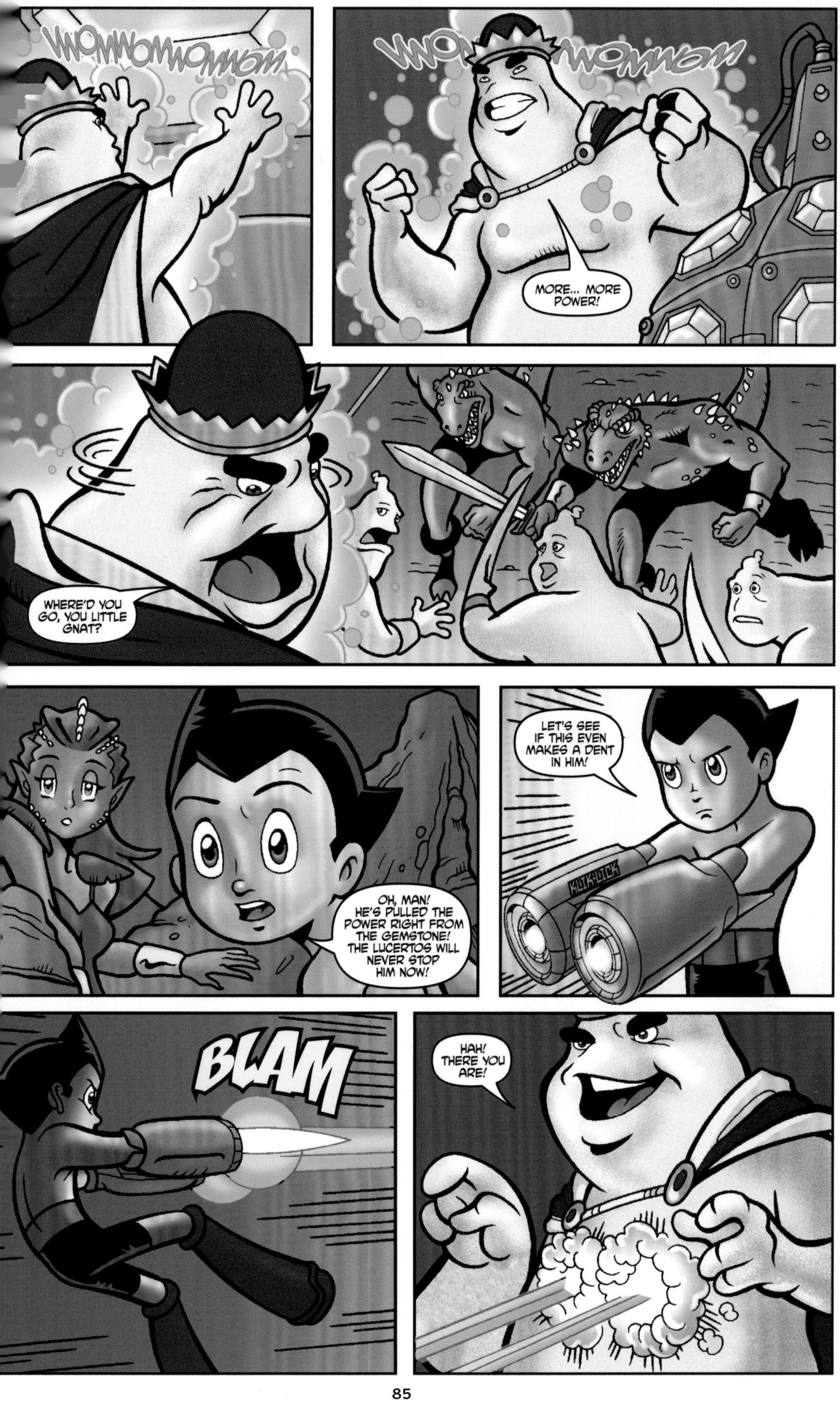
MORE... MORE POWER!
WHERE'D YOU GO, YOU LITTLE GNAT?
OH, MAN! HE'S PULLED THE POWER RIGHT FROM THE GEMSTONE! THE LUCERTOS WILL NEVER STOP HIM NOW!
LET'S SEE IF THIS EVEN MAKES A DENT IN HIM!
BLAM
HAH! THERE YOU ARE!

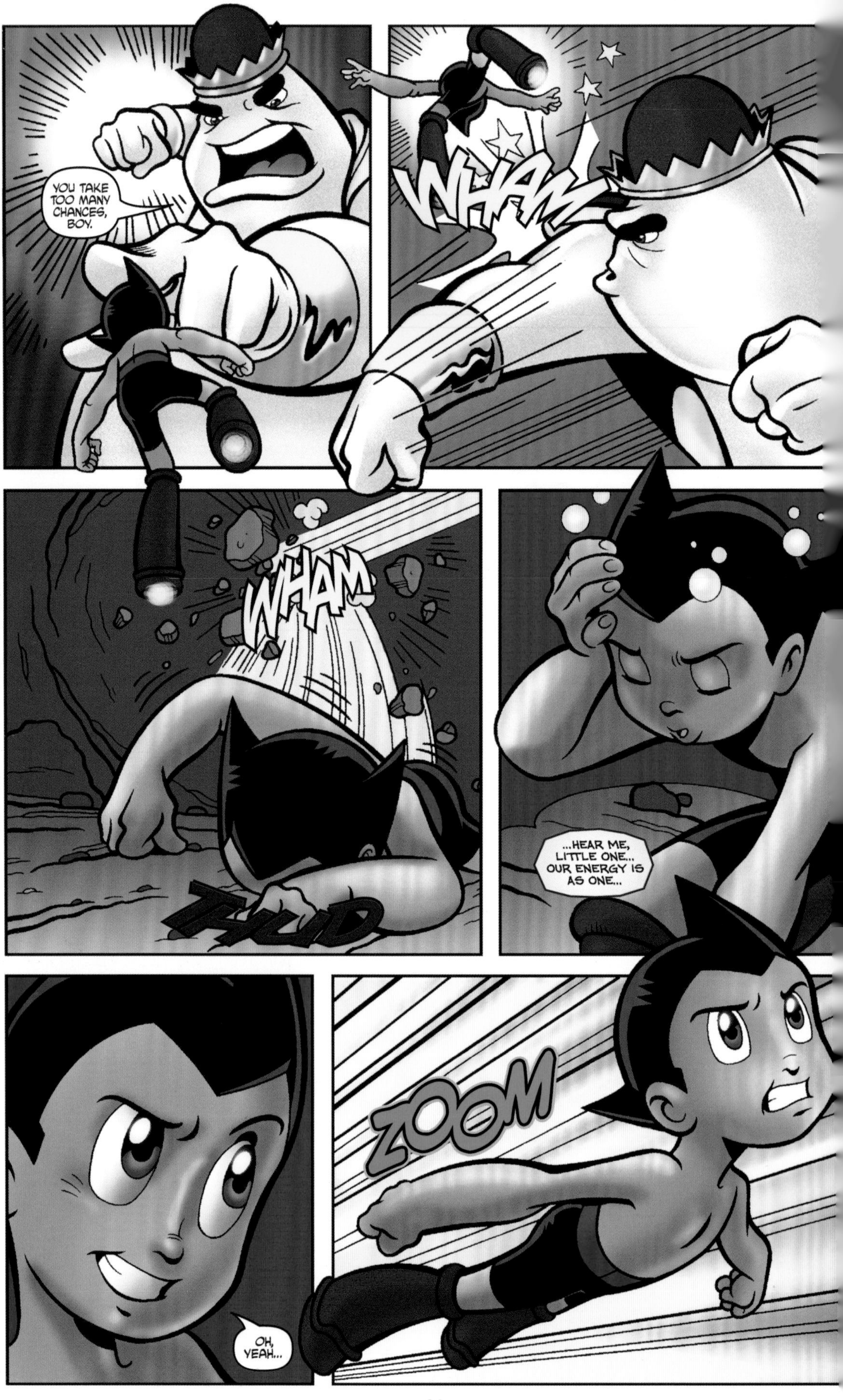
YOU TAKE TOO MANY CHANCES, BOY.
WHAM
WHAM
THUD
...HEAR ME, LITTLE ONE... OUR ENERGY IS AS ONE...
OH, YEAH...
ZOOM

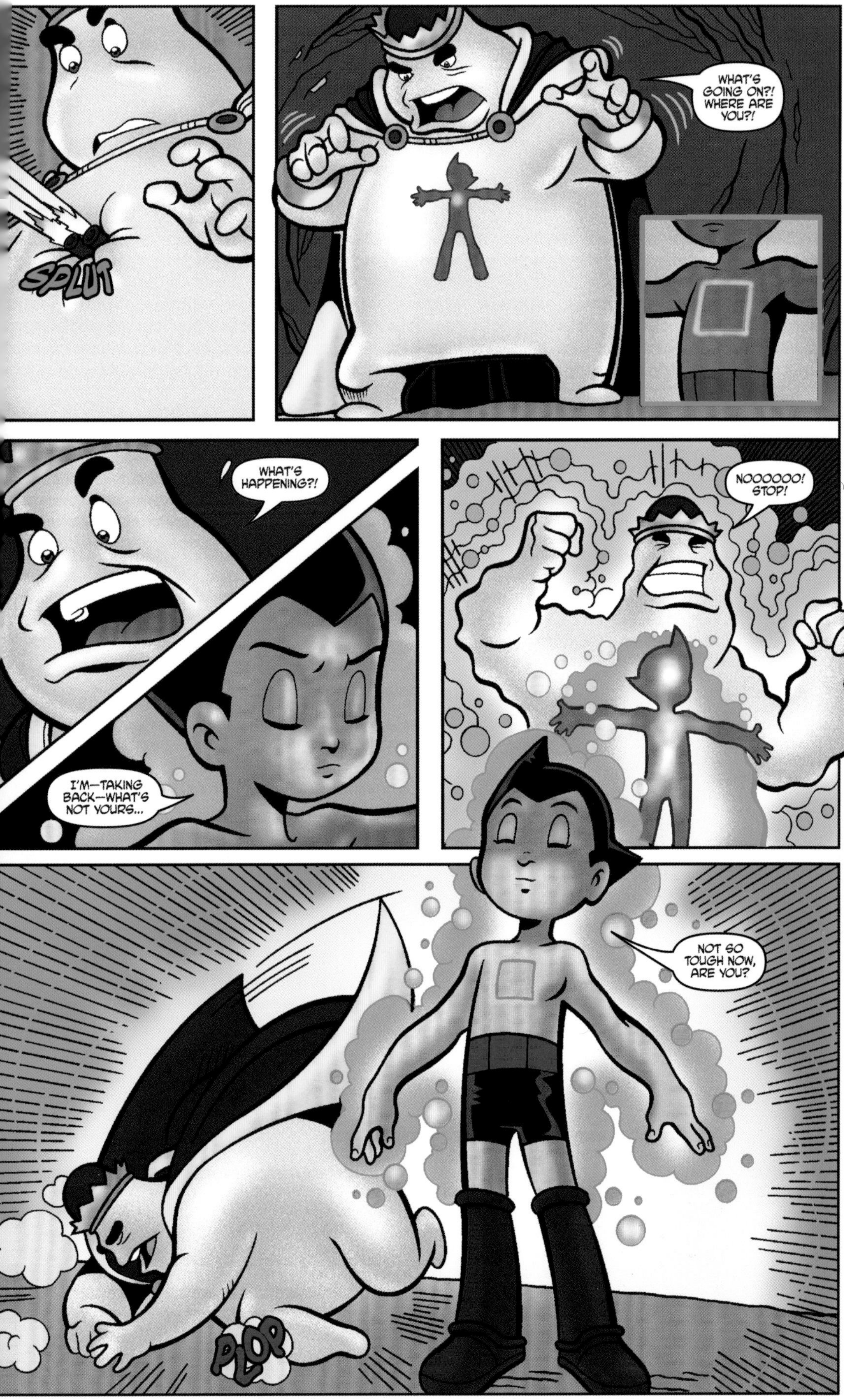
SPLUT
WHAT'S GOING ON?! WHERE ARE YOU?!
WHAT'S HAPPENING?!
I'M—TAKING BACK—WHAT'S NOT YOURS...
NOOOOOO! STOP!
NOT SO TOUGH NOW, ARE YOU?
PLOP

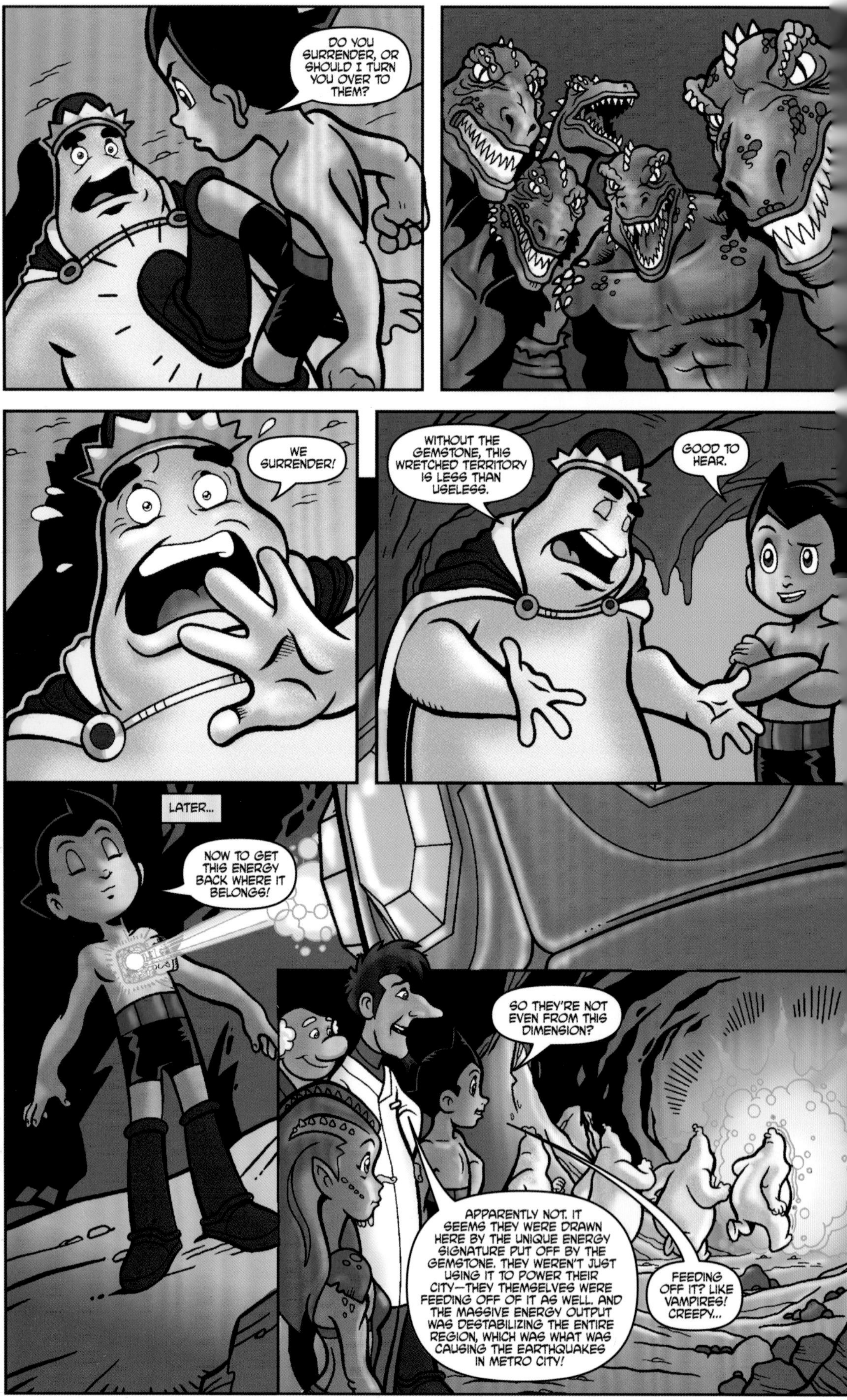
DO YOU SURRENDER, OR SHOULD I TURN YOU OVER TO THEM?
WE SURRENDER!
WITHOUT THE GEMSTONE, THIS WRETCHED TERRITORY IS LESS THAN USELESS.
GOOD TO HEAR.
LATER...
NOW TO GET THIS ENERGY BACK WHERE IT BELONGS!
SO THEY'RE NOT EVEN FROM THIS DIMENSION?
APPARENTLY NOT. IT SEEMS THEY WERE DRAWN HERE BY THE UNIQUE ENERGY SIGNATURE PUT OFF BY THE GEMSTONE. THEY WEREN'T JUST USING IT TO POWER THEIR CITY—THEY THEMSELVES WERE FEEDING OFF OF IT AS WELL. AND THE MASSIVE ENERGY OUTPUT WAS DESTABILIZING THE ENTIRE REGION, WHICH WAS WHAT WAS CAUSING THE EARTHQUAKES IN METRO CITY!
FEEDING OFF IT? LIKE VAMPIRES! CREEPY...

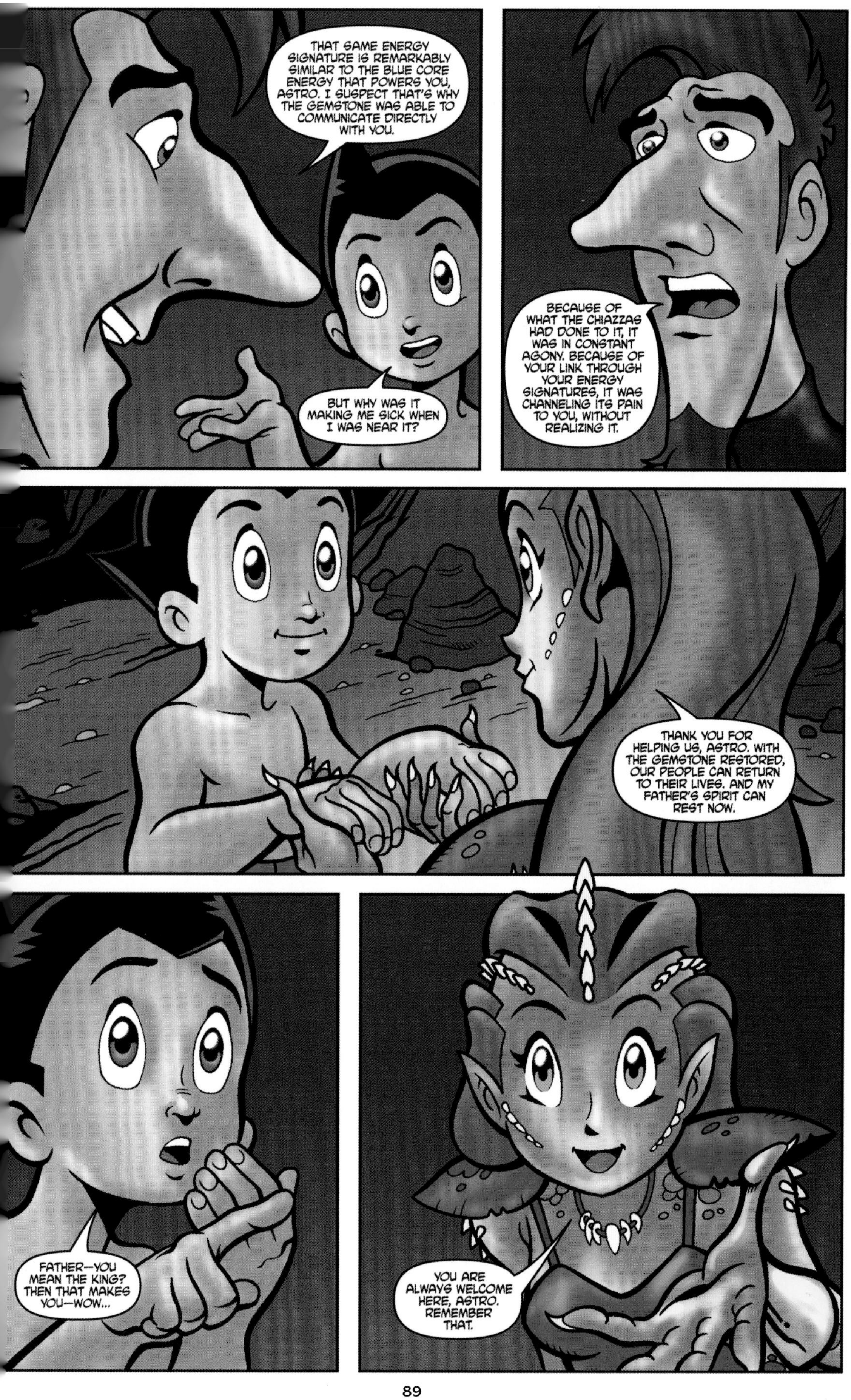
THAT SAME ENERGY SIGNATURE IS REMARKABLY SIMILAR TO THE BLUE CORE ENERGY THAT POWERS YOU, ASTRO. I SUSPECT THAT'S WHY THE GEMSTONE WAS ABLE TO COMMUNICATE DIRECTLY WITH YOU.
BUT WHY WAS IT MAKING ME SICK WHEN I WAS NEAR IT?
BECAUSE OF WHAT THE CHIAZZAS HAD DONE TO IT, IT WAS IN CONSTANT AGONY. BECAUSE OF YOUR LINK THROUGH YOUR ENERGY SIGNATURES, IT WAS CHANNELING ITS PAIN TO YOU, WITHOUT REALIZING IT.
THANK YOU FOR HELPING US, ASTRO. WITH THE GEMSTONE RESTORED, OUR PEOPLE CAN RETURN TO THEIR LIVES. AND MY FATHER'S SPIRIT CAN REST NOW.
FATHER—YOU MEAN THE KING? THEN THAT MAKES YOU—WOW...
YOU ARE ALWAYS WELCOME HERE, ASTRO. REMEMBER THAT.

AHEM... ASTRO, WE'D BETTER GET BACK TO METRO CITY.
HUH? OH, RIGHT!
AFTER ALL, ELEFUN AND I HAVE A MINISTRY OF SCIENCE TO REBUILD!
SO LONG, EVERYONE!
LOOK AT THESE READINGS FROM THE SEISMIC SENSORS, TENMA. IT'S VERY, VERY PROMISING DATA...
BRRRVVRRTT
THE END.

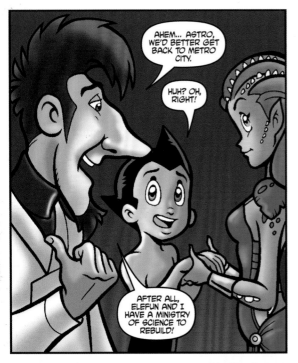

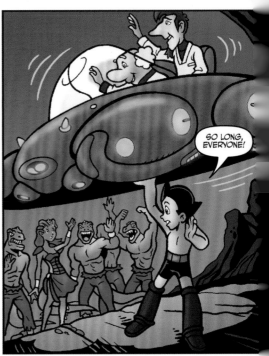

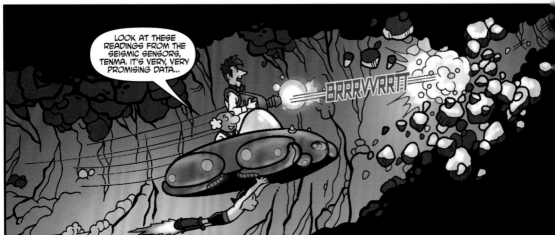

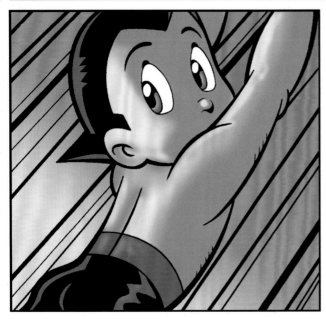

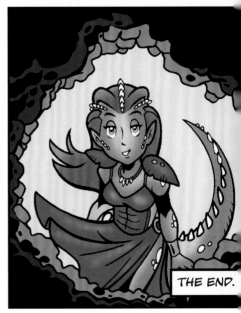

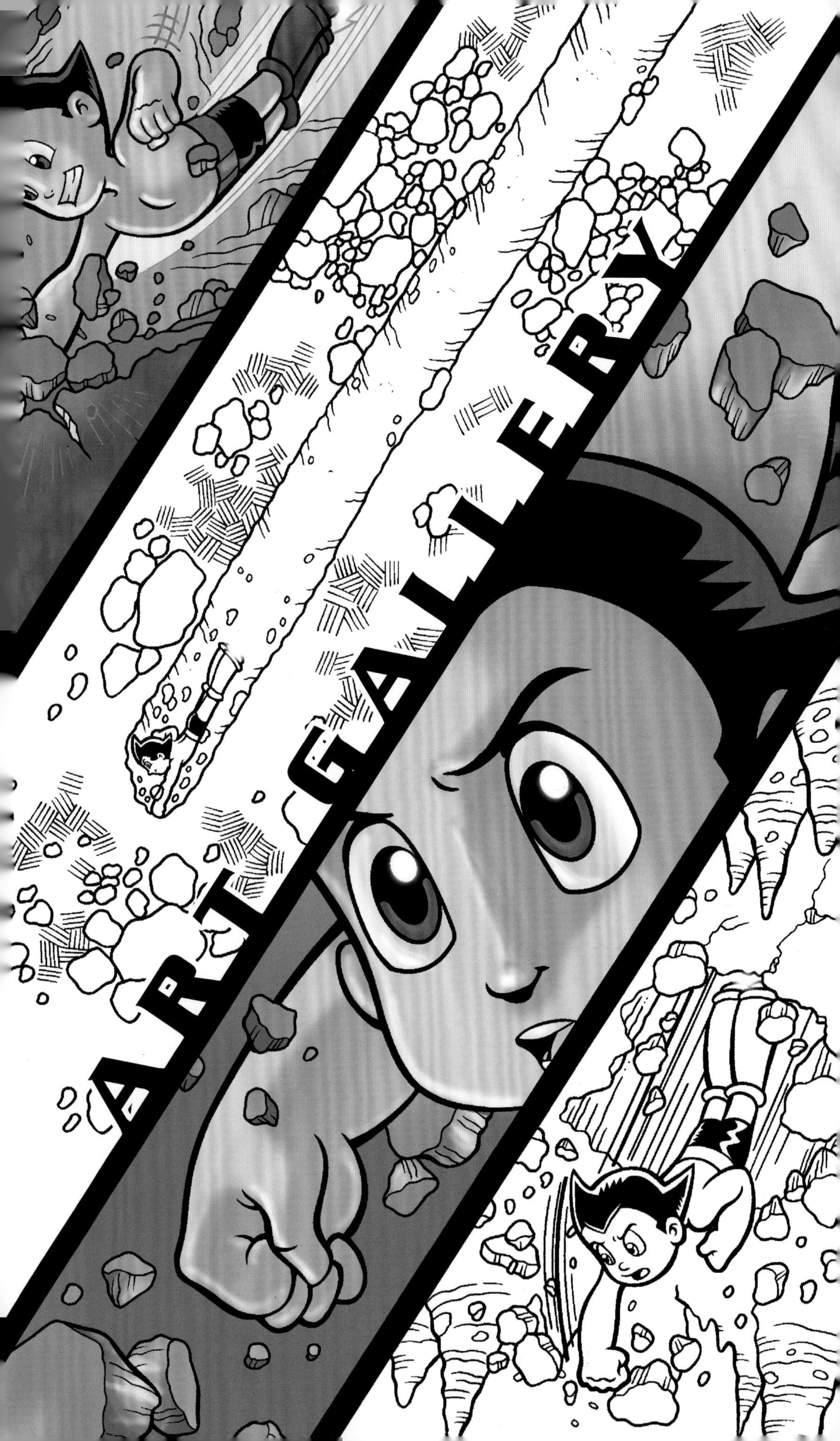
ART GALLERY

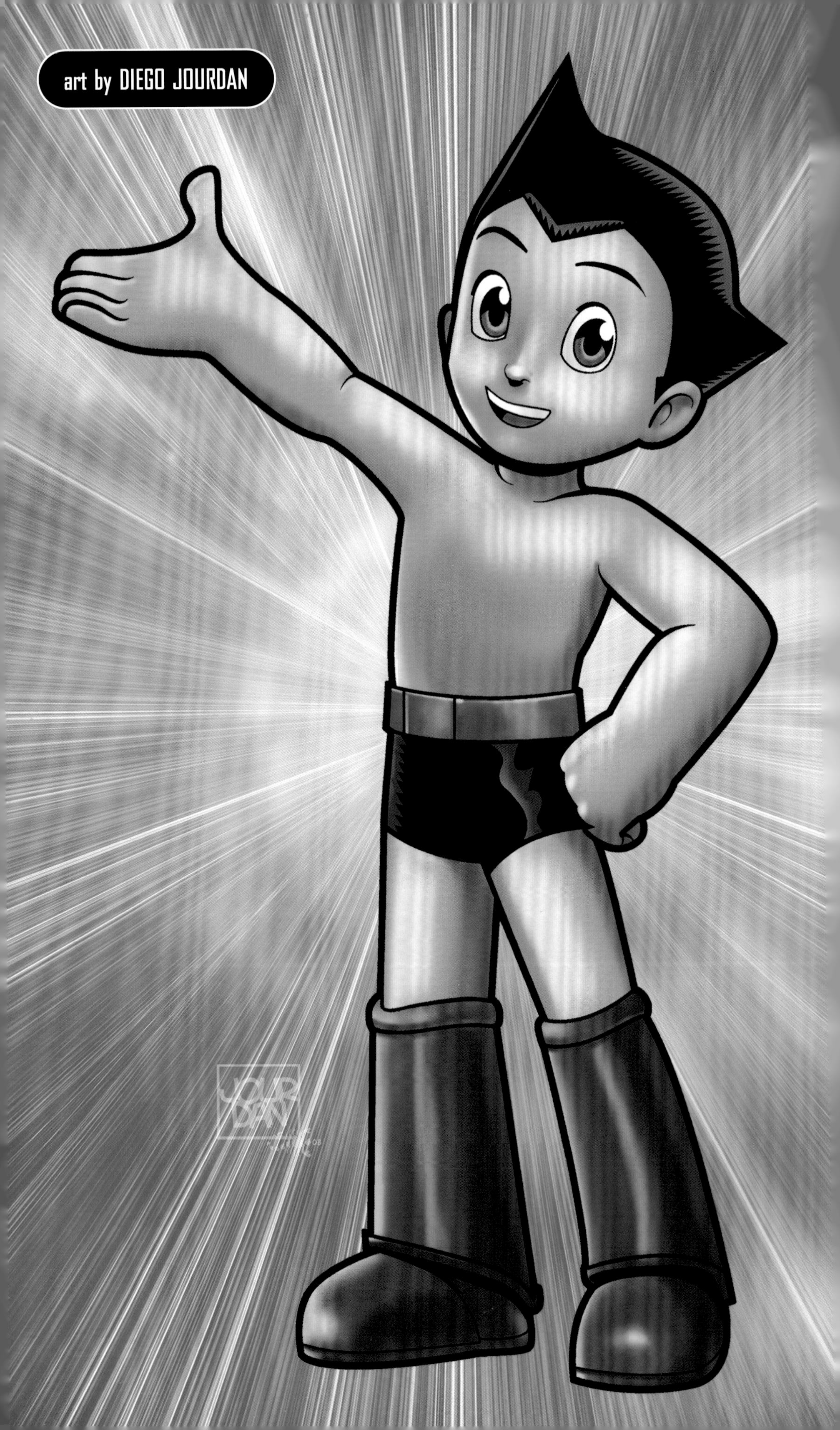

art by DIEGO JOURDAN

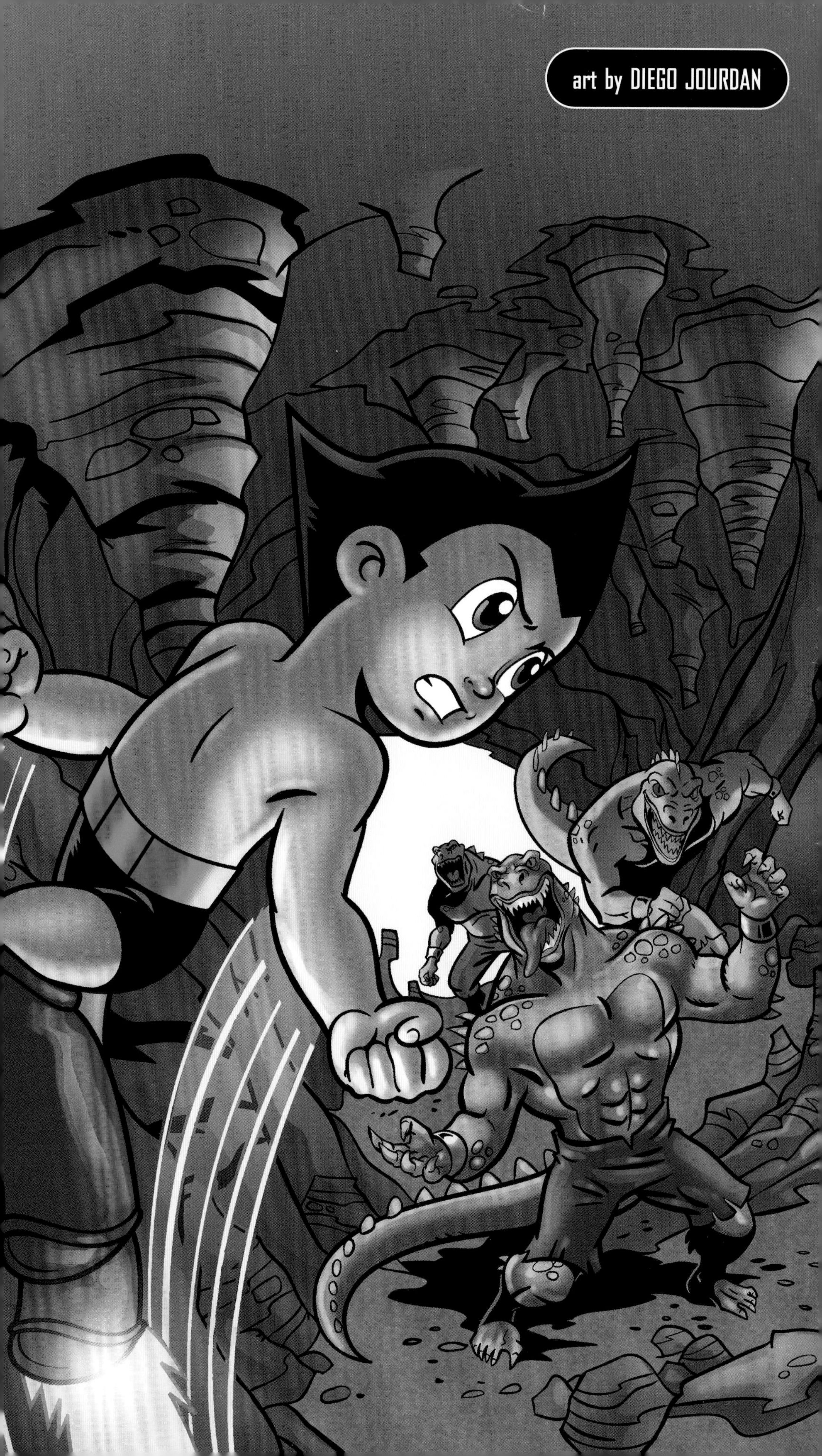
art by DIEGO JOURDAN

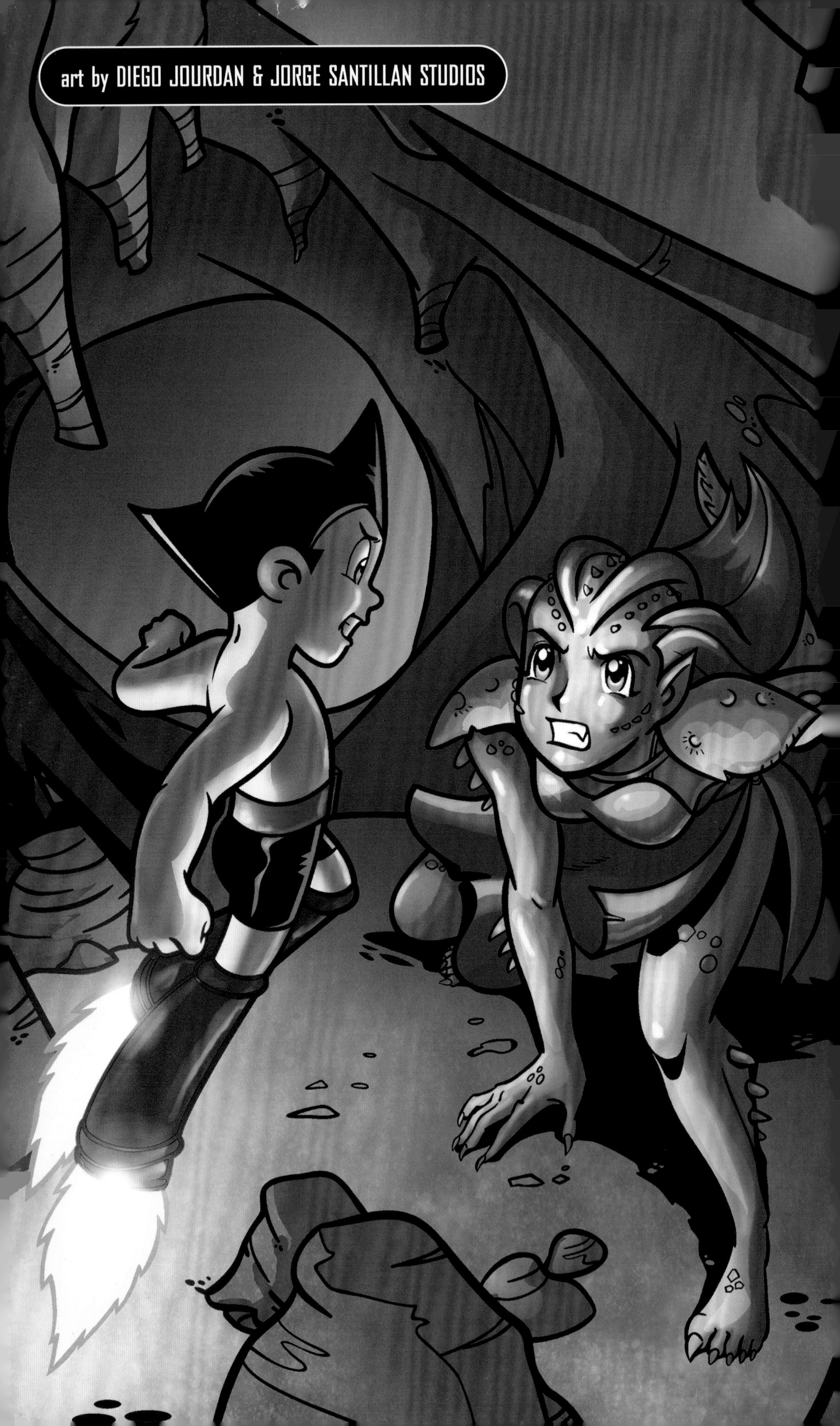
art by DIEGO JOURDAN & JORGE SANTILLAN STUDIOS

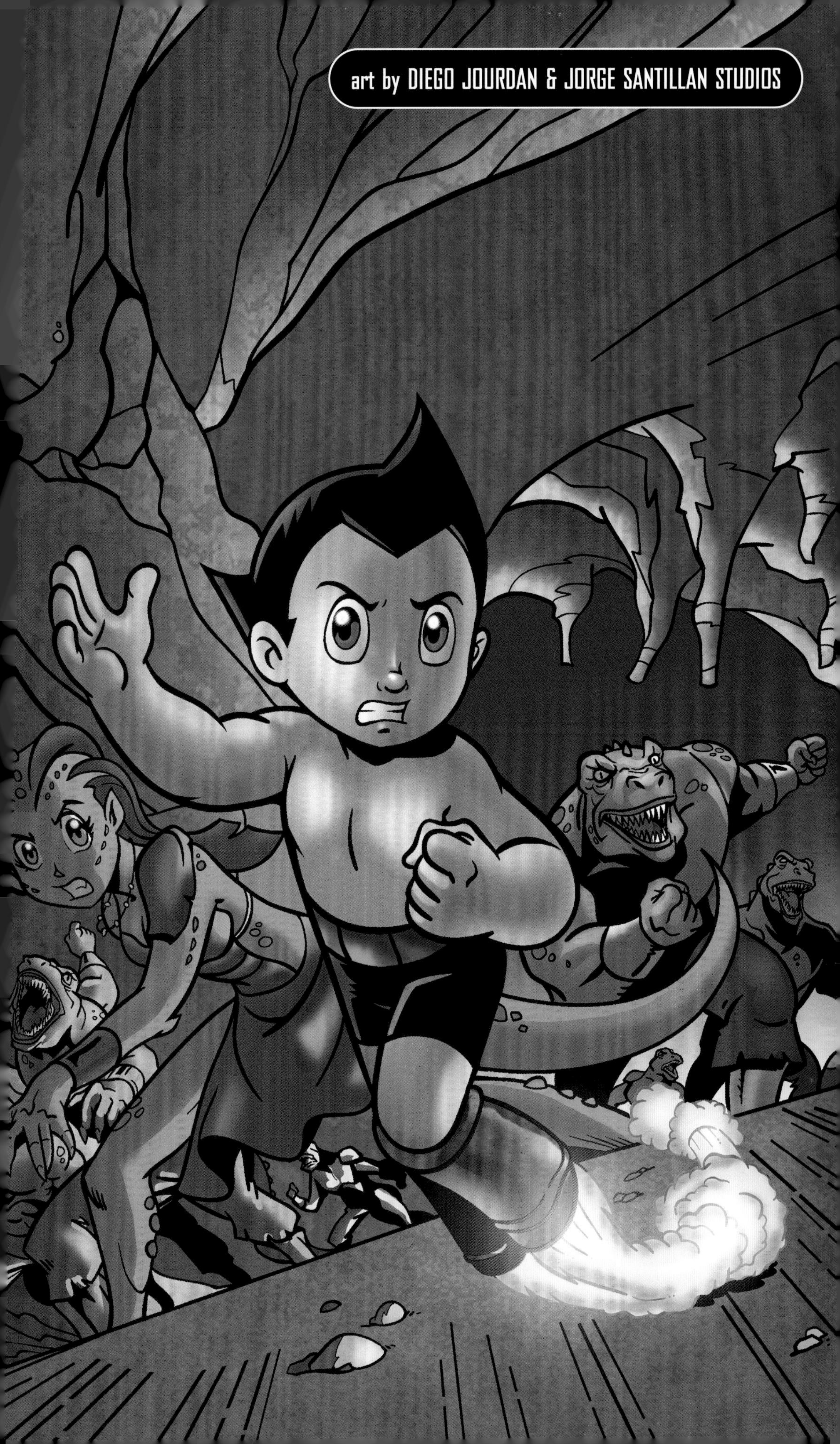
art by DIEGO JOURDAN & JORGE SANTILLAN STUDIOS

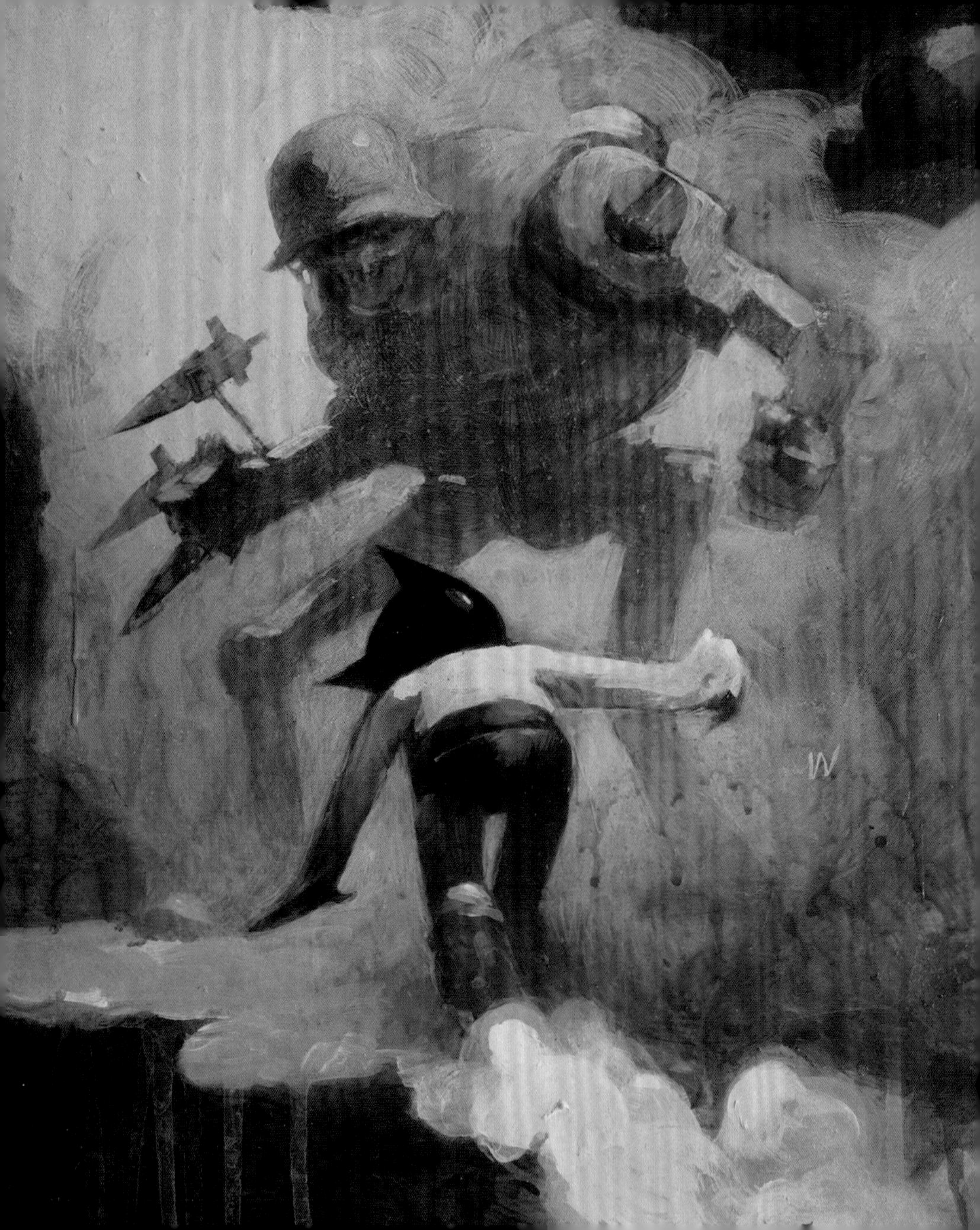

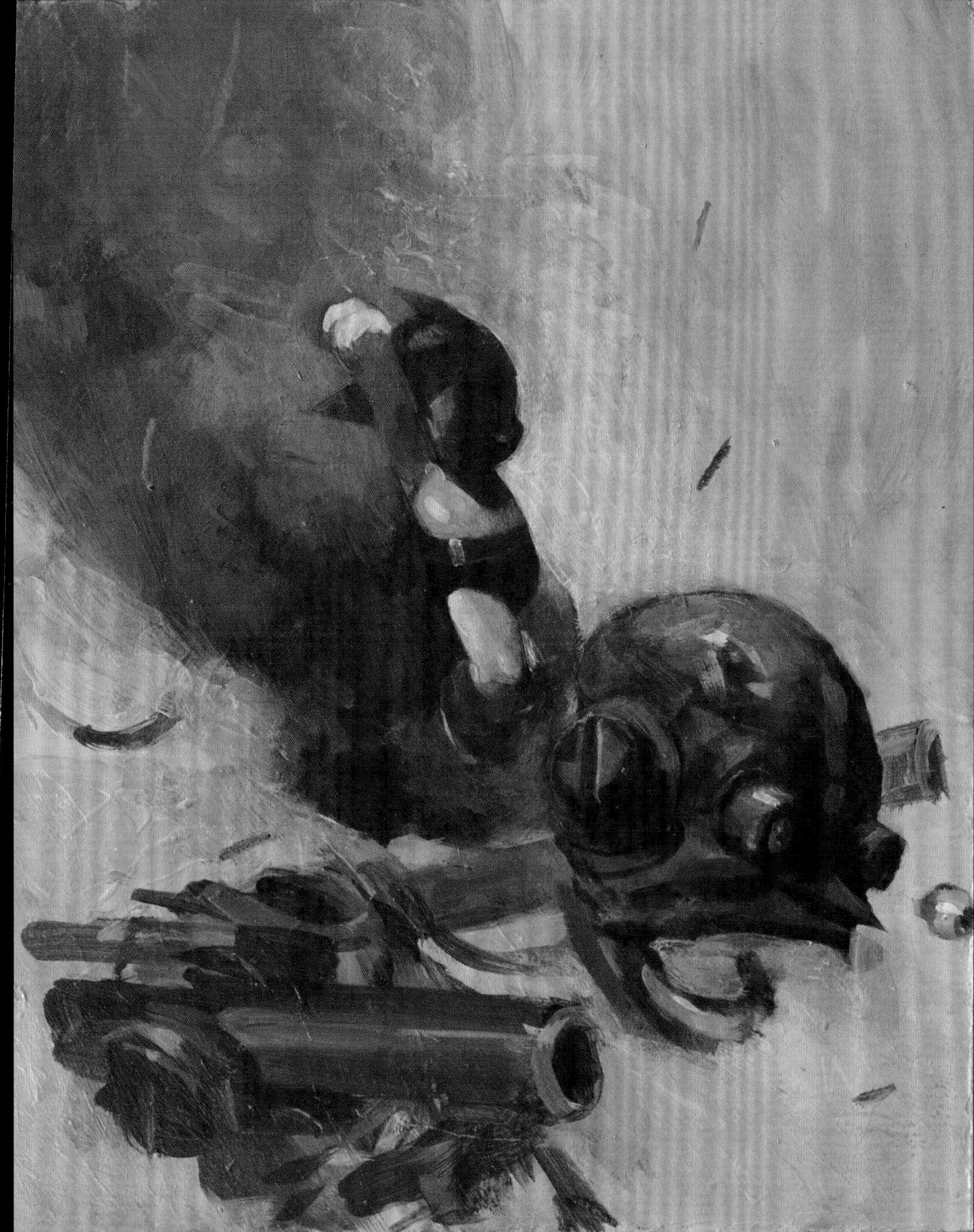

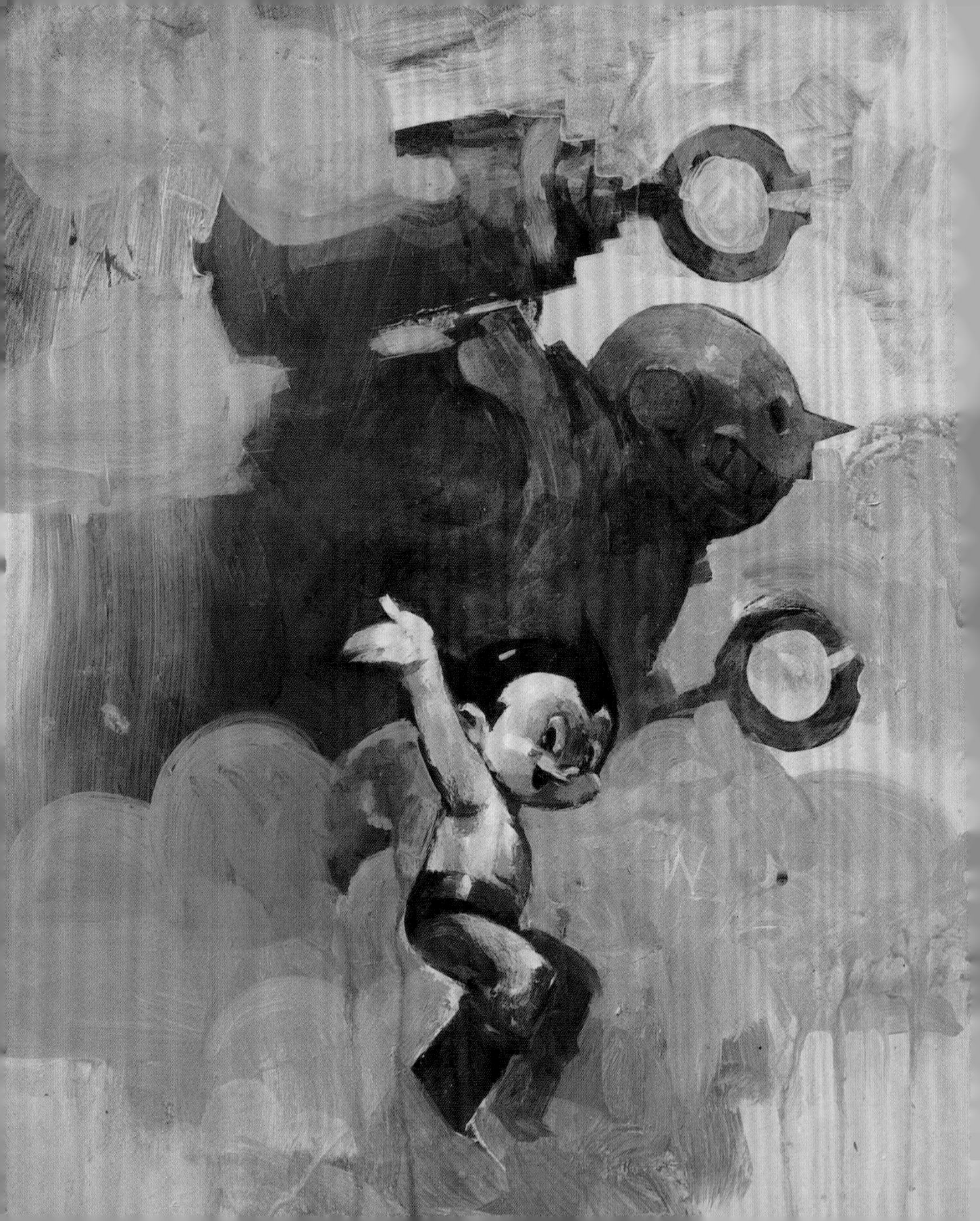

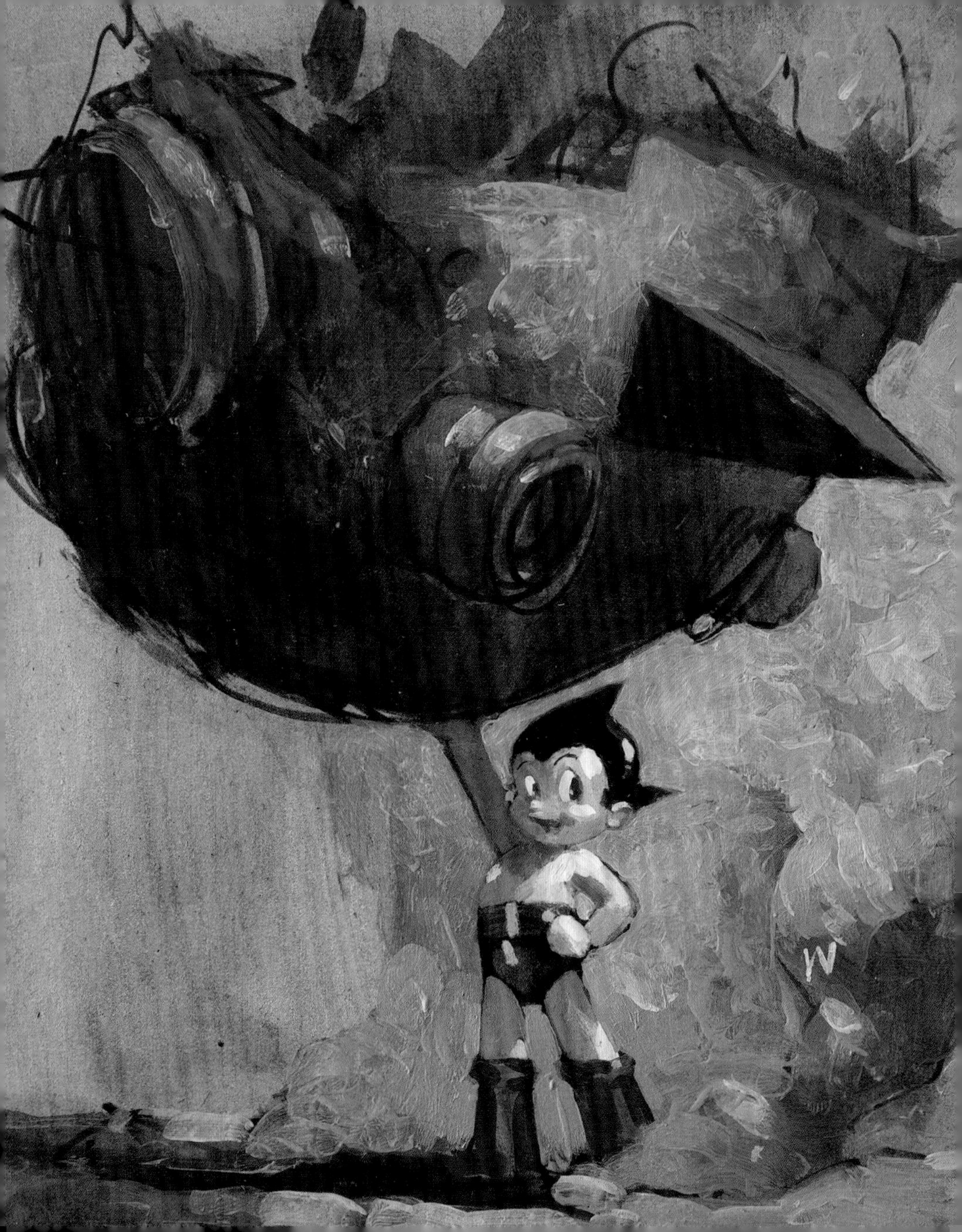

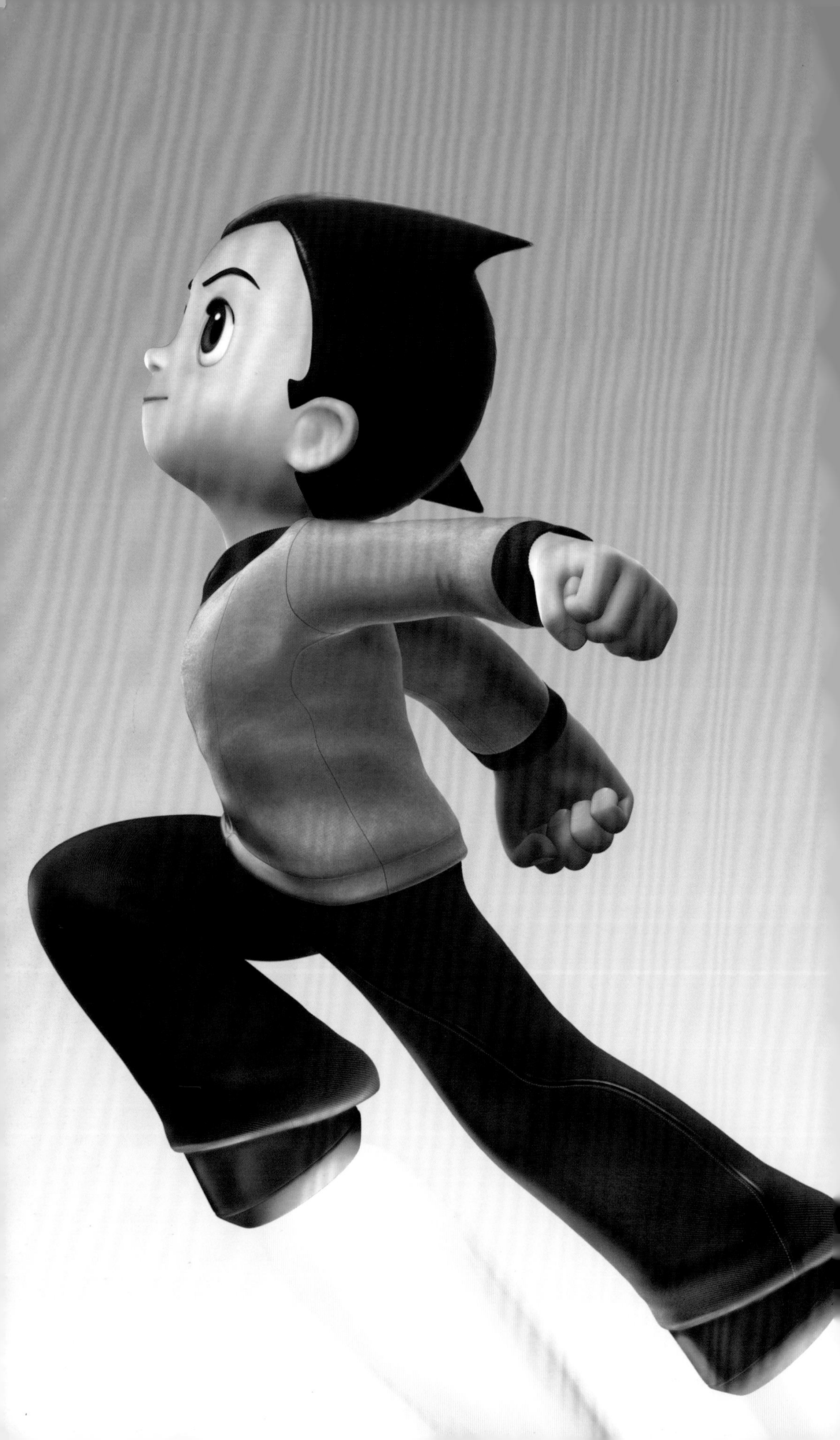

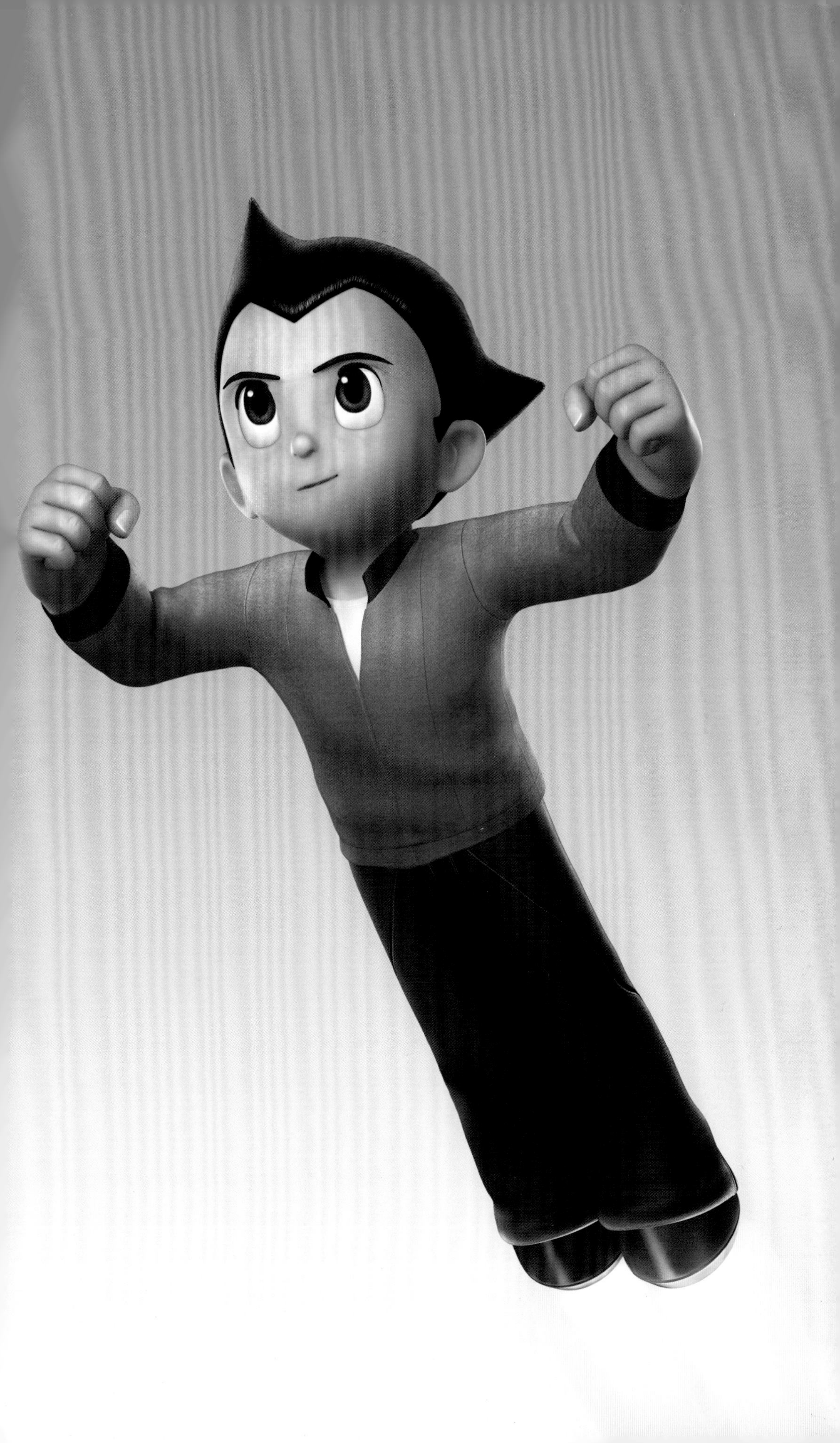

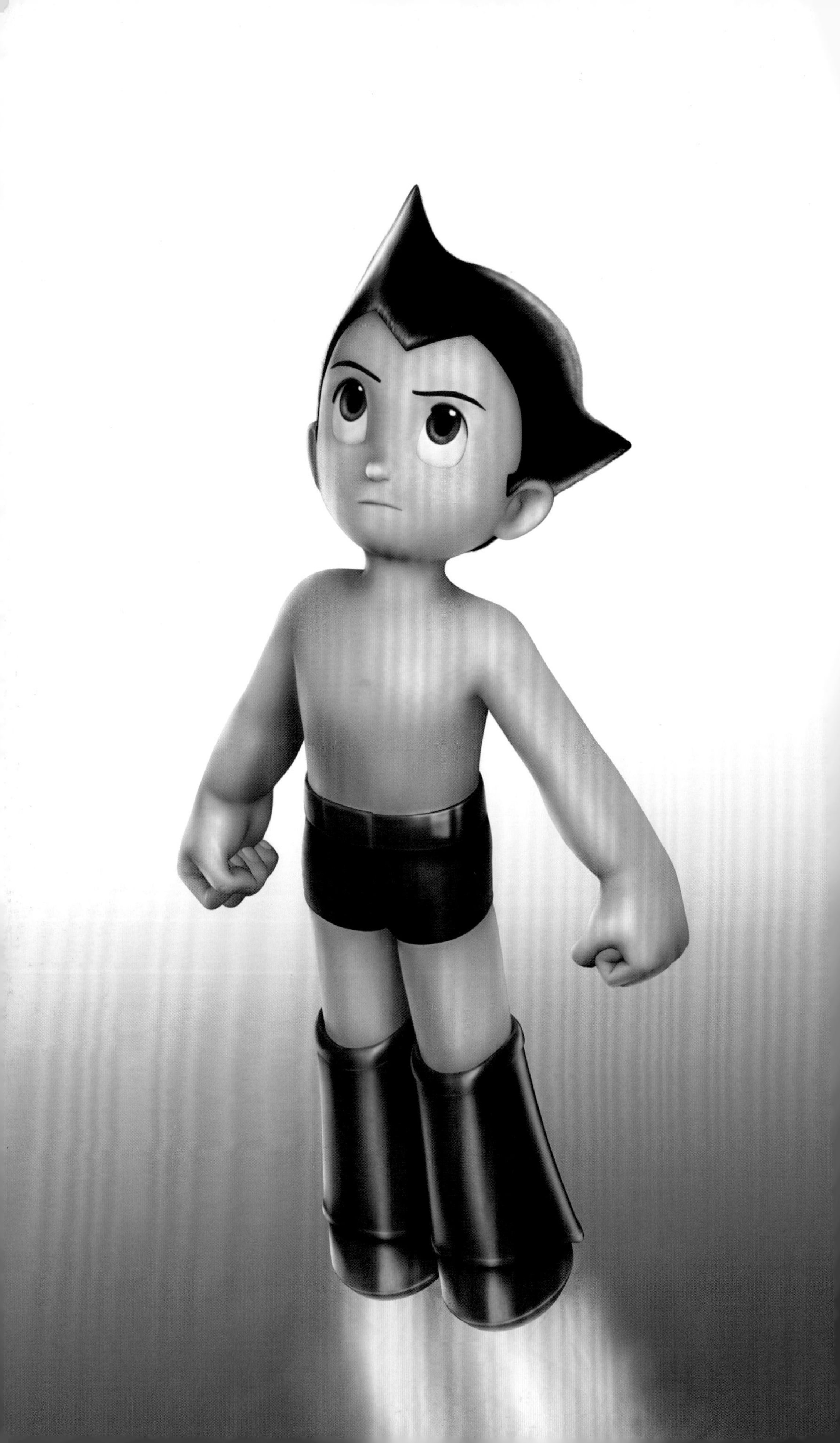

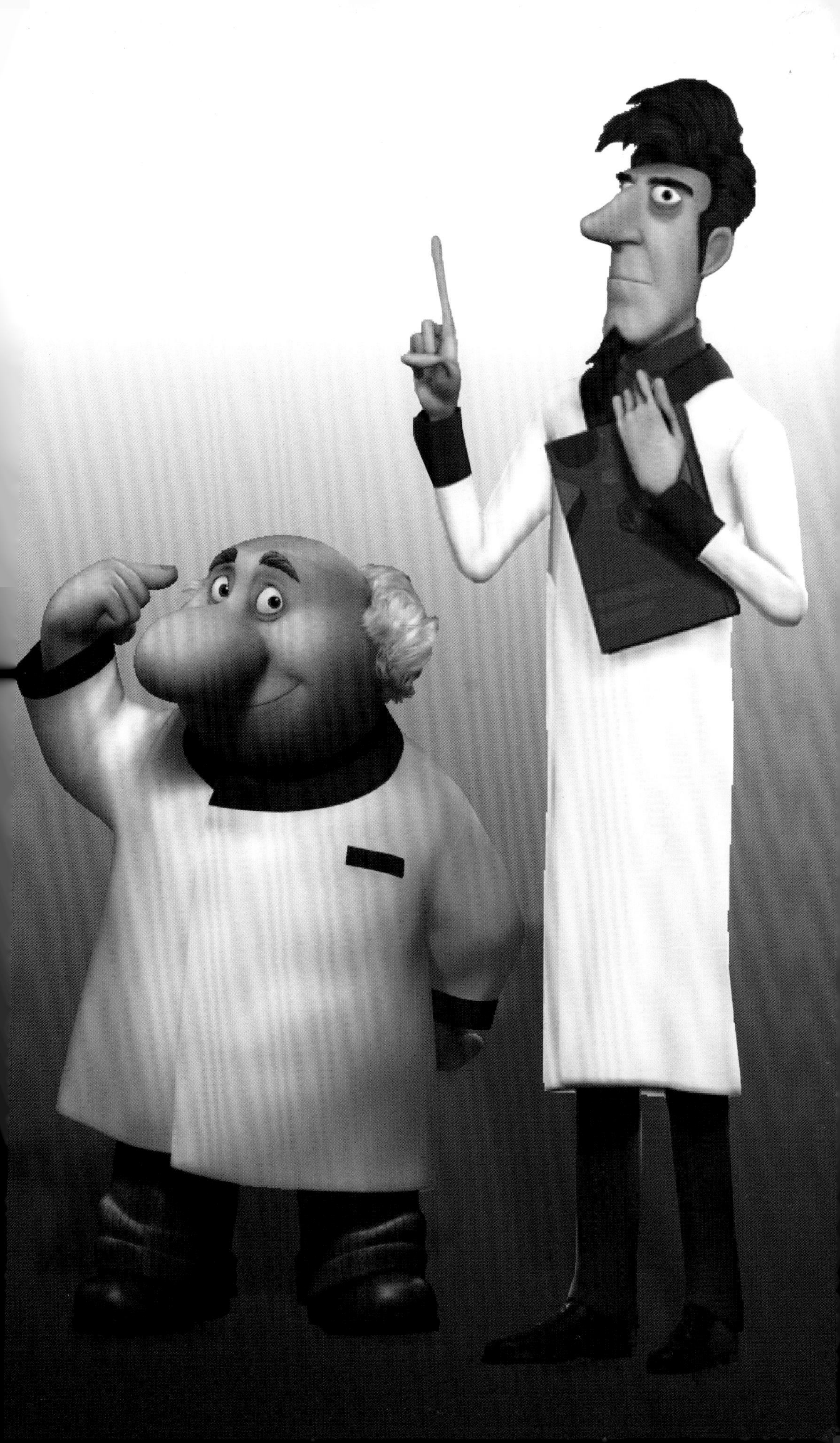

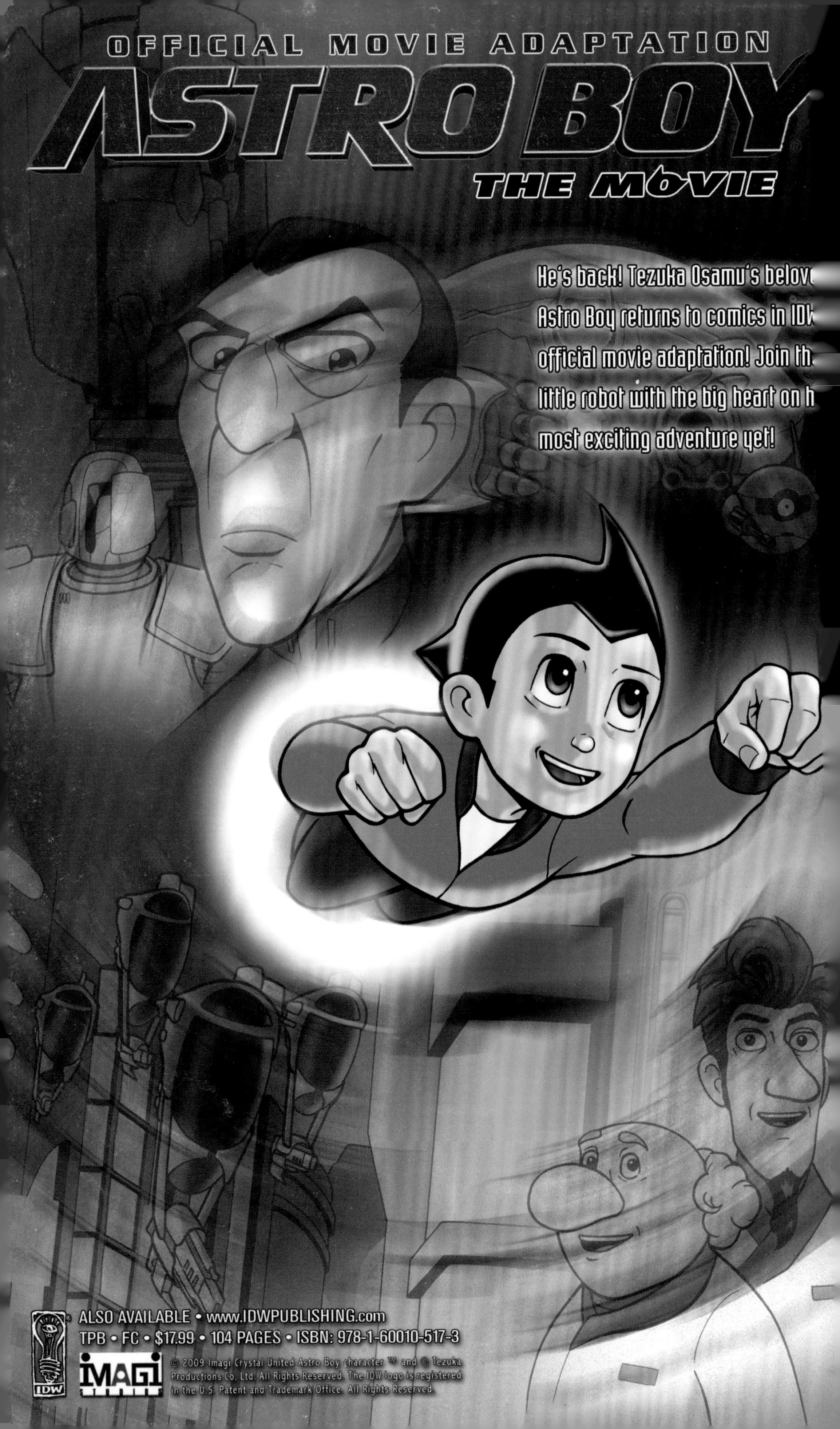
OFFICIAL MOVIE ADAPTATION
ASTRO BOY
THE MOVIE
He's back! Tezuka Osamu's belov
Astro Boy returns to comics in IDV
official movie adaptation! Join th
little robot with the big heart on h
most exciting adventure yet!
ALSO AVAILABLE • www.IDWPUBLISHING.com
TPB • FC • $17.99 • 104 PAGES • ISBN: 978-1-60010-517-3
IDW
IMAGI
© 2009 Imagi Crystal United Astro Boy character ™ and © Tezuka Productions Co. Ltd. All Rights Reserved. The IDW logo is registered in the U.S. Patent and Trademark Office. All Rights Reserved.